Race and Racism in C̶o̶n̶t̶...

Ma
Te:

Also by John Solomos

Racism and Equal Opportunity Policies in the 1980s (editor, with
  Richard Jenkins)
The Roots of Urban Unrest (editor, with John Benyon)
Black Youth, Racism and the State

Race and Racism in Contemporary Britain

John Solomos

Lecturer in Politics
Birkbeck College
University of London

MACMILLAN

First published 1989
Reprinted 1990

Published by
MACMILLAN EDUCATION LTD
Houndmills, Basingstoke, Hampshire RG21 2XS
and London
Companies and representatives
throughout the world

Typeset by Elite Typesetting Techniques, Southampton

Printed in Hong Kong

British Library Cataloguing in Publication Data
Solomos, John
Race and racism in contemporary Britain
1. Great Britain. Racism
I. Title
305.8'00941
ISBN 0–333–42141–8 (hardcover)
ISBN 0–333–42142–6 (paperback)

To the memory of Cleopatra, Solomos, Styliani and Yiannis, who missed out on the opportunities I have enjoyed, but whose experiences remain with me

Contents

Acknowledgements

I would like to thank all the colleagues, students and friends who have helped me to articulate arguments which are developed in this book. Since 1982 I have taught a number of courses on the politics of racism and related issues, and this has allowed me to test out some of the early versions of chapters included in this volume. I also owe a special debt to my former colleagues at the Centre for Research in Ethnic Relations, University of Warwick, who provided support and a challenging intellectual environment in the initial stages of writing. My present colleagues in the Department of Politics and Sociology at Birkbeck College have given me the space and encouragement to complete this study, and without their support it would have been much delayed. A number of other academic colleagues have given me help and support, in particular Bob Benewick, John Benyon, Mike Cowen, Andrew Gamble, Clive Harris, Bob Jessop, Michael Keith, Bob Miles and Solomos Solomou. Equally I have benefited from the superb collection of materials on race relations brought together by Heather Lynn at Warwick, which has no doubt saved me many hours of searching. At Warwick I received valuable administrative and secretarial support from Rose Goodwin, Gurbakhsh Hundal, and Charlotte Wellington. At Birkbeck I have benefited from the invaluable secretarial support of Audrey Coppard and Harriet Lodge. My students at Birkbeck during 1987–8 were the unknowing recipients of some parts of this book in the form of lectures, and their comments helped me to sharpen my ideas and to organise this volume somewhat differently.

I owe a deep debt to Steven Kennedy, my publishing editor, for his support of the project despite unforeseen delays. At a personal level my family has provided me with necessary emotional support. Friends in Birmingham and London have seen the project develop and helped me to relax when I needed to. George and Ian were good company on our various trips to watch West Bromwich Albion, and they and the 'Baggies' deserve a special thanks. Christine Dunn helped to keep me going even when the labour got too much. This book is dedicated with much love to my grandparents.

JOHN SOLOMOS
Birkbeck College, London

A Note on Terminology

Contemporary social theorists are not agreed about the meaning of the concepts of 'race' and 'racism', and often use them in a haphazard fashion. Indeed in recent years a lively debate has developed around the terminology that social scientists use in discussing these issues. It is necessary, therefore, before launching into the substantive chapters to clarify how these concepts will be used in the course of this book.

To take the concept of 'race' first. It has long been recognised that, notwithstanding the long history of scientific debates about this category, races do not exist in any scientifically meaningful sense. Yet it is also clear that in many societies people have often acted and continue to act as if race exists as a fixed objective category, and these beliefs are reflected in political discourses and at the level of popular ideas. Common-sense conceptions of race have relied on a panoply of classificatory variables as skin colour, country of origin, religion, nationality and language.

What are the consequences of racial categorisation for politics, ideology and social action? How does the meaning attached to race as a social category generate political debate and discourses? These are the questions that this book addresses. My central focus, then, is on the construction and changing meanings attached to the category of race in British society, and on how in specific contexts it becomes a signifier for a range of social problems and conflicts.

I move on to the concept of 'racism'. In this study racism is broadly defined, in the sense that I use it to cover those ideologies and social processes which discriminate against others on the basis of their putatively different racial membership. There is little to be gained from seeing racism as a signifier for ideas of biological or cultural superiority, since it has become clear in recent years that the focus on attributed biological inferiority is being replaced in contemporary forms of racist discourse by a concern with culture and ethnicity as historically fixed categories.

xiii

A central theme in this book is the argument that racism is not a static phenomenon. In societies such as Britain racism is produced and reproduced through political discourse, the media, the educational system and other institutions. Within this wider social context racism becomes a integral element of diverse social issues, such as law and order, crime, the inner cities, urban unrest, etc.

1 Theories of Race and Racism: An Overview

Introduction

The aim of this book is twofold. First, to provide a critical introductory political analysis of the post-Second World War history of race and racism in Britain. This will involve a detailed overview of the historical context of race and immigration in British politics, the political responses to black immigration in the immediate post-war period, the pressures for legislative controls and restrictions, national and local policy developments in relation to such issues as racial discrimination and racial disadvantage, and the shifts in racial ideologies that took place during the period from the 1940s to the 1980s.

The second aim is to analyse the most important aspects of the racialisation of contemporary British politics. This will be done through an analysis of the growth of ideologies which focused on race as an important political symbol, the role of anti-racist and black political mobilisation, and of the impact of social and economic restructuring on racial and national identities in British society. This part of the book will include a detailed account of the possibilities for social reform and change within the current context of socio-economic restructuring and political crisis management, and look forward to likely developments in the 1990s.

Focus of study

The political dimension of racial relations in British society has, until recently, received little serious attention from social science scholars. While sociological studies abound there has not emerged as yet a

1

major body of research on the various aspects of the interrelationship between race and politics in the period since 1945.

This neglect is hard to understand, given the relatively high profile occupied by racial questions on the political agenda during this period. A clear manifestation of the importance of race to any rounded analysis of contemporary British politics has been provided, however, by the impact of the outbreaks of urban violence which occurred in many inner city areas in 1980–1 and again in 1985. In addition, recent developments in the Labour Party have led to important changes in the role of race issues and black politicians at both a local and national level. Similar trends seem to be at work in the other major political parties. It has also become clear over the years that questions about employment policy, welfare provision, local government, policing, housing, and youth provision have a strong racial element which needs to be taken more fully into account.

All of these issues help to explain why, particularly from the late 1960s onwards, race came to play an increasingly important role in public political debates and official policy analysis. For many on the Right, immigration and race are important issues because of their supposed impact on the cultural and political values of British society. Statements made by politicians, press commentators, the police and government agencies have helped to build up the view that without drastic steps to control immigration and to help deal with the internal impact of race at local and national levels, the whole fabric of British society could come under threat. For the Left too, the emergence of race as a theme in political debate represents a challenge to many received wisdoms about working class politics and processes of class formation. While rejecting many of the most extreme images of the impact of immigrants and race on British society, for example, the Labour Party found itself during the 1960s and 1970s caught within a political language in which its stance on this question resonated with elements of the discourses developed by the right, and no less ambiguous about the position of black minorities within traditional working class politics.

In the context of the late 1980s and 1990s it is clear that the changing form of the politics of racism needs to be situated against the background of wider changes in the political economy of post-war Britain and the social and cultural transformations which are being faced at the present time.

This book will develop a framework for a political analysis of race and racism in contemporary Britain, and suggest some avenues for more research and analysis. The prime focus of this study will not therefore be on the description of all post-1945 debates about immigration and racial issues but on developing a critical analysis of the major processes which can help us to understand the usage of race as a political symbol and the growing importance of debates about racism and anti-racism in contemporary Britain.

Before moving on to the substance of this account, however, it is necessary to say something about the basic features of some of the most influential theories of race and racism and their relevance to the study of racial relations in contemporary British society. This will help to clarify some of the broader questions that we shall address in the rest of this book, and situate the conceptual framework which has shaped the arguments developed in the substantive chapters. A number of the themes of this chapter are ones to which we shall return in Chapter 10.

Approaches to the study of race and racism

In the past two decades, many social scientists have been increasingly preoccupied by the issues surrounding the question of race and ethnic differences in various historical, social, political and economic contexts. Theoretical and political debates have raged during this time, and have sometimes led to bitter conceptual and political arguments. At the same time the question of race has become an established field of study in a number of social science disciplines, most notably in sociology, anthropology and political science. The literature emanating from all these areas of study has multiplied over the years, not only in Britain but also in the United States, Europe, and other societies such as South Africa.

Such developments are certainly a step forward, particularly in a context where the role of state agencies and Government policies is increasingly important to any full understanding of the dynamics of race and racist ideologies in contemporary British society. Certainly this volume would not have been possible without the growing interest in the politics of race and racism over the last few years, and the growth of theoretical and empirical investigations around this issue. The distinctive contribution of this book, however, lies in its attempt to construct a political analysis of contemporary racism which goes beyond the narrow boundaries of existing political science literature on the subject and uses insights from a critical theoretical framework which draws on the approaches of a number of disciplines and scholarly traditions in order to fathom the complex meanings attached to race and politics within contemporary Britain.

Rather than attempt to cover all aspects of theoretical debates about racism the focus of this chapter will be on some of the strands that are of particular interest to this study. Each strand will be analysed in its own terms and with particular emphasis on the fundamental theoretical questions which are associated with it. This will then allow us to explore some of the main criticisms of each strand, particularly as exemplified in some of the recent standard works which have been produced within each framework. From this critical review will follow a discussion of the alternative analytic framework which will be developed in the rest of this book.

Whilst not wishing to spend too much time on the intricate details of theoretical debates about the social analysis of race and racism, it does seem that some clarification of concepts, terminology and differences in methodology is necessary. In particular, we have chosen in the rest of this chapter to look at three main dimensions of contemporary theoretical debates:

(a) sociological studies of race relations and racial inequality in the USA and Britain;
(b) studies of the politics of racism and the role of the state;
(c) neo-Marxist theories of racism in advanced capitalist societies.

There are other dimensions which can be looked at, but these three are the ones which link up most directly with the concerns of this book. After looking at the context and implications of these perspectives we shall then return to the question which we raised at the beginning of this chapter; namely, what are the questions which we should be asking when analysing the politics of racism in contemporary Britain and other advanced capitalist societies.

It is of course possible to analyse and categorise the various theoretical approaches to the study of race and racism from a number of angles. To take just one example Michael Omi and Howard Winant have argued that there are basically three identifiable paradigms in the literature on race: (a) ethnicity-based theories; (b) class-based theories; and (c) nation-based theories. Within each paradigm they identify other sub-divisions and methodological differences (Omi and Winant, 1986: 9–54). Other writers have distinguished between Weberian, Marxist, Neo-Marxist, and World-System theories of racial and ethnic differentiation. The list of paradigms and different approaches seems to be endless (see for example the papers in Rex and Mason, 1986).

(a) The sociology of race relations

The study of racism and racialised social structures can be traced back to the work of classical social theorists and nineteenth-century political thinkers. But as a field of social scientific inquiry and research the analysis of race relations can be seen as originating in the work of a number of American social theorists, including most notably Robert E. Park, Lewis Wirth, Charles S. Johnson, and E. Franklin Frazier. From a different perspective the work of black writers, most notably W.E.B. Du Bois, helped to establish the centrality of race to the analysis of American society. During the period from the 1920s to the 1950s the works of this group of writers helped to establish what came to be defined as the study of race relations, particularly through their studies of segregation, immigration and race consciousness in the United States. During the inter-war period the works of these authors helped to develop a body of sociological concepts which were later to be refined into a sociology of race relations.

Many of the American studies of race up to the 1960s were influenced by the ideas of this group of writers and concentrated on the analysis of the social and economic inequalities suffered by blacks, their cultural and psychological make-up, family relations and political isolation. Following Park, the dominant assumption seemed to be that race relations were types of social relations between people of different racial characteristics, particularly morphological features. In his classical definition of the notion of race relations Park had argued that the main feature of such relations was consciousness of racial differences:

> Race relations, as that term is defined in use and wont in the United States, are the relations existing between peoples distinguished by marks of racial descent, particularly when these racial

differences enter into the consciousness of the individuals and groups so distinguished, and by so doing determine in each case the individual's conception of himself as well as his status in the community. (Park, 1950: 81)

Although in some of his, and his students, work there is an acknowledgement of the economic and social conditions which can help produce race consciousness the focus is on the nature of relationships between races. Thus Park and his followers tended to see the development and perpetuation of racial conflicts in terms of the ways in which phenotypical differences came to be understood in terms of racial definitions and identities. The emphasis was on a cycle of race relations, leading to the assimilation of different racial groupings into a common culture. The cycle was seen as consisting of four stages of contact, conflict, accommodation and assimilation (Park, 1950: 82–4).

While Park's work was by and large descriptive and untheorised it was instrumental in leading to the development of a distinct sub-field of sociological studies of race relations in the United States. This trend was helped by the publication of Gunnar Myrdal's *An American Dilemma* in 1944, which documented the history of black inequality and racial prejudice in the United States. Arguing forcefully for the integration of blacks into mainstream American life, Myrdal predicted that the process of integration and assimilation would eventually replace the processes of conflict and segregation (Myrdal, 1969a; Myrdal, 1969b).

From the late 1940s to the 1960s this model of assimilation became a dominant influence on research in this field in the United States. Pierre L. van den Berghe, for example, characterised the American studies of race in the following way:

The field has been dominated by a functionalist view of society and a definition of the race problem as one of integration and assimilation of minorities into the mainstream of a consensus based society. (1967: 7)

Sociological theorising on race and racism in the United States thus developed around notions of race relations and the race problem as an outcome of processes of group contact and social interaction. Race was considered a relevant empirical referent only to the extent to which cultural and social meanings were attached to the physical traits of a particular social group. This in turn helped to popularise notions about the origins of racial conflicts and prejudice which concentrated on situations of cultural contract. The emphasis in sociological studies of the race problem during these decades was on the origins of race prejudice, the interplay between prejudice and conflict, the impact of assimilation on the life of Black Americans and the processes through which racial conflicts could be mediated or overcome.

Sociological studies of other race relations situations in a number of societies were influenced from the beginning by various aspects of the American literature, as well as by the experience of racial differentiation in South Africa. This was certainly the case in the British context, where the study of race began to establish itself during the 1940s and 1950s. At this time the emergent field of race studies in Britain was dominated by two main themes. First, the issue of coloured immigrants and the reaction to them by white Britons. Second, the role of colonial history in determining popular conceptions of colour and race within British society. Most studies of this period concentrated on the interaction between specific groups of coloured immigrants and whites in local situations. Little theorising was attempted as such, and writers such as Sheila Patterson and Ruth Glass were in fact critical of attempts to subsume the situation of the black migrants under generalised categories of race relations (Glass, 1960; Patterson, 1963).

An early attempt to construct a theoretical framework was Michael Banton's book on *Race Relations*, which was published in 1967. This study looked at race relations from a global and historical perspective, concentrating particularly on situations of cultural contact, beliefs about the nature of race, and the social relations constructed on the basis of racial categories. By looking at the experience of changing patterns of interaction historically he argued that six basic orders of race relations could be delineated: namely institutionalised contact, acculturation, domination, paternalism, integration and pluralism (Banton, 1967: 68–76). From this theoretical framework Banton then sought to analyse the situation in post-war Britain within this framework, and to examine the pertinence during the 1950s and 1960s.

During the 1950s and 1960s there was a great variety of both popular and academic usages of the terms race and race relations, and this was reflected in the debate about whether West Indian and Asian migrants could be defined as a racial group, coloured immigrants or immigrant workers. The concentration on the interplay between colour and immigration reflected the dominant preoccupations not only of academic researchers but of public opinions about the consequences of the arrival of black workers in Britain. Thus during the 1950s and 1960s a number of studies of various situations of contact between black and white communities were published (Little, 1947; Banton, 1955; Glass, 1960; Patterson, 1963), along with studies of how to improve relations between the two communities (Banton, 1959).

Perhaps the most influential body of sociological writing on race, however, is that produced by John Rex. Over the past two and a half decades Rex has produced two major empirical and a number of theoretical accounts of what he calls race relations situations. In his classical study of *Race Relations in Sociological Theory* he attempts to define the field of race relations in the following terms:

> Race relations situations and problems have the following characteristics: they refer to situations in which two or more groups with distinct identities and recognisable characteristics are forced by economic and political circumstances to live together in a society. Within this they refer to situations in which there is a high degree of conflict between the groups and in which ascriptive criteria are used to mark out the members of each group in order that one group may pursue one of a number of hostile policies against the other. Finally, within this group of situations true race relations may be said to exist when the practices of ascriptive allocation of roles and rights referred to are justified in terms of some kind of deterministic theory, whether that theory be of a scientific, religious, cultural, historical, ideological or sociological kind. (1983: 159–60).

According to Rex's analytic model the definition of social relations between persons as race relations is encouraged by the existence of certain structural conditions: e.g. frontier situations of conflict over scarce resources, the existence of unfree, indentured, or slave labour, unusually harsh class exploitation, strict legal inter-group distinctions and occupational segregation, differential access to power and prestige, cultural diversity and limited group interaction, and migrant labour as an underclass fulfilling stigmatised roles in a metropolitan setting. From this perspective the study of race relations is concerned with situations in which such structured conditions interacted with actors' definitions in such a way as to produce a racially structured social reality (Rex, 1986: 74).

In developing his own empirical work on Britain Rex was particularly interested in two fundamental questions. First, he posed the question of how far the black migrants to Britain were equally incorporated into welfare state institutions and enjoyed equal access to housing, education and employment. Second, he explored the consequences of the development of racial inequality for the development of a 'racialised' consciousness among both the white and black and white working class. In one way or another those were the questions which were the focus of his studies of Sparkbrook and Handsworth, and his work on general aspects of race relations policies (Rex and Moore, 1967; Rex and Tomlinson, 1979).

Other attempts were made during the late 1960s and 1970s to develop a generalised sociological framework for the analysis of race and racism. Spurred by the increasing politicisation of racial issues in the United States, Britain and elsewhere a mass of sociological theorising, monographs and case studies was produced during this period. It is notable, for example, that it was during this period that British sociologists began to show a serious interest in this subject, both as it concerned Britain and as a global phenomenon.

With a few notable exceptions, however, most sociologists working in the field of race relations during the 1950s and 1960s did not analyse questions of power and political intervention in any detail. Zubaida wrote in 1972, of the a-theoretical and a-historical nature of many sociological studies of race relations during this period, which led them to ignore the political context of political parties, trade unions, local and central government in their analysis of the British situation:

In spite of the great importance of this issue, this political area of race relations appears to be little researched at any significant level. There is a plethora of studies . . . which are concerned with 'attitudes', 'prejudice' and 'discrimination'. They are remarkably uninformative; for the most part, they tell us about the relative readiness of sections of the population to subscribe to one set of verbal formula rather than another. What we need are studies of

the way the race relations issues enter into the structures, strategies
and ideologies of political parties and trade unions and governmental bodies. (Zubaida, 1972: 141)

The work of authors such as Rex did raise the issue of politics and
power, but it remained a secondary influence on the mainstream of
sociological studies of race relations. Moreover, few of the influential
studies of this period analysed the political context which structured
the meanings attached to race and racism in contemporary Britain.
At a descriptive level some of the issues which Zubaida mentions were
analysed, but they were not integrated into the wider conceptual
debates about the theory of racism or into the analysis of processes of
racialisation in contemporary Britain.

There are of course a number of other aspects of the sociological
and anthropological analysis of races which need to be taken into
account in any rounded overview. This is, however, not our aim in
this study. Rather we want to move on to the contribution of other
analytic frameworks: in the following section we outline the main
contribution of political analysis in this field.

(b) Politics, power and racism

The most important thing to say about the literature on the politics of
racism in Britain is that it is very underdeveloped, both theoretically
and empirically. Whether Marxist, or non-Marxist, most existing
political theory has concentrated almost entirely on the class and
status determinants of political ideology and behaviour, in the belief
that the logic of politics in advanced capitalist societies springs from
the nature of the social structure. Questions about issues such as
gender, race, environmental policy and novel forms of political
organisation have received relatively little attention, and even then
they have generally been added on to existing analytic models. This
neglect is even more noticeable when compared to the voluminous
literature on the sociology of race relations and the social
anthropology of migrant and black communities, fields of study
which have expanded greatly over the last two decades.

Nevertheless, what is also clear is that the dominant focus of the
texts that have looked at the politics of racism has been a limited set of
issues relating only to some aspects of the integration of black
minorities in the established political institutions. Since the early

studies of the impact of immigration and race on the 1964 and 1966 General Elections, the majority of political analyses of race have concentrated on the following main issues:

1. accounts of the electoral politics of immigration and race;
2. analysis of the role of specific politicians, lobby groups and individuals in articulating forms of racialised political discourse;
3. accounts of the history of various racist, anti-immigrant and neo-Nazi groupings;
4. case-studies of particular policy areas or issues;
5. the role of the police and other law and order agencies in relation to black communities;
6. the local politics of racism;
7. studies of legislation on immigration and race relations;
8. studies of the politics of urban disorder;
9. studies of black political action and the role of anti-racist politics.

Over the last two decades all of these issues have received some attention, although not always from a political science perspective, and have led to a small but growing body of literature on each subject. Many of the questions asked in these studies have related narrowly to the role of political parties, Parliament and interest groups. The pre-occupation of much of the literature on British politics with what John Dearlove and Peter Saunders call a 'narrow view of politics and power' (1984: 3–4) has thus been reproduced in the literature concerned with the politics of racism.

In this body of work, produced since the early 1960s, surprisingly little attention has been paid to the question of the substance of the state interventions in this field and who benefited from them; the causes of changes in ideology and policy; the interrelationship between policy changes in the race sphere and other areas of economic, social and welfare policy; and, perhaps more importantly, the mediations between state and society which bring about changes in political and ideological relations within the race field.

Apart from these blind-spots, however, there seems to be a genuine ambiguity about how best to come to grips with the impact of race on British political life. The historical importance of racism in British political discourses and ideologies has hardly been reflected in the mainstream or radical and neo-Marxist accounts of British politics. According to Zig Layton-Henry:

Political scientists have been strangely remiss in neglecting the political consequence of New Commonwealth immigration, despite the political controversy it has aroused and the important implications for integration that are involved. (Layton-Henry, 1984: xi)

Until very recently most standard text books on British politics contained no reference to racism, despite the massive historical and sociological evidence that at different stages of development questions about nationalism, chauvinism, race and ethnicity have played a central role in the social definition of British political culture (Solomos, 1986).

The relative absence of race from the agenda of mainstream political analysis needs to be contextualised against the background of a number of factors. First, as a number of writers have pointed out (Leys, 1983: ch. 1; Coates, 1984; Moran, 1985) political science in Britain has developed along conventional lines, and often did not link up directly with the changing realities of political life in contemporary Britain. Dearlove has pointed out that, unlike most other social science disciplines, British political science was left largely untouched by the intellectual unrest of the 1960s. It was only the acute economic, social and ideological crisis of the 1970s that resulted in a period of soul searching and critical self-evaluation among political scientists, that the discipline experienced the intellectual turmoil and strife which other disciplines had experienced during the 1960s. It was this turmoil that led to a strong feeling among many political scientists that 'the established discourse is no longer an adequate basis for understanding contemporary British politics' (Dearlove, 1982: 437), and a lively debate about the theoretical and empirical basis for the study of the political context of economic, social and political inequalities.

Within this broader context of the development of post-war political science it is possible to begin to make sense of how the encounter with race was dealt with, an encounter which broadly covers the two periods of Dearlove's periodisation. For it was during the 1960s and early 1970s that the political study of racism remained noticeably underdeveloped, particularly when compared with the massive growth of the sociology of race relations over this same period. Having produced little in the way of textbooks and monographic studies during the previous two decades, political science approaches to race issues got a further boost by the growth of the National Front during the late 1970s and the series of violent disorderly protests which took place during 1980–1 and 1985. With the break-up of what Dearlove has called the 'established understandings' of British political life, issues such as gender and race also began to receive more serious attention from within the mainstream of political science, even if only at the margins of established political issues such as inner city policy and unemployment.

A number of sociological and neo-Marxist writings on racism provide a useful starting point for rethinking the interrelationship of race to power relations and political structures, but there are few analytically clear studies of this aspect of racism. During the 1960s and 1970s some studies of voting behaviour, immigration and race relations legislation, were carried out within the framework of political science. But what is interesting is that few of these studies became part of the teaching syllabus in politics departments or attracted the attention of non-race specialists, whether in the mainstream or in the radical sections of the discipline. This gap has been bridged in recent years by the attention given to race issues in some of the new politics textbooks, though this is by no means the case in all of them.

A number of recent texts provide a hint of the value of rigorous political analysis for the understanding of racism as an ideology, the function of state policies, the role of racist political groups, black political organisations, and of the role of race in the urban unrest that Britain has experienced in the 1980s. David Coates, for example, while emphasising the primacy of class in relation to all aspects of British society and politics, also argues that racism, sexism and religion should be seen as relatively autonomous forces in the processes determining the form and content of political action in contemporary Britain. Talking of the distribution of the black population in the white class structure he argues:

> Their incorporation into mainly the lower section of the working
> class initially as migrant labour and their incorporation there,
> because of the racism of society as a whole, means that their
> situation is not reducible to that of white class membership.
> Instead it has a definite 'racial' dimension that shapes its interests

and politics in a way that parallels white class politics, and yet establishes for itself a space of its own. (Coates. 1984: 177)

Examples of this relative autonomy that are mentioned by Coates include the attempts by black workers to organise themselves to defend their common interests, the resistance of black youths to police efforts aimed at criminalising them, and the growth of black feminist ideologies (ibid., 179ff). In essence then Coates is suggesting that the role of the racial dimension of British politics needs to be explored further through an analysis of the interplay between class and non-class determinants of political action.

Dearlove and Saunders adopt a somewhat different angle initially, although they come to the same conclusion about the importance of race and gender divisions in contemporary British society. Rejecting completely any idea that domination on the basis of gender, race or ethnicity can be reduced to a more fundamental form of class domination, they argue that there are in fact different (though related) systems of domination, and that 'the capitalist system of private property and wage labour is only one of them'. From this starting point they go on to look at various forms of non-class power and domination, including (apart from racial divisions) gender, age, religion, and divisions between public and private sector workers (Dearlove and Saunders, 1984: 183ff).

Studies such as these, have made some important contributions to the political analysis of racism in contemporary Britain. But there remain many gaps which can only be filled if the contribution of the studies referred to above can be integrated within a theoretically rigorous and empirically grounded political analysis of racism. Such theoretical and empirical clarification of the roots of racism has not been forthcoming, however. Indeed, racism remains a sadly neglected issue in most discussions of British politics, even in those that are influenced by radical Marxist and feminist ideas. This is despite the attention given to this issue in other disciplines.

This is a more general problem with political science, which has been characterised by Dearlove as a discipline which is closed to influence from other disciplines. His call for a more open analysis of British politics is worth recalling:

We need to be self conscious, sceptical and tentative about our theory, opening ourselves up to a serious and sympathetic consideration of rival problematics and rejecting the philosophers' stone of a simple key to understanding; we need to be alive to the place of our work in politics and sensitive to the implications of the social context within which we work; and we need to be interested in disputes about all these matters within the social sciences, within the sociology of knowledge and within the philosophy of social science. (Dearlove, 1982: 453)

In many ways it seems to be this lack of openness which has held back the serious consideration of racism as a political issue along with complex questions such as the nature of state power and ideology in capitalist societies. If this is the case then there needs to be a more fundamental change then simply adding such issues to an already existing agenda for research and teaching. This can be seen more clearly if we explore the question of the politics of racism in relation to social change and political power, which we shall do later on in this chapter. But before we move on to this dimension it is important to clarify what we mean by a political analysis of racism.

The term is often used to delineate an analysis of a question from a narrow perspective of analysing the actions of governments and political institutions to deal with a specific issue. But the main concern of this volume is not to develop a discrete account of the political aspects of race in contemporary Britain as such. Rather, we are particularly interested in the complex totality of forces in British society which have produced racialised political ideologies and practices, whether these forces be political or not. The interplay of these forces in relation to particular areas of policy provides the substantive content of the following chapters – which look at the development of racialised politics from a variety of angles and within the context of particular policy networks.

One of the paradoxes is that the relatively underdeveloped analysis of the politics of racism in Britain is not so evident in the United States, where social scientists working on racial questions from a number of disciplinary backgrounds have provided a more detailed historical account of racialised political issues. The experience of the race riots during the 1960s, the civil rights movement, black power movements, and the emergence of a black political elite have all formed issues of concern not only for political scientists, but also for sociologists and economists. Additionally, there are by now numerous historical and contemporary case studies of the political context of racism and racial ideologies, which have done much to illuminate the understanding of the political dilemmas faced by American blacks.

Manning Marable (1981) explains this emphasis on the politics of racism on a number of factors, but he emphasises particularly the role of black intellectuals and radical white intellectuals who have emphasised in their work the importance of politics in determining the social and economic position of blacks in American society. Additionally, he cites the experience of the riots during the 1960s as an important source of research on political power and powerlessness in relation to racism. A number of other studies of the U.S. situation have highlighted similar processes, albeit from divergent analytical perspectives (Preston *et al.*, 1982; McAdam 1982).

It is also worth mentioning that a number of the writers on race issues in Britain have been American, most notably Ira Katznelson, Donley Studlar, David Kirp and Anthony Messina (Katznelson, 1976; Studlar, 1978 and 1980; Kirp, 1979; Messina, 1985 and 1987). They have used their training in America to analyse the British experience, and sometimes to theorise about the similarities and differences between the two situations. The work of Katznelson provides examples of the kind of comparisons that can be made between the British and the American situation, as well as a powerful analysis of the role of the interplay between politics and social change in the formation of racialised politics (Katznelson, 1976: xxii–xxiv).

(c) Marxism, racism and class theory

The other main conceptual framework we want to look at in this chapter is Marxism. Marxist discussion of the interrelationship of class relations and forms of social differentiation based on racial and ethnic categories has become intense over the last two decades. This explosion of Marxist debate on this issue certainly contradicts the oft-cited argument that the preferred response of Marxism to non-class forms of social division is either silence or an attempt to force a complex reality into narrow and deterministic models. But what advances have been made through these debates? To what extent have the problems encountered been due to a failure to move beyond economistic interpretations of class?

A number of key questions have dominated recent debates. First, there is the issue of Marx's and Engels' views on the subject, or rather their supposed failure to analyse it systematically. Second, there is the problem of how Marxist concepts of class can help us understand the dynamics of societies that are structured by racial and ethnic categorisation. Third, there is the question of how recent Marxist debates on ideology, hegemony and over-determination can help us understand the development of racism as an important ideological force in contemporary societies. Fourth, there is the question of how the important debates about the class position of women and about sexism interlink with the analysis of race. Finally, a lively discussion has taken place on the alleged 'Eurocentric' bias of Marxist theory.

The starting point of the majority of recent Marxist studies of the dynamics of race and class is that classical Marxism contains no systematic treatment of this question. It has been pointed out, for example, that although the works of Marx and Engels contain a number of scattered references to the pertinence of racial and ethnic relations in certain social formations, e.g. the reference to race as an economic factor in the slavery of the United States, they contain little historical or theoretical reflection on the role of such processes in the capitalist mode of production as a whole. Perhaps even more damaging, a number of critics have argued that several statements on race by Marx and Engels reveal traces of the dominant racial stereotypes of their time and an uncritical usage of common sense racist imagery (Robinson, 1983). Additionally, a number of critics of Marxism have argued that the reliance by Marxists on the concept of class has precluded them from analysing racial and ethnic phenomena in their own right, short of subsuming them under wider social relations or treating them as a kind of superstructural phenomenon (Parkin, 1979; Banton, 1983).

In the writings of Marx and Engels, references to racial and ethnic divisions, along with related issues of religious differences, regional identity and nationality, are organised around two central themes. The first is the question of internal divisions within the working class. A good example of this strand is the question of the Irish workers who migrated to England and Scotland in search of employment. Both Marx and Engels commented at various points in their work on the impact of this division on the consciousness of the English working class and the manner in which it was perpetuated. The second theme to be found in the works of Marx and Engels is the issue of the nation and the national question. They frequently drew attention to the significance of national identities and their interrelationship with class relations. For example, they initially highlighted the effect that the development of Irish nationalism had on the consciousness of the English proletariat. Later, they came to perceive the development of a nationalist movement in Ireland as essential to the emergence of a strong labour movement in England. Their historical works are suffused with references to the emergence, development or demise of nationalities. The analysis provided is by no means as detailed as it could have been, but (a) it does allow us to question the notion that Marx and Engels were silent on forms of extra-class differentiation, and (b) provides a basis for later attempts by Marxists to analyse the impact of nationalism and racism within the working class.

Early Marxist work on racial and ethnic divisions concentrated particularly on race and class as modes of exploitation. Oliver Cox's *Caste, Class and Race* (1948) is an early example of this focus. Cox was primarily interested in the economic interests which produce racist exploitation and ideologies historically, and explained racial inequality as an outcome of the interest of the capitalist class in super-exploiting sections of the working class. Since he saw class divisions as the fundamental source of exploitation in society, the main thrust of his work was to conceptualise racial exploitation as a special form of class exploitation. This model was subsequently to exercise a deep influence on the work of Marxist writers on race in the United States, and to a more limited extent in European and other societies.

New life was breathed into this question during the 1960s, particularly as a result of the regeneration of Marxist debates on class and historical materialism which sought to transcend economic reductionism and partly through increasing political awareness that contemporary racial inequalities were being reproduced in a complex manner which could not be reduced to economistic notions of class. This rethinking of class theory and the historical context of race/class relations is evident in new research on slavery in the United States, studies of racism and labour market segmentation, the analysis of state racism in South Africa and the large body of work on the economics of migrant labour. Out of this large body of research and historical writing since the 1960s a number of main themes have emerged. These have centred on: (1) the question of the autonomy of racism from class relations; (2) the role of the state and political institutions in relation to racial and ethnic issues; (3) the impact of racism on the structure of the working class and dynamics of class struggle and political organisation; (4) the processes through which racist ideologies are produced and reproduced.

The question of autonomy in relation to race and class introduced into this field theoretical problems which had been posed through the analysis of class formation and the capitalist state by radical and neo-Marxist writers. The focus of these writers has been particularly on the interplay between class forces and political strategies (Jessop, 1982; Evans *et al.*, 1985; Alford and Friedland, 1985; Dunleavy and O'Leary, 1987), but in recent years some attempt has been made to utilise the insights of these studies to analyse the politics of racism in Britain and elsewhere.

This influence is particularly clear in the work of Stuart Hall and other Marxist writers in Britain, the writings of a number of American scholars, and the work of several writers on European migration. The starting point of Hall's work is the assertion that it is incorrect to counterpose race to class in a simple manner, since it is the articulation between two in historically specific situations that is the core issue. For example, in a study of Jamaica, he stresses the manner in which class is overdetermined by race, colour and culture. Thus, Hall argues, while one cannot reduce racism to class or other social relations, he also maintains that it cannot be adequately understood in abstraction from wider economic, political and ideological forces (Hall, 1977; 1980; 1985a).

Recent studies in the USA and Great Britain have focused more specifically on the role of the state as a site for the reproduction of racially structured situations (CCCS Race and Politics Group, 1982; Omi and Winant, 1986). Drawing partly on recent Marxist debates on the nature of the capitalist state, a number of studies have analysed the interplay between politics and racism in specific historical settings. Studies of the role of state institutions in maintaining racialised structures in a number of societies, particularly the USA and South Africa, have highlighted the importance of the political context of racism. This has raised important questions and problems: what is the precise role of the state in the reproduction of racially structured social relations? How far can the state be transformed into an instrument of anti-racist political actions? These, and other questions, are currently being explored and debated.

As mentioned earlier, the claim that racism is a source of division within the working class was central to the work of early Marxist writers such as Cox. This theme has once again become central to contemporary debates about racism and class formation, partly as a result of the growth of working class support for racist political groups and the emergence of black politics. In their study of immigrant workers in the class structure of Western Europe, Castles and Kosack deal with the way in which the state has intervened to create two distinct strata within the working class through the system of contract labour, which denies political rights to the essentially foreign lower stratum. This lower stratum is said to perform the function of a reserve army of labour (Castles and Kosack, 1985). In Britain, the work of Miles and Phizacklea on working class racism represents another strand of the debate. Their writings reflect a deep concern with overcoming the potentially divisive impact of racism on class organisation and radical political action (Phizacklea and Miles, 1980; Miles and Phizacklea, 1984). In the United States similar questions have been raised and given the political climate in many advanced capitalist societies this is bound to be of concern for some time to come (Marable, 1985; Omi and Winant, 1986).

The final theme to emerge from the debates on race and class is that of ideology. The development of racist ideologies, and the various forms such ideologies have taken at different stages of capitalist development, has not been an issue which has received much attention among Marxists. But the renewed interest in the analysis of ideology has helped to overcome this neglect, and questions have begun to be asked about the historical, cultural, literary, and philosophical roots of ideologies of race. Specifically, questions are being asked about the role that ideological relations can play in providing a basis for the articulation of racists ideologies and practices (Gates, 1986).

A final aspect of recent debates about the pertinence of Marxism to the analysis of race and racism is the question of whether there is an intrinsic Eurocentric bias in the core of Marxist theory. This is a theme which has been taken up in recent years by a number of critics of Marxism and by others who profess to be sympathetic to the Marxist tradition (Banton, 1983; Rex, 1983; Gilroy, 1987). Perhaps the most important statement of this position is Cedric Robinson's *Black Marxism* (1983) which argues forcefully that Marxism is inextricably tied to Western European philosophical traditions which cannot easily incorporate the experience of racism and ethnic divisions. This and other studies seem certain to raise questions which will play a part in Marxist discussions for some time to come.

What seems clear is that Marxist discussion of the question of race and class is searching for a new agenda for the analysis of the dynamics of racial categorisation, and there are some encouraging signs of development and renewal (Solomos, 1986). Important contributions are being made to this debate from a number of countries, and these are helping to fashion new perspectives on Marxist theory and practice. Above all, recent advances have been made in our understanding of the role of racial ideologies and the function of racialised state institutions, e.g. in South Africa (Bozzoli, 1987; Wolpe, 1987). Much more theoretical and historical analysis remains to be done.

This would be aided by a recognition that the analysis of classical Marxism offers us a method rather than a doctrine and that there can be no simple 'reading off' of theoretical concepts into concrete social formations (Hirst, 1985). If we are to understand the complex interplay between race and class in both historical and contemporary capitalism, the advances over the last decade need to be used imaginatively, since this is clearly an issue of crucial importance both for Marxist theory and practice.

What kind of alternative?

Given the critical tone of the above discussion of existing approaches to the study (or non-study) of the politics of racism, the question arises about what kind of alternative analysis will be offered in this book. There are, in fact, two basic elements which make up the distinctive contribution to the study of the politics of racism offered here. The first is the insistence on the need to look at the impact of racism as it affects politics and ideology in contemporary Britain beyond the scope of conventional politics. This is reflected in the theoretical and historical concerns of Chapters 2 and 3 and the linkage in Chapters 5 and 6 between the politics of racism and the wider socio-economic transformations of British society.

The second distinctive feature of this book is the detailed analysis in Chapters 8 and 9 of the impact of racist ideologies and nationalist discourses, anti-racist discourses, and black political action on political institutions and forms of political mobilisation. Over the last four decades political discourses of race and nation have become a central component of British political culture, a phenomenon which is only partially understood if one looks merely at the role of extreme right-wing groups or the ideologies of the new right. Much more central, and of vital importance for future political change, are the complex interrelationships of power which are represented through the political language of race.

It is not the aim of this book to provide a detailed analysis of all the issues that will be raised, since the main channel for a historical and multi-dimensional conception of the politics of racism must be a critical and more reflexive debate among scholars, researchers and practitioners. There are areas of the political analysis of racism which have still to be analysed and yet others that need to be understood more fully. But such work must be part of a longer-term project which aims to comprehend the 'concrete historical work which racism accomplishes under specific historical conditions–as a set of economic, political and ideological practices' (Hall, 1980: 338–42).

Although much of the recent work on the politics of racism can be seen as a contribution to such an understanding, there are a number of areas which need to be analysed more fully, including (1) the politicisation of racism from the post-war conjuncture to the growth of Powellism and the institutionalisation of racist discourse; (2) the growth of popular racism and its relationship to the broader economic and legitimation crisis of the British state; (3) the role of black politics in redefining the terms of political discourse about race; (4) finally, the politics of policing and disorderly protest in relation to black communities and their environment.

A number of recent studies have addressed these issues in some form or other. Robert Miles and Annie Phizacklea, for example, have attempted to analyse the racialisation of British political culture in the post-1945 period as an outcome of the complex intermingling of economic, political and ideological relations (Miles and Phizacklea, 1984). Zig Layton-Henry has provided a detailed narrative history of the politics of race, particularly in relation to party politics and electoral strategies (Layton-Henry, 1984). Gary Freeman has analysed the differences in the responses of the British and French labour movements to immigration through an intricate account of shifting political ideologies and economic conditions (Freeman, 1979). A number of recent studies have analysed the role of black political mobilisation through the mainstream political parties and in relation to specific policy issues (Fitzgerald, 1984; Anwar, 1986; Jacobs, 1986). More provocatively, and perhaps too abstractly, some authors have talked of the emergence of a new racism, which is defined by the way it mobilises notions of culture and nation to construct a definition of the British nation which excludes those of a different cultural, ethnic or racial background from the national collectivity (Barker, 1981; CCCS Race and Politics Group, 1982; Reeves, 1983; Miles and Phizacklea, 1984; Gilroy, 1987).

The narrow focus of these studies, however, has meant that they have not addressed two core questions. The first focuses on the general characteristics of racism in British society and asks, How do political structures and institutions in Britain function in relation to race and in what ways do they produce/reproduce or help overcome racism? The second question points to a related but more concrete set of concerns about how racism is formed and transformed historically, asking, How does racism shape the ways in which class, gender and other social relations are actually experienced and how do they structure political action?

In the chapters that follow, we shall set down some of the major perspectives which have been used to account for the racialisation of British politics, and evaluate them against each other on the basis of these two fundamental questions. This will lead to a critical analysis of the racialisation of politics at specific points in British history and the substantive content of state interventions to manage race relations in contemporary Britain.

Plan of the book

Chapter 2 examines the migration process in the immediate post-war conjuncture, and looks at the relevance of arguments that the genesis of post-war racist politics can be traced back to developments during this period. This account is taken forward in Chapter 3 through an analysis of the pressures to introduce controls on migration through legislative measures and the genesis of state agencies which regulated the entry of black labour into Britain. This chapter pays particular attention to the debates among political parties about immigration and the reasons why a political consensus in favour of regulation was established.

Chapters 4 and 5 explore the history, mechanisms and outcomes of state interventions aimed at regulating and managing race relations through equal opportunity and anti-discrimination policies. This is done through a detailed critical review of the experience of such policies over the last three decades, both at the national and local political levels. As well as dealing with the actual policies pursued over this period, particular emphasis will be given to shifts in political ideologies.

Chapter 6 attends to the importance of the riots during the 1980s, and the political and policy responses which they gave rise to. Much of the recent political debate on race related issues has been dominated by the experience of violent street disorders in 1980–1 and 1985, and this chapter provides a critical analysis of the actual events and their wider impact.

The focus of the book moves on in Chapter 7 to the analysis of the impact of ideologies of race and nation on political mobilisation. By analysing the continuities and discontinuities between various forms of racist ideologies and mobilisation it illustrates the material basis for the reproduction of racism in contemporary Britain and the implications this has for struggles against racism. Chapter 8 takes up the question of the role of black political mobilisation, anti-racist politics and oppositional social movements and their impact on the political agenda.

As well as dealing with the current forms of this mobilisation this chapter also explores the historical antecedents and the reasons for the limited success of anti-racist strategies in challenging entrenched racist practices. This is followed in Chapter 9 by a more detailed discussion of the limits and possibilities of radical changes in the fundamental structures of racism in British society, and the role of wider social and economic relations in shaping the course of such change.

The book concludes with a discussion of the main theoretical arguments and empirical evidence reviewed in earlier chapters in an attempt to provide an overview of the changes which are currently affecting the politics of racism in contemporary Britain. The particular emphasis of this concluding chapter is on the emergence of new forms of state intervention and new meanings in racist ideologies during the 1980s and how these interrelate to wider changes in society.

Taken together these chapters will hopefully, provide an introduction to the fundamental theoretical and political questions which make up the politics of racism in contemporary Britain. As such this study will no doubt give rise to a number of questions which cannot be fully answered in a single book. But then this book will have achieved its task if it convinces the reader of the need for a critical approach to the analysis of the politics of racism, and the urgency for more theorisation and research.

Summary and conclusion

This chapter has outlined some of the basic theoretical concerns that have guided the writing of this book. The guidelines proposed are basically research criteria that will be developed and expanded upon in the rest of this book, particularly in relation to the history and contemporary forms of racialised politics in Britain. The main emphasis in this book will be on the identification and analysis of the historical context of the politics of race and racism in British society, the role of the state and political institutions in the formation of a racialised politics, and the interplay between racist political action, anti-racism and social movements.

From this starting point, the book aims to develop a critical assessment of existing theoretical approaches to the study of racism. This will be done specifically through an analysis of some of the most important facets of political debates about race and immigration since 1945, and a critical assessment of the role of political ideologies and practices in framing the racialisation of British politics and society.

A volume of this size cannot hope to take up all the themes which have occupied us in this chapter in any great detail. But the following chapters, taken together, are intended as a critical and historically grounded introduction to the politics of racism in contemporary Britain. Each chapter will explore the question from a specific angle, but they will all be linked up by the theme which resonates through the volume as a whole: namely, that the analysis of racism in its various forms requires us to move beyond both abstract generalisations and reductionist assertions, recognising first and foremost the historical specificity and autonomy of racialisation as a political process.

The study of race and racism has clear political consequences, whether intended or unintended. Any analysis of this issue must therefore have a clear theoretical understanding of the questions to be asked, methods to be used, and the political climate within which the research is to be carried out. This is precisely what this chapter has attempted to do. But many of the questions it has raised will perhaps become clearer after reading the substantive chapters, and so we shall return to them for further reflection in the concluding chapters.

2 Race and Immigration in British Politics: The Historical Context

Introduction

This chapter is concerned with providing a historically specific overview of the politics of race and immigration in the period from the late nineteenth century to 1945. This is necessary because it is impossible to fully comprehend the politicisation of racial questions in Britain since 1945 without a historical perspective, despite the tendency in many recent studies of this subject to ignore this dimension.

In particular we shall examine three dimensions of this historical background: (1) the history and political response to Irish migration; (2) the politics of Jewish migration; and (3) the history of the migration of black and other colonial peoples to Britain, particularly in the early twentieth century. These three aspects are the ones which link up directly with the politics of race and immigration in the post-1945 period.

All three aspects are deserving of more detailed analysis, and some important work on the history of these issues has already been carried out. An interesting overview of the major migratory processes since the nineteenth century can be found in Colin Holmes's *John Bull's Island*, which covers the history of immigration and British politics from the late nineteenth century to the 1970s (Holmes, 1988). The history of black settlement in Britain is analysed in some detail in Peter Fryer's *Staying Power*, which contains a wealth of original sources (Fryer, 1984).

The historical context of racism in Britain

In terms of the arguments developed in the previous chapter, an understanding of processes which produce and reproduce social distinctions based on racial and ethnic divisions requires an analysis of both the historical context and contemporary social relations. Only by analysing the way the historical context overlaps with the present is it possible to understand the continuities and discontinuities between contemporary racial ideologies and previous forms.

There is by now a rich comparative literature on the complex historical forms which racial ideologies and structures have taken in different societies over time and space (Greenberg, 1980; Fredrickson, 1981; Wolf, 1982). This body of work includes studies of the development of racial ideologies and institutions in the United States and in South Africa, the two situations that have attracted most attention over the years. But increasingly attention is turning to the history of racial categorisation in other societies, and comparative research is being broadened out to include the situation in societies such as Britain.

Yet it is clear that much of the analysis of race relations in Britain during the post-1945 period has been dominated by perspectives which lack a historical and comparative dimension. There are, of course, some notable exceptions to this trend, and a number of useful monographs have analysed the complex history of racial thought, of immigration and of anti-Semitic and other racist political trends in British society (Holmes, 1978 and 1979; Lunn, 1980; Fryer, 1984). Such studies have highlighted two interrelated issues. First, the complex variety of migratory processes which have occurred at various times in British history. Second, a number of studies have looked at aspects of the continuities and discontinuities between the political and social responses to these waves of migration.

As we argued in Chapter 1, however, the relative neglect of racial and ethnic issues in the study of British politics has had a negative effect on the development of a detailed political analysis of migration and racial categorisation in British society. Thus while in the past decade there has been a renewed interest in analysing contemporary political conflicts over race, particularly in the aftermath of the urban unrest during the 1980s, this has not resulted in rigorous attempts to analyse the main trends in the historical development of racism in British society.

Anglo-Saxons and Celts

The story of Irish migration to Britain and the political responses to it
represents an important, but often ignored, aspect of the historical
background to contemporary debates about race and immigration.
While an Irish presence in Britain can be traced back over several
centuries, the issue of Irish migration is usually considered separately
from other migrations, since in the words of James Walvin it is seen as
a 'special case' (Walvin, 1984: 48–60). More recently, however, the
theoretical work of Bob Miles on migrants has served to emphasise
the historical importance of Irish migration and its relevance to any
rounded political analysis of this issue (Miles, 1982: 121–50). A
number of detailed historical studies of migration from Ireland to
Britain and responses to it have helped to focus more attention on this
question (Gilley 1978 and 1980; Curtis, 1984; Swift and Gilley, 1985).

The history of Irish migration to Britain can be traced back to the
late eighteenth and early nineteenth century (Hechter, 1975). This
was a period of important economic and social changes in both
Ireland and Britain. During this time the migration of Irish labour to
Britain seems to have been largely determined by the uneven
interdependence between the two societies and the pace of economic
and social transformation within them. The genesis of Irish migration
can therefore be traced to a period of rapid economic change,
urbanisation and class formation within British society. According to
the account developed by Miles it was precisely this process of rapid
social change that led to the demand for labour and a search for new
sources of labour (Miles, 1982: 121–50). At the same time within
Ireland, a process of land consolidation was occurring in the north
and east as part of the process of development of capitalist agriculture
(Hechter, 1975; Redford, 1976).

The objective was to produce grain, meat and dairy products as
commodities for exchange in Britain and the result for sections of the
Irish population in these regions was dispossession and ejection from
the land. In the south and west, dominated by small peasant
landowners or small tenant producers, a process of extensive
subdivision of plots was underway, in a context where the population
was increasing and the potato had been introduced as the main crop
and means of subsistence. The consequent 'freeing' of sections of the
population from the land coincided with attempts to establish
capitalist industrial production within Ireland, especially around

Belfast, where a demand for labour was developing. Following the Act of Union, and the subsequent abolition of protective tariffs in Ireland, the development of capitalist agriculture was intensified while the flow of cheap manufactured goods from Britain stemmed the rise of industrial production within Ireland (Miles, 1982; Swift and Gilley, 1985).

During this early period Irish migration to Britain tended to be seasonal, especially on the part of small peasant producers who sought a cash income to meet increasing rent demands. The potato was planted early in the year and then men of the family unit migrated to Britain to sell their labour to British farmers, especially during harvesting (Jackson, 1963; Lees, 1978). In 1841, approximately 60 000 seasonal migrants came to Britain from Ireland but the numbers declined from the 1850s, although demand for their labour power remained high in certain areas. However, seasonal migration was only a serious option for those who retained access to land in Ireland. Thus, in combination with a growing demand for semi-and unskilled wage labour in British urban areas, a second consequence was the development of an emigration from Ireland which resulted in settlement in Britain.

The appearance of potato blight in 1845, and the resulting starvation, intensified a migration that was therefore already well-established (Jackson, 1963: 7–9). The 1841 Census indicated that there were more than 289 404 Irish people living in England and Wales, and 126 321 in Scotland. By the 1851 Census, and largely as a consequence of the famine migration the Irish population increased to 519 959 in England and Wales and 207 367 in Scotland. The peak was evident in the 1861 Census which gave the total Irish-born population resident in England and Wales as 601 634, although in Scotland it had declined somewhat to 204 083. After this there was a slow decline. In 1901, the Irish-born population was 426 565 in England and Wales, and 205 064 in Scotland (Holmes, 1988: 20–1). As a proportion of the total population, the 1851 figures constituted 2.9 per cent for England and Wales and 7.2 per cent for Scotland (Jackson, 1963:11).

There were, as is clear from the above account, two main areas of Irish settlement. In England, the main areas of Irish settlement were London and Lancashire, with smaller concentrations in the West Midlands and Yorkshire (Jackson, 1963; Lees, 1978; Gilley, 1980; Waller, 1981; Miles, 1982; Swift and Gilley, 1985). In Scotland, the main areas of settlement were in various parts of the West, and particularly around Glasgow. This migration and settlement led to the formation of distinct communities, identifiable by cultural differences, notably religion (O Tuathaigh, 1985).

In purely numerical terms the number of Irish migrants to Britain over the past two centuries has been far in excess of any other migration. Yet, as a number of studies have shown, there has been little direct state intervention to regulate this migration and settlement, particularly when this is compared to the response to later Jewish and black migrations to Britain. Part of the explanation for this relative absence of state regulation of Irish migration lies in the fact that in 1800 an Act of Union incorporated Ireland into the United Kingdom. In practice, and then in law, therefore the population of Ireland has been incorporated into a larger political unit within which it had the status of common citizenship and within which it circulated in response to economic and political circumstances, within constraints imposed by the British state (Hechter, 1975; Miles, 1982).

This situation was maintained even after the formation of the Republic of Ireland in 1922, because citizens of the Irish Republic retained the right to freely enter and settle in Britain. Even after the Irish Republic left the Commonwealth in 1947, the British Nationality Act accorded citizens of the Republic the unique status of being free to enter, settle, work and vote in Britain (Evans, 1983: 61). Though there seems to have been some opposition to the continuation of this status in Cabinet during the 1950s (DO 35/5219, 1957), there was no change in the policy of non-intervention in relation to Irish migration.

This laissez-faire approach to Irish migration did not mean that there was no hostile political response to Irish migration. There is in fact a long history of anti-Irish stereotypes and images in British culture (Curtis, 1968 and 1971; Lebow, 1976; Dangerfield, 1976). At various points during the nineteenth century there was a hostile response to Irish migrants to Britain, and this was helped by popular images which stereotyped them in terms of their Catholicism as well as their supposed biological inferiority (Gilley, 1978; Miles, 1982: 135–45; O Tuathaigh, 1985: 20–3). There was also widespread use of violence against Irish migrants (Waller, 1981; Millward, 1985; Gallagher, 1985).

The widespread nature of anti-Irish images in popular culture during the late nineteenth century has been illustrated both in studies of working class and of elite culture. Holmes (1988), for example, argues that in towns such as Liverpool 'a particularly fierce anti-Irish sentiment existed which was capable of combining various complementary strands of antipathy and susceptible to political exploitation' (Holmes, 1988: 60). Drawing on a study of popular images of the Irish in Victorian England Curtis (1968) argued that not only were such images widespread among the working class but that 'many educated Victorians actually believed in the existence of a wide racial and cultural gap between themselves and Irish Celts' (Curtis, 1968: 121). Some aspects of these images were to persist well into the twentieth century.

One final point about such beliefs is important to note, and we shall return to it in later chapters. Images of the racial or cultural inferiority of the Irish were based not only on particular ideological constructions of the Irish but on a self-definition of 'Englishness' or Anglo-Saxon culture in terms of particular racial and cultural attributes. In later years such images of the uniqueness and purity of 'Englishness' were to prove to be equally important in the political debates about black migration and settlement (Reeves, 1983; Rich, 1986).

Political and ideological responses to Jewish migration

From the late nineteenth century a significant factor in the politics of immigration was the arrival of large numbers of largely Jewish migrants from Eastern Europe. The political and ideological responses to this migration have often been compared to the post-1945 politics of black migration. This interest in comparing the two periods is partly the result of the relative importance of political debates about immigration during these two periods. It is also because the Aliens Order of 1905 was a radical departure from previous policies on immigration and formed the foundation for subsequent legislation on this issue up until after the Second World War (Garrard, 1971; Gainer, 1972; Gartner, 1973; Holmes, 1979).

The context of the politicisation of Jewish immigration during the late Victorian and Edwardian periods was the arrival of a new group of Jewish settlers from Eastern Europe, but as Lebzelter (1981) has pointed out it was the response of broad sections of British political opinion to these new arrivals that provides the key to understanding this process. She argues that:

> In the 1880s and 1890s as well as in the post-war period, anti-Semitism in England served as an explanatory model to account for objective problems–unemployment and poverty in the first instance, opposition against British authority in the Empire in the second–by attributing them to the outsider, the Jew. (Lebzelter, 1981: 102)

As an example of how this process worked she gives the example of how in the context of economic crisis and high unemployment the slogan 'England for the English' became a popular slogan for both Conservatives and trade union leaders (ibid., 90).

What is interesting in this context is that the level of political opposition to Jewish migration was not simply related to the number of migrants. The pressure to restrict Jewish migration contrasts sharply with the continuing and unrestricted entry of Irish migrants into Britain, who represented numerically a much larger group. In the late nineteenth century, there were approximately 60 000 Jewish people living in Britain, more than half having been born in Britain. The majority of this population were shop-keepers and merchants, but a smaller proportion constituted a part of the capitalist class and another section were artisans of various kinds (Lipman, 1954: 27–9, 79–81). Between 1870 and 1914, some 120 000 Jewish people migrated to and settled in Britain (Gartner, 1973: 30) and by 1914 the Jewish population had grown to about 300 000 persons (Pollins, 1982: 130). This was relatively small when compared to the size of the Irish community in Britain, but throughout the period from the 1880s to the first world war and afterwards Jewish migration remained a bitterly controversial issue (Lee, 1980; Kennedy and Nicholls, 1981).

The political debates and state actions in response to this migration were partly influenced by the processes of social and economic change of the particular localities of Jewish settlement. For example in the East End of London the political debates about Jewish migration were structured by the context of competition for jobs, housing and amenities. Gainer argues that:

> 'Immigrant' and 'Jew' became synonymous terms because of the extraordinary concern for the social problems of the East End of

London which emerged roughly at the time of the first great wave of immigration. (Gainer, 1972: 3)

Holmes (1979) has shown that this wider social context was an important element in trade union agitation for immigration controls. These demands were recognised in resolutions passed at Trades Union Congresses in 1892, 1894 and 1895, although that section strongly in favour of restrictions on entry was small and weak (Garrard, 1971: 71, 174) because the economic consequences of Jewish migration were experienced by only certain sections of the working class. But the more significant reflection of this opposition was evident in Parliament because a small number of Conservative MPs took up the issue in order to attract working class votes. Their support for restrictions on entry was logically and politically consistent with Conservative demands for state intervention for, for example, the protection of domestic industry (Gainer, 1972: 144; Pollins, 1982: 140). The Liberal Party, on the other hand, remained opposed to restrictive legislation because of its support for free trade and therefore the free movement of human beings as well as commodities (Garrard, 1971: 90).

Parliamentary support for immigration controls was linked with extra-Parliamentary action. In 1901, a Conservative MP for an East London constituency formed the British Brothers League to agitate against Jewish migration and settlement. It organised mass protest rallies and attained a membership of around 45 000 people (Gainer, 1972: 60–73; Holmes, 1979: 89–97). The activities of the British Brothers League gave wider public prominence to the demand for control within Parliament, and agitation within Parliament made Jewish migration a national political issue. The ideological form in which the political issue was expressed, and the motivation for some of the agitation, was explicitly racist (Gainer, 1972: 113) and articulated with nationalism (Garrard, 1971: 56).

The progress of the demand for restrictive legislation within Parliament is well documented (Garrard, 1971; Gainer, 1972; Alderman, 1983: 66–85). Demands for legislation were first raised in 1887, but could not be realised until the election of a Conservative government. But even after this happened in 1895, political circumstances obstructed their realisation until 1905 when the Aliens Order was passed. The legislation applied to the entry into Britain of all non-United Kingdom subjects, to those otherwise defined as aliens. The most important provisions of the legislation were, first, that aliens could be refused permission to enter Britain if they did not have, or did not have the means to obtain, the means of subsistence in adequate sanitary condition; and, second, that an alien could be expelled from Britain without trial or appeal if he or she were found to be receiving poor relief within a year of entering Britain, if he or she were found guilty of vagrancy, or were found to be living in insanitary conditions due to overcrowding. Other provisions of the Order were that the Home Secretary was given the power to expel 'undesirable' immigrants, and that an immigrant refused permission to enter Britain could appeal to an Immigration Board. But the Order also embodied in law the provision that an immigrant could not be refused permission to enter Britain where it could be shown that he or she was the subject of political or religious persecution (Gainer, 1972: 190; Macdonald, 1983: 8; Bevan, 1986: 71–2).

Soon after the Aliens Order became law, the Conservative Government was replaced by a Liberal Government which, although it failed to repeal the legislation, implemented it in a non-restrictive manner. Until 1914, approximately 4000/5000 Jews entered Britain annually (Lebzelter, 1978: 9). But it was the outbreak of war which initiated further legislation on immigration. The Aliens Restriction Act, 1914, passed through Parliament in a single day and gave the government considerable powers to control immigration through Orders in Council, the justification for such powers being in terms of 'national security' in circumstances of war. The legislation applied to aliens whom the government could prohibit from entering Britain, whom could be deported and who could be subject to restrictions on where they lived and travelled.

After the end of the war, the Aliens Restriction (Amendment) Act 1919 repealed the 1905 legislation and extended the 1914 Act for one year, despite the fact that the original justification for the Act no longer applied. In the following year a new Aliens Order was passed and thereafter the Acts of 1914 were renewed annually under the Expiring Laws Continuance Acts. Under the Aliens Order 1920, immigration officers could refuse entry to an alien who was considered to be unable to provide for his or her own support and were given increased powers to deal with aliens who had evaded immigration control. Aliens had to register their residence and any change thereof. The Home Secretary gained the power to deport any alien whose presence was not considered to be 'conducive to the public good'. Finally, if an alien wished to work in Britain, he or she could only do so following the issue to an employer of a permit by the Ministry of Labour, the permit being issued only when it was shown that no British labour was available (Evans, 1983: 10–12; Macdonald, 1983: 8–9; Gordon, 1985: 9–11; Bevan, 1986: 72–4).

It is important to note that it was partly within the terms of this legislation that the British state responded to the growing numbers of Jewish and other refugees fleeing from Germany following the installation of a fascist government (Hirschfeld, 1984; Berghahn, 1984; Holmes, 1988). It is important to recall that the substance of that legislation was that aliens considered to be without the means to sustain themselves could be refused permission to enter Britain while poverty was not sufficient grounds to refuse entry to those claiming to be fleeing religious or political persecution. Events demonstrated that other circumstances were cited as reasons for denying entry to Britain to political refugees. Throughout the period 1933–9, the British government asserted that Britain was not a country of immigration because of its large population and high level of unemployment, and therefore the admission of Jewish (and other) refugees from Germany could only be on a limited scale (Sherman, 1973: 259). In this period of time, about 55 000 refugees from Germany, Austria and Czechoslovakia were admitted to Britain (Sherman, 1973: 271). But despite the evidence of the consequences of events in Germany for the Jewish community there was a political reluctance to act decisively to help refugees from Germany because of the widespread anti-Semitism within British society.

Race and labour in the early twentieth century

As mentioned above the historical presence of black communities within Britain can be traced back over several centuries. Black communities and individuals were a feature of British society and culture for centuries before the arrival of Asian and Afro-Caribbean migrants in the period after 1945. By the end of the nineteenth century black seamen were either settled or a migrant population in Liverpool, London, Cardiff, Bristol and other port towns. This is not the place to go into the details of this history, which has recently been the subject of a number of important and insightful studies (Walvin, 1973; Shyllon, 1974; Fryer, 1984; Ramdin, 1987). But we do want to

look at some aspects of the politics of black migration and settlement
in Britain in the period of the early twentieth century, since it was
during this period that the terms of political debate and domestic
ideologies and policies towards coloured workers and their
communities were formed in an embryonic fashion.

Indeed, it was during this period that the issue of racial difference
begun to play a central role in the politics of immigration. This was
the case despite the relatively small size of the black population, and
the fact that they possessed the formal rights of citizenship.
According to Harris (1988) a central theme in debates about the black
communities during the inter-war period related to the supposed
social problems which their presence gave rise to:

> Social decay was supposed to be connected with the presence of a
> 'Negro' population of Somalis, Arabs, West Indians, West
> Africans and so on who constituted an almost insignificant
> percentage of the population of the seaport towns. (1988: 18)

Such issues were to become a more central feature of political debate
in the post-1945 period, yet it is clear that their origins can be traced,
to some extent, to the inter-war era and the common sense images of
black communities in the seaport towns and beyond.

Part of the history of this period is being recovered by the research
of scholars such as Fryer, Rich and Harris, and by the increased
interest in the history of the black presence in British society (Walvin,
1984; Ramdin, 1987). Much more research needs to be done on this
period of British history, but its importance for any rounded analysis
of the politics of race and racism in British political life is already
clear.

Yet the preoccupation of the bulk of studies in this field remains
with the period since 1945 and is stubbornly ahistorical, even when
written from a radical perspective. This means that many important
connections and continuities in the history of race and racism in
British society are hardly discussed (Cohen, 1988).

Let us take an example of the consequences of such an approach,
and its limitations. In the preceding section, we have been concerned
with the policy of the British state towards the entry into Britain of
people who were, by law, aliens, that is non-British citizens. Yet it is
also clear that the legislation effected by the state was also used to deal
with, and contained provisions concerning, certain categories of

British subjects, specifically seamen recruited in different parts of the Empire, particularly from India and the Caribbean. Despite being British subjects, Indian seamen (widely known as lascars) had been subject to discriminatory treatment by the state since the nineteenth century, if not before, partly in order to limit their settlement in Britain when the passage that they had worked terminated in Britain.

An Act of 1813 required the East Indian Company to provide subsistence for Indian sailors in Britain until they returned to India, while an Act of 1823 stipulated that Indian seamen were not British subjects and prohibited seamen as British subjects, however. These powers were consolidated in the Merchant Shipping Act 1894 which set out articles of agreement to be signed by Asian seamen and masters which bound the former to return to their country of origin and gave the Secretary of State the power to repatriate those who attempted to become resident in Britain (Hepple, 1968: 42–4; Joshua, *et al.*, 1983: 14–16; Gordon, 1985: 5–6). These attempts were only partially successful, as the continuous presence of Asian and Caribbean people in British seaports proved (Fryer, 1984: 294–5; Visram, 1986: 34–54; Ramdin, 1987).

After 1918, the British state reinforced discriminatory practices and made further efforts to prevent British subjects considered to be of a different 'race' settling in Britain. This occurred in the context of the ending of the First World War, during which there had been an increase in the number of British subjects from the Empire employed as seamen. Concerning discriminatory practices, Section 5(2) of the Aliens Restriction (Amendment) Act 1919 legalised different rates of pay for British subjects employed as seamen according to their race (Hepple, 1968: 44–5; Joshua *et al.*, 1983: 16). Additionally, there was a slump in employment in the shipping industry after 1918 and the relevant trade unions campaigned to restrict employment to white seamen. In the resulting competition for work, Indian, Chinese and Caribbean seamen resident in Britain became the victims of racist violence in Cardiff, Liverpool and Glasgow (May and Cohen, 1974; Evans, 1980, 1985; Jenkinson, 1985). In Cardiff, the police sought to 'repatriate' these seamen (Evans, 1985: 73–4). The Home Office pointed out that they were British subjects and therefore were not liable to enforced expulsion from Britain, but also made arrangements for the return of as many seamen who might be 'persuaded' to do so. This initiative by the state was largely unsuccessful (Joshua *et al.*, 1983: 31–2).

Subsequently, a further initiative was made using Article 11 of the
Aliens Order 1920. By reference to this Article, the Special Restrictions (Coloured Alien Seamen) Order 1925 was effected (Hepple,
1968: 45; Joshua *et al.*, 1983: 32–5; Gordon, 1985: 7; Evans, 1985:
80–1; Rich, 1986: 122–30). The Order formally applied to colonial
seamen, previously entitled to sign off from a ship in a British port
and to seek residence there, who did not possess satisfactory
documentary evidence of being British subjects. These seamen were
required to obtain permission of an Immigration Officer before
landing and were subject to removal from Britain. In practice, the
police, Aliens Department and Immigration Officers forced coloured
British subjects possessing the required documentation to register
under the Order, an action that deprived them of the legal status of
British subjects and thereby rendered them liable to the powers of the
Alien Restriction (Amendment) Act 1919 and the Aliens Order 1920,
including the requirement that they register with the police, to whom
they were required to report any change of address, and the
possibility of deportation. Joshua *et al.* comment that:

> The Order was specifically designed to restrict the entry and
> settlement of black colonial British citizens. But, because the
> Conservative Government did not wish to undermine the notion
> of a British subject which was at the heart of the Empire, the Order
> could achieve its ends through a series of legalistic contortions and
> double standards. (1983: 32)

The concern of the state, both at the local and national level, was
multi-faceted. It was responding to local racist agitation and violence
against those defined as coloured seamen, action that was grounded
in the inability of the economic system to provide full employment
(Lunn, 1985). But it was also grounded in a wider, racist concern that
followed from the settlement of these seamen in Britain, specifically
the growth of a population that resulted from sexual relations
between these seamen and indigenous women (Rich, 1986: 120–44;
Ramdin, 1987).

As in the period after 1945 the two most common responses to
black migration and settlement were reflected in political debates
about the need to control the arrival of this group of migrants, and
even in calls for the repatriation of those who were already settled in
Britain. Partly through the violent conflicts which occurred with

some regularity in some of the port towns, but largely through the mobilisation of images of the black communities as a source of social problems, even the relatively small-scale black settlements that took shape in the inter-war period were perceived as alien and a possible threat to the British way of life.

Summary and conclusion

In the light of the story we have told in this chapter, it becomes difficult to sustain the notion that the politicisation of immigration and racial issues is somehow a unique feature of political life in the post-1945 period. By the Second World War there was already a long historical experience of political debate and mobilisation around issues of ethnicity, race and religion. The complex history of these processes has, indeed, only barely been touched in this chapter.

In part the responses of the state and political institutions to Irish, Jewish and black colonial and other migrants before 1945 were the product of the specific social, economic and political conditions prevalent at the time. Yet the experience of the past four decades cannot be completely separated from this longer historical experience of racial and ethnic categorisation in British society. Indeed, it can be argued that we can best understand aspects of the more contemporary experience of racism in British society if we look back at this historical background, and compare the processes through which racialised political action developed in different periods. This is a point to which we shall return once we have analysed the history of race and migration in the post-1945 period.

3 The Politics of Immigration since 1945

Introduction

The story of the politics of migration from the nineteenth century onwards that we have told in the previous chapter has shown us that migration and race were contested issues long before the arrival of large numbers of black colonial migrants in the period since 1945. From the response to Irish, Jewish and early black migration we have seen that the response of political institutions to the arrival of these groups was complex and not uniform. The response to Irish migration, despite a degree of opposition and violent confrontations was markedly different from the attempts to exclude and control Jewish and black migrants. There was also a more limited political mobilisation in defence of the interests of these groups.

In this chapter we shall look at the history of ideological and political responses to the arrival and settlement of black migrants in the period since 1945. Of course migrants from a variety of racial and ethnic backgrounds have continued to come to arrive and settle in Britain, and it is important to any rounded account of migrant labour to look at their experiences (Holmes, 1988). For the purposes of this study, however, we shall now concentrate on the politics of black migration and settlement since 1945.

This period has attracted the attention of most researchers on racial issues in Britain, and there is by now a voluminous literature on most aspects of this phenomenon. Looking specifically at the politics literature, two main themes have been highlighted above all else. First, a number of studies have sought to analyse how the question of immigration per se has become inextricably linked to black immigration, that is the arrival of migrants from the new Commonwealth and Pakistan (Katznelson, 1976; Freeman, 1979; Layton-Henry, 1984).

This body of work has looked particularly at the political debates about black migration and the role of changing political ideologies in the construction of racial issues.

Second, other research has shown how the successive governments have attempted to regulate and eventually to halt the arrival of black migrants through immigration legislation and other means (Sivanandan, 1982; Macdonald, 1983; Miles and Phizacklea, 1984). According to this body of work arguments about the supposed problems created by the arrival of too many black migrants have been used to legitimise legislative measures which have had the effect of institutionalising controls on black migrants, thereby excluding potential migrants on the basis of the colour of their skin.

Both these interpretations have been the subject of much controversy and debate, to which we shall refer in the course of this chapter. The main focus of this chapter, however, will be to analyse and explain the political and ideological responses to the arrival of migrants from the West Indies, India, Pakistan and other new Commonwealth countries. The first section provides a critical review of the development of political opinions and policy response in the immediate post-war conjuncture. We then move on to assess the impact of state intervention on the patterns of black migration, and to look at how immigration became a focus of political discourses and conflict from the 1940s to the 1980s.

The tensions evident in political debates about immigration since 1945 are ones to which we shall return later on, in Chapters 7 and 8. There we shall explore the various ways in which political mobilisation around racial symbols took place, both in the form of racist political actions in the political mobilisation of the black communities themselves. For the moment we shall concentrate on the processes of political debate and decision making.

The post-1945 conjuncture and European migration

During the Second World War the issue of black settlement in Britain became an issue in a number of related, but distinct ways. As a result of the war black workers and soldiers arrived from the colonies to fight in the British army or to help with the war effort (Richmond, 1954; Sherwood, 1984). Additionally, black American soldiers also arrived and attracted a variety of responses (Smith, 1987). At the same time there was concern about two issues. First, the social consequences of the arrival of new groups of black workers and soldiers on the older black seaport settlements. Second, there was increased concern that the arrival of new black migrants could lead to conflict and the institutionalistion of a colour bar in a number of towns.

Despite evidence of increased concern about black immigration both during and immediately after the war, debate about immigration in the immediate post-1945 period was not primarily focused on the arrival of black colonial migrants. Despite the arrival of the SS Empire Windrush in 1948 with some 400 British subjects from the Caribbean, there was no large-scale migration from the colonies and dominions at this stage. Most of the migrants arriving in Britain during the immediate post-1945 conjuncture were from other European countries.

The most important source of migrants to Britain from 1945 to 1954 was Europe. Between 1945 and 1951, between 70 000 and 100 000 Irish people entered Britain. Although some concern was expressed later about the entry of Irish migrants, there was surprisingly little debate about this issue at this stage (PREM 11/1409, 1956; Jackson, 1963; Holmes, 1988).

In addition, the Labour Government was instrumental in encouraging the settlement of Polish soldiers and their families in Britain (Zubrzycki, 1956: 36; Lunn, 1980). In 1940, the Polish Government and Armed Forces in exile (a total of 30 500 persons) were allowed to enter Britain. Additionally, the Polish Second Corps, which joined the British Command in 1942, was brought to Britain in 1946, followed by families and dependants of members of the Polish armed forces. The latter were subsequently disbanded through the Polish Resettlement Corps in the case of those who were unwilling to return to Poland and who were given the option of settlement in Britain. It has been estimated that, in 1949, the resident Polish population in Britain consisted of 91 400 members of the Polish Resettlement Corps, 31 800 dependants of Polish ex-servicemen, 2400 distressed relatives and 2300 additional ex-members of the Polish armed forces. These groups totalled 127 900 persons, to which one can add 29 400 European Volunteer Workers of Polish origin (Zubrzycki, 1956: 62).

The other significant group of migrants which the Government encouraged was recruited by the British state specifically to resolve labour shortages in certain sectors of the economy. On the European mainland, there were several camps for displaced persons or political refugees who were unable or did not wish to return to their country of birth following the redrawing of political boundaries after the defeat of Germany, and the Labour Government decided to send Ministry of Labour officials to them to recruit workers. The occupants of these camps were or had been, in law, nationals of other countries and were therefore aliens as far as the British state was concerned. But the procedures for admission under the Aliens Order 1920, concerned as they were with the admission of single persons, were not appropriate for what was to become a considerable migration. The result was, in the British context, a unique scheme, the British state undertaking to meet all the costs of recruitment, transport and repatriation on behalf of those capitalists short of labour power and, in a number of respects, it anticipated the contract migrant labour system set up by a number of Western European states in the 1950s and 1960s (Castles and Kosack, 1985; Castles *et al.*, 1984; Miles, 1986). The total cost of the scheme up to October 1948 was £2.75 million (Tannahill, 1958: 56).

Those displaced persons who came to Britain were required to sign a contract, the terms of which stated that they would accept work selected by the Minister of Labour and that they could only change that employment with the permission of the Ministry of Labour. Therefore, they became European Volunteer Workers (EVWs). Following health checks, they were admitted initially for one year, an extension being dependent upon the individual complying with the conditions of the contract and behaving 'as a worthy member of the British community' (Tannahill, 1958: 123 8). Many of those recruited were not initially eligible to bring their dependants with them, although most of those who eventually settled in Britain were subsequently joined by their families. The conditions of placement of EVWs in employment varied but usually included the requirements that no British labour was available, that in the event of redundancy EVWs would be the first to be made unemployed, that EVWs should join the appropriate trade union and that they should receive the same wages and conditions as British workers (Tannahill, 1958: 57).

EVWs were recruited during 1947 and 1948 under a number of different schemes, the most important being the Balt Cygnet and Westward Ho schemes. In total 74 511 persons (17 422 women and 57 089 men) were recruited by those two schemes. Most originated from Estonia, Latvia, Lithuania, Poland and Yugoslavia. In addition 8397 Ukranian prisoners of war were brought to Britain for political reasons in 1947 and it was subsequently decided to treat them as EVWs. Under the North Sea and Blue Danube schemes, 12 000 German and Austrian women were recruited on a distinct temporary contract for two years, most returning to Germany and Austria on the termination of the contract. Under a similar arrangement, 5000 Italians of both sexes were also recruited (Tannahill, 1958: 5–6, 30–3). Although approximately 85 000 refugees were recruited as workers for employment in the late 1940s, this total was lower than that orginally envisaged. For example, it was anticipated that 100 000 workers would be recruited in 1948 alone.

The encouragement given to these two groups of migrants to settle in Britain contrasted with the concern of the Government with the social and political consequences of the relatively small-scale migration from the colonies during this period. What recent research has made clear is that even at this early stage black migration and settlement was politically perceived in a different way from European migration. Privately the Government was considering the most desirable method of discouraging or preventing the arrival of coloured British citizens from the colonies.

Migration, colonial labour and the State: 1945–62

At the end of the Second World War the British state had legislative powers in the form of the Aliens legislation to control the entry into Britain of non-British subjects and their access to the labour market. However, the vast majority of British subjects in the colonies and dominions retained a legal right to enter and settle in Britain. This legal right was confirmed by the British Nationality Act of 1948 which, in response to the granting of independence to India, made a formal distinction between British subjects who were citizens of the United Kingdom and Colonies and those who were Commonwealth citizens, both categories of people having the right to enter, settle and work in Britain (Evans, 1983: 59–62; Bevan, 1986: 112–13). Additionally, citizens of the Republic of Ireland retained the right of unrestricted entry and settlement.

As we have seen already, despite the fact that the vast majority of British subjects from the colonies and independent Commonwealth countries retained the right to enter and settle in the UK, the concern of the state was to encourage the use of migrant labour from Europe to meet the demand for labour. Some British subjects from the colonies did arrive during this period, particularly from the West Indies, but almost as soon as they began to arrive they were perceived as a problem.

The relatively liberal attitude towards the arrival of European workers contrasted sharply with the fears expressed about the social and racial problems which were seen as related to the arrival of coloured colonial workers who were British subjects. Both the Labour Governments of 1945–51 and Conservative Governments throughout the 1950s considered various ways to stop or reduce the number of black migrants arriving and settling in Britain (Joshi and Carter, 1984; Carter, Harris and Joshi, 1987; Dean, 1987).

It was during the period from 1945–62 that the terms of political debate about coloured immigration were established, leading to a close association between race and immigration in both policy debates and in popular political and media discourses.

Contrary to the arguments of some scholars it seems quite inadequate to see this period as an age of innocence and lack of concern about black immigration into the UK (Rose *et al.*, 1969; Patterson, 1969; Deakin, 1970). Throughout this period an increasingly racialised debate about immigration took place, focusing on the supposed social problems of having too many black migrants and the question of how they could be stopped from entering given their legal rights in the 1948 British Nationality Act.

Although much publicity was given to the arrival of 417 Jamaicans on the Empire Windrush in May 1948, and subsequent arrivals by large groups of West Indian workers, the focus on coloured immigration helped to obscure the fact that the majority of immigrants continued to come from the Irish Republic, from white Commonwealth countries and other European countries (Patterson, 1969: ch. 1; Miles and Phizacklea, 1984: 45–8). The concentration on the number of West Indian immigrants, and later on the number of immigrants from India and Pakistan, has been shown to have been an issue of debate within the Cabinet during the period 1950–5, when various measures to control black immigration and to dissuade black workers from coming to the UK were considered. On the basis of a careful analysis of Cabinet and Ministerial debates about immigration from the colonies a recent study has concluded that the period from 1948 to 1962 involved the state in complex political and ideological racialisation of immigration policy (Carter, Harris and Joshi, 1987).

The period between the 1948 Nationality Act and the 1962 Commonwealth Immigrants Act is frequently characterised as one in which the principle of free entry of British subjects to the UK was only relinquished with great reluctance and after considerable official debate. This was not the case. On the contrary, the debate was never about principle. Labour and Conservative Governments had by 1952 instituted a number of covert, and sometimes illegal, administrative measures to discourage black immigration (Carter, Harris and Joshi, 1987).

Additionally, throughout the 1950s the debate about immigration in Parliament and the media began to focus on the need to control black immigration. Although both in public debate and in private policy discussions attention was sometimes focused on the behaviour of undesirable black migrants, such as those involved in crime or prostitution, the terms of political debate through the 1950s were also about the desirability of letting into Britain a sizeable number of West Indian or Asian migrants.

The 1958 riots in Notting Hill and Nottingham may have helped to politicise this process further (Miles, 1984; Pilkington, 1988). But it is clear that both before and after the riots themselves the question of control was being integrated into the policy agenda.

With the growing emphasis on the control of coloured immigration the terms of ideological and policy debates about the future of black migration turned on two themes which were to prove influential later on. First, a vigorous debate took place in and out of Parliament about the possibility of revising the 1948 Nationality Act so as to limit the number of black workers who could come and settle in the UK. The terms of this debate were by no means fixed purely by political party ideologies, and there was opposition from both Conservative and Labour politicians to the call for controls and the abandonment of the free entry principle. Second, a parallel debate developed about the problems caused by too many coloured immigrants in relation to housing, employment and crime. This second theme became particularly important in the period 1956–8, and in the aftermath of the 1958 riots (*Hansard*, Vol. 596, 1958: Cols 1552–97).

By linking immigration to the social aspects of the colour problem a theme was established which was later to prove influential in shaping both the immigration control legislation and the Race Relations Acts. This was the argument that it was necessary to use direct state intervention to halt the gathering momentum of black migration and to resolve the social problems which were perceived as linked to it.

Controls on coloured immigration had been discussed as early as the late 1940s, and were seriously discussed again in 1954 and 1955. A number of arguments were used in opposition to such controls, and it was not until 1961 that a Bill to control Commonwealth immigration was introduced by the Government. The reasons for the reluctance to introduce controls remains to some extent a matter of speculation, although the release of Government documents for the period of the early 1950s has shed some light on this non-decision making process (Joshi and Carter, 1984: 55–63; Rich, 1986: ch. 7). But at least part of the reluctance to introduce controls seemed to result from a concern about whether legislation which excluded black people could be implemented without causing embarrassment to Britain's position as head of the Commonwealth and Colonies, the fear that it would divide public opinion, and a doubt about the legality of controls based on colour in both British and international law (Deakin, 1968: 26–30; Miles and Phizacklea, 1984: ch. 2).

What is clear, however, is that the period from the late 1940s to the late 1950s was not a period of laissez faire in relation to black migration. Rather it was one of intense debate within Government departments and in public circles about the impact of black immigration on housing, the welfare state, crime and other social problems.

It is important to note, however, that these debates were not purely about the supposed characteristics of black migrants. They were also about the effect of black immigration on the racial character of the British people and on the national identity. Harris (1988) makes this point clear when he argues that the debates about black immigration during the 1950s reinforced a racialised construction of 'Britishness' which excluded or included people on the grounds of race defined by colour:

> When individuals like the Marquis of Salisbury spoke of maintaining the English way of life, they were not simply referring to economic or regional folk patterns, but explicitly to the preservation of 'the racial character of the English people'. We have

developing here a process of subjectification grounded in a racialised construction of the 'British' Subject which excludes and includes people on the basis of 'race'/skin colour. (Harris, 1988: 53)

This process was still in its early stages in this period, but it is impossible to understand the legislation passed to control black immigration during the 1960s and 1970s without referring to the genesis and articulation of political discourse about black immigration during the period from 1945 to 1962.

Immigration and racialised politics

The 1958 race riots, in Nottingham and Notting Hill, are commonly seen as an important watershed in the development of racialised politics in Britain. It is certainly true that the events in these two localities helped to bring to national prominence issues which had previously been discussed either locally or within government departments.

The riots themselves consisted of attacks by whites on blacks but this did not prevent them being used as examples of the dangers of unrestricted immigration. By the time of the 1958 riots, however, the mobilisation of opinion in and out of Parliament in favour of controls was well advanced, and the disturbances in Nottingham and Notting Hill were used by the pro-immigration controls lobby to support calls for the exclusion or even the repatriation of 'undesirable immigrants'. They were also used in support of the argument that black immigration was a threat to the rule of law in the inner cities and endangered the 'English way of life'. Lord Salisbury used the riots to justify his claim that controls should be imposed on black immigration, and he argued that 'he was extremely apprehensive of the economic and social results, for Europeans and African alike, that were likely to flow from an unrestricted immigration of men and women of the African race into Britain' (*The Guardian*, 3 September 1958).

It is noticeable that between these events and the introduction of the Commonwealth Immigrants Bill in 1961 a number of important debates on immigration control took place in Parliament and at party conferences. (Patterson, 1969; Freeman, 1979: 49–52; Miles, 1984). In Parliament a number of Conservative MPs, including Cyril

Osborne, organised a campaign in favour of immigration controls, though they made their case against coloured migrants largely through coded language. The Labour Party, along with the Liberals, generally argued against controls, though this was by no means the case for all Labour MPs and local councillors (Reeves, 1983: ch. 7; Layton-Henry, 1984: 31–43).

Outside Parliament there was widespread coverage in both the popular and serious newspapers of stories relating to race and immigration issues. There was a flowering of popular debate about housing and social conditions in areas of black settlement, about aspects of employment and competition for jobs, and a resurgence of extreme right groups which sought to use immigration as a basis for political mobilisation. The interplay between these processes produced a wide variety of stereotypes and popular images about black people. In September 1958 *The Times* reported that in the areas affected by the riots:

> There are three main charges of resentment against coloured inhabitants of the district. They are alleged to do no work and to collect a rich sum from the Assistance Board. They are said to find housing when white residents cannot. And they are charged with all kinds of misbehaviour, especially sexual. (*The Times*, 3 September 1958)

It was precisely around such concerns that the extreme right groups focused much of their propaganda during and after the riots. There was no need in this context for such beliefs to be substantiated by evidence, but it proved equally difficult to counteract such stereotypes. This weakened the attempts to resist the pressures for immigration controls.

The ambiguities in the presence for controls became even more pronounced during the early 1960s, the period of the passage of the first legislative measures controlling the immigration of citizens of the United Kingdom and colonies, the 1962 Commonwealth Immigrants Act. It is to this period that we now turn.

Immigration controls and state racism

In the previous section we argued that the racialisation of the immigration issue during the 1950s laid the basis for the move towards the control of black immigration, an objective which was first implemented through the 1962 Commonwealth Immigrants Act. Part of the dilemma faced by the Conservative Government of the time was how to legitimise a policy which aimed to control black immigration as a more universal measure. William Deedes, who was a Minister without Portfolio at the time, recalls that

> The Bill's real purpose was to restrict the influx of coloured immigrants. We were reluctant to say as much openly. So the restrictions were applied to coloured and white citizens in all Commonwealth countries – though everybody recognised that immigration from Canada, Australia and New Zealand formed no part of the problem. (Deedes, 1968: 10)

The racialisation of the immigration issue was in other words done through coded language: 'commonwealth immigrants' were seen as a 'problem', but 'race' itself was not always mentioned as the central issue. The politicisation of such terms was later to lead to a situation where, despite the continuing scale of white immigration, popular common sense perceived all immigrants as black, and 'immigration' became a coded term for talking about racial questions.

Two competing explanatory models have been used to explain the move towards immigration controls. Some scholars have seen this shift as a response by the state to the pressure of popular opinion against black immigration (Foot, 1965; Rose *et al.*, 1969). This is also the main line of argument used by some of the main political figures involved in the crucial debates about control of black immigration (Butler, 1971; Macmillan, 1973). Yet others have argued that the state was responding to the economic interests of the capitalist class, which required the adoption of a migrant labour system which undermined the right of black workers to migrate and settle freely in the UK (Sivanandan, 1982: 101–26).

Both explanations have been widely used in the extensive literature on the politics of immigration, but as we have indicated already it seems inadequate to view the role of the state as purely responsive, whether to popular opinion or to economic interests. Throughout the period 1948–62 the state was actively involved in monitoring and regulating the arrival of black workers, and helped to articulate a definition of the immigration question which was suffused with racialised categories. Additionally, as recent research seems to indicate the Conservative Government came close to agreeing on a policy of controls on black immigration in 1955–6 (Carter, Harris and Joshi, 1987).

The genesis of the demand for the control of black immigration during the early 1950s matured during the period 1955–62 into a concerted campaign within the Cabinet, Parliament, the media and political parties, in favour of action to 'curb the dangers of unrestricted immigration'. This in turn led to the policy debate which developed in the period leading up to the introduction of the Commonwealth Immigrants Bill in 1961 about the formulation of legislation which could exclude black labour from entry and settlement. This process can hardly be interpreted as a move from laissez faire to state intervention, since the state and its institutions were already heavily involved in defining the terms of the debate about the problems caused by black immigration.

The 1962 Commonwealth Immigrants Act

The acceptance of the need to extend administrative controls on black immigration into legislative action was formally announced in October 1961, when the Conservative Government announced the introduction of the Commonwealth Immigrants Bill. The controls announced under the Bill were legitimised by arguments about the need for a halt to black immigration because of the limited ability of the host society to assimilate coloured immigrants. Even though some MPs and commentators were reluctant to accept that the Bill was simply a way of dealing with the immigration of coloured workers, the Labour Party and sections of the media identified the Bill as a response to crude racist pressures. Hugh Gaitskell, as Leader of the Labour Party, led a particularly strong attack on the Bill in Parliament and its crude amalgamation of immigration with race (Patterson, 1969: 17–20; IRR Newsletter: May 1962). But despite strong criticism from the Labour Party and sections of the press, the collective pressures against the entry of black British succeeded when the Commonwealth Immigrants Act became law in 1962.

Since it was the outcome of the sustained political campaign against black immigration, it is not surprising that despite claims to the contrary, the main clauses of the Act sought to control the entry of black Commonwealth citizens into the UK. The Act introduced a distinction between citizens of the UK and Colonies and citizens of independent Commonwealth counties. All holders of Commonwealth passports were subject to immigration control except those who were (a) born in the UK; (b) held UK passports issued by the UK Government; or (c) persons included in the passport of one of the persons excluded from immigration control under (a) or (b) (Macdonald, 1983: 10–12). Other Commonwealth citizens had to obtain a Ministry of Labour employment voucher in order to be able to enter the UK. The Act initially provided for three types of vouchers:

CATEGORY A: Commonwealth citizens who had a specific job to come to in Britain.
CATEGORY B: Applicants who had a recognised skill or qualification which was in short supply in Britain.
CATEGORY C: All other applicants, priority treatment being given to those who had served in the British forces during the war.

The creation of these different categories was legitimised in coded terms as a way of controlling the number of immigrants entering the country, but it was clear in both the parliamentary and the media debates about the Bill that it was widely seen as a piece of legislation specifically aimed at black migrants. In this sense the 1962 Act can be seen as the climax of the campaign for the control of black immigration which was launched from both within and outside government during the 1950s.

Public debate about the Act reflected a variety of views and was by no means all in favour of it. In fact, a number of lead articles in the press during 1961–2, along with sections of the Labour Party, expressed opposition to the racist thinking behind the Act. Concern was also expressed about the possible consequences of the passage of the Act for Britain's standing in the black Commonwealth countries (Deakin, 1968).

The changing terms of political debate

Almost as soon as the Act became law there was a widespread political debate about its effectiveness. During the period from 1963 to 1972, when the voucher system was abolished, there was pressure to cut back the number of vouchers allocated, and this was reflected in a fall from a level of 30 130 vouchers in 1963 to 2290 in 1972. Significantly, no controls were imposed on the entry of citizens of the Irish Republic into Britain. Nevertheless opponents of immigration were quick to call for even tighther controls, and in the political climate of the mid 1960s their voices were a major influence on the terms of political debate about race and immigration.

The opposition of the Labour Party to the 1962 Act was not sustained. When Harold Wilson took office as Labour Prime Minister in 1964 he announced that the Commonwealth Immigrants Act would be maintained. In 1965 the Government issued a White Paper on *Immigration from the Commonwealth* which called for controls to be maintained in an even stricter form, along with measures to promote the integration of immigrants. The White Paper represented a shift in the direction of what some have called a 'Little England' policy (Rose *et al.*, 1969: 229), and signalled a convergence of the policies of the Conservative and Labour Parties in favour of immigration controls (Wilson, 1971). This was to be exemplified by the nature of the political debate about race and immigration during the period from 1964 to 1970, when the Labour Party was in power. Three events that represent good examples of this debate are the controversies over the electoral contest in Smethwick in 1964 and the East African Asians during 1968–9, and the political turmoil caused by Enoch Powell's intervention in this debate from 1968 onwards.

Smethwick and immigration

The impact of events in Smethwick during 1964 on the terms of national political debates about race and immigration is sometimes forgotten in hindsight. Yet it is no exaggeration to say that the political turmoil around the issue of immigration in Smethwick and the surrounding area had a deep impact on both the local and national political scene. Popular debate and media coverage was aroused by the contest between the Labour candidate, Patrick Gordon Walker, who was widely seen as a liberal on immigration, and the Conservative Peter Griffiths who fought the election largely on the basis of defending the interests of the local white majority against the 'influx of immigrants' (Foot, 1965; Deakin, 1972). In the volatile political climate of the time one of the slogans commonly heard during the election campaign was 'If you want a nigger for a neighbour vote Labour', and Griffiths was later to defend the use of this slogan as 'a manifestation of popular feeling' about immigration in the area, and refused to condemn those who used it (*The Times*, 1968: 139; Griffiths, 1966).

The debate about the implications of Griffiths' victory in Smethwick carried on for some time and was influential on both the Labour Party (*The Economist*, 7 August 1965; Deakin, 1965; Wilson, 1971; Crossman, 1975) and the Conservative Party (Berkeley, 1977; Layton-Henry, 1980). Within the West Midlands region in particular the events in Smethwick helped to shift political debate and attitudes in both major parties towards a stance which emphasised their support for strict controls on black immigration (Lenton, *et al.*, 1966; Deakin, 1972).

East African Asians

One of the features of the 1962 Act was that citizens of the United Kingdom living in independent Commonwealth countries were exempt from control provided they had a UK passport. This included a large number of European settlers as well as a sizeable number of East African Asians in Kenya and Uganda. During the period from 1965 to 1967 a steady flow of this group began to arrive in Britain and when sections of the media and MPs started to call for action to be taken to stop their arrival a heated political debate ensued in late 1967 and early 1968.

The political debate about the right of East African Asians to enter Britain reached its high point in February 1968. As noted above the Labour Party had moved towards acceptance of the need for firm immigration controls during the period from 1963–5, and so it came as no surprise when it responded to this political campaign by introducing the second Commonwealth Immigrants Act in early 1968. This Act sought to control the flow of East African Asians by bringing them under immigration control. Under the new law any citizen of the United Kingdom or colonies, who was the holder of a passport issued by the UK Government, was subject to immigration control unless they or at least one parent or grandparent was born, adopted, naturalised or registered as a citizen of the United Kingdom and colonies in the UK.

The political context in which the Act was passed made it difficult to argue that it was non-racial, as to some extent had been claimed by the Conservative Government which had passed the 1962 Act. *The Times* contrasted the behaviour of the Labour Government to the attitude of the Labour opposition in 1962 and went so far as to call the Act a 'colour bar' and 'probably the most shameful measure that the Labour members have even been asked by their whip to support' (27 February 1968).

The transformation of the political climate between 1962 and 1968 was, however, clear enough for all to see in the Parliamentary debates about the 1968 Act. Given the highly politicised nature of the debate around the Act and the defensive stance taken by the Government, only a few MPs and newspaper commentators saw fit to question the racism which underlay the legalisation (Freeman, 1979: 56; Miles and Phizacklea, 1984: 59–67). Indeed the period between the 1968 Act and the 1970 election, which saw the return of a Conservative Government, saw a further racialisation of the immigration issue. Even though it was difficult to see how immigration could be cut even further than the controls imposed by the 1962 and 1968 Acts, it was precisely during the period 1968–70 that immigration and race relations became issues of partisan political debate on a larger scale than before.

Powellism and political debate

During this period the Labour Government was forced on the defensive by Enoch Powell's famous 'rivers of blood' speech in Birmingham in April 1968, which helped to popularise the common sense racial message that even tighter controls on immigration were not enough to deal with the race problem. In this speech, and in a succession of others over the next few years, Powell sought to warn of what he saw as (a) the dangers of immigration leading to a 'total transformation to which there is no parallel in a thousand years of British history, and (b) the longer term of danger of increasing racial tensions manifesting themselves in Britain on the American model. In the most infamous section of his Birmingham speech Powell said that as he looked into the future he felt deep forebodings about the fate of the nation if present trends were continued, and went on:

> As I look ahead, I am filled with foreboding. Like the Roman, I seem to see 'the River Tiber foaming with much blood'. The tragic and intractable phenomenon which we watch with horror on the

other side of the Atlantic, but which there is interwoven with the history and existence of the States itself, is coming upon us here by our own volition and our own neglect. (*The Observer*, 21 April 1968).

According to Powell's argument the long-term solution to the immigration issue went beyond the issue of immigration controls and was likely to involve the repatriation of immigrants already settled in the UK. Such a line of argument helped to push political debate beyond controls as such and established repatriation as part of the political agenda. Indeed in the same speech Powell used all his rhetorical powers to construct an image of white Britons increasingly becoming isolated and strangers in their own country:

> They found their wives unable to obtain hospital beds in childbirth, their children unable to obtain school places, their homes and neighbourhoods changed beyond recognition, their plans and prospects for the future defeated. (*Ibid.*)

Against this background Powell was able to argue that it was the failure of successive Governments to act decisively to halt immigration in the 1950s that had led to a situation where more drastic measures were required to solve the problem.

The furore caused by the speech was such that Powell was forced out of the Shadow Cabinet, and there was extensive media coverage of the issues he raised throughout 1968 and 1969, and in the period leading up to the 1970 General Election (IRR Newsletter, April/May 1968 and April 1969). It acted as a focus for those calling not only for tighter controls on black immigration but for action to facilitate the repatriation of those black migrants already settled.

Institutionalising immigration controls

Within the political climate created by Powell's interventions and the ensuing political debates the continued arrival of the dependants of Commonwealth migrants already settled in the UK helped to keep the numbers game alive, leading to increasing calls in and out of Parliament, and the media for more action to halt immigration and to deal with the problems that were popularly seen as associated with it.

The combined effect of those two pressures, and the use of immigration as an electoral issue, opened up the possibility of further legislative measures. In 1969 the Labour Government introduced the Immigration Appeals Act, which was officially based on the report of the Committee on Immigration Appeals headed by Sir Roy Wilson (Macdonald, 1983: 269). This report accepted the need for restrictions on immigration, but argued that a system of appeal ensured that the restrictions were applied fairly. Although this Act is sometimes interpreted as a positive measure, it institutionalised a process of deportation for those breaking conditions attached to entry. It also legitimised restrictions on the right of entry of those who were legally entitled to settle in the UK through the obligation that dependants seeking settlement in Britain had to be in possession of an entry certificate. Such certificates had to be applied for by an interview at the nearest British High Commission. Applicants had to prove their claimed relationship to the person legally resident in Britain, and if they were unable to do so they could be denied entry. It is under this system that many recent controversial cases have arisen (Moore and Wallace, 1975; CRE, 1985b).

The marked shift of the Labour Party towards the idea of firm immigration controls was part of a wider political process, which led to the introduction of the 1971 Immigration Act by the Conservative Government. During the 1970 election campaign the Conservative Party had promised them there would 'be no further large-scale permanent immigration'. When the Immigration Bill was introduced in February 1971 it was legitimised on this basis, but as a number of speakers pointed out during the debates on the Bill it was difficult to see how it would actually reduce the number of primary immigrants further. In essence the 1971 Act qualified the notion of citizenship by differentiating between citizens of the United Kingdom and colonies who were 'patrial' and therefore had the right of abode in Britain, and non-patrials did not. The most important categories of patrials were:

(a) citizens of the United Kingdom and colonies who had the citizenship by birth, adoption, naturalisation or registration in the United Kingdom or who were born of parents, one of whom had United Kingdom citizenship by birth, or one of whose grandparents had such citizenship.
(b) citizens of the United Kingdom and colonies who had at any time settled in the United Kingdom and who had been ordinarily resident in the United Kingdom for five years or more.

Under the Act all aliens and Commonwealth citizens who were not patrials needed permission to enter Britain. Whilst before, Commonwealth citizens entering under the voucher system could settle in Britain, after the 1971 Act came into force they entered on the basis of work-permits. They thus became subject to control by annual work-permit, and thus to the non-renewal of the permit. This change of status has been defined by some scholars as a move towards the migrant worker system of other European countries, with Commonwealth workers who were not patrials (and by definition almost certainly black) reduced to the effective status of short-term contract workers rather than settlers (Castles and Kosack, 1985; Sivanandan, 1982: 108–12).

During the Parliamentary debates on the 1971 Immigration Act the amalgamation of immigration with race became an issue of dispute between the Conservative and Labour parties. Although during the late 1960s the Labour Party effectively accommodated itself to a 'White Britain Policy', in 1971 it felt moved to question the treatment of Commonwealth immigrants along the same lines as aliens and the overtly racial criteria which underlay the notion of partiality. Despite the fact that the new Act was rightly seen as racialist because it allowed potentially millions of white Commonwealth citizens to enter under the patriality clause and settle in Britain, a right denied to almost all non-white Commonwealth citizens, successive Immigration Rules issued by the Home Secretary to supplement the 1971 Act have emphasised the intention of the Act to keep out black Commonwealth citizens as opposed to whites (Macdonald, 1983: 25–30). With the exception of the Ugandan Asians who were expelled by Idi Amin in 1972, and some of whom were allowed to settle in Britain during 1972–3, this policy has been consistently pursued ever since. Additionally such measures have emphasised the essentially sexist nature of immigration controls (WING, 1985).

The decade between 1961 and 1971 had seen the introduction of three major pieces of legislation aimed largely at excluding black immigrants. The 1971 Act eventually took away the right of black Commonwealth immigrants to settle, and thus represented an important step in the institutionalisation of racist immigration controls.

Immigration and race in the Thatcher years

The amalgam of immigration controls and race relations policies as a solution to the problem was fostered under the Labour administration between 1974–9. But in the lead-up to the 1979 election sections of the Conservative Party, including its leader Margaret Thatcher, chose to emphasise the dangers posed to British social and cultural values by the black communities already settled here. Thatcher's famous 'swamping' statement in 1978 was part of a wider campaign to use race as a symbol for the neo-Conservative ideology of Thatcher's wing of the party (Barker, 1981). Even though the political language used still referred to immigrants, the main reference point of this campaign were the black communities already settled in Britain. Immigration control remained an issue of public and policy debate, particularly in relation to dependants and the marriage partners of those settled legally (Gordon, 1985).

The policies pursued by the Conservative Government since 1979 represent a further stage in the development of immigration policy. This has involved two main policy changes. First, a number of changes to the Immigration Rules issued under the 1971 Immigration Act have been introduced, with the explicit intention of tightening controls even further. Second the 1981 British Nationality Act was passed under the first Thatcher administration, and came into force in 1983. Debates in Parliament on both these issues give a clue to the attempt by the Government to further circumvent the rights of those black Commonwealth citizens with a legal right to enter Britain and to construct the question of nationality along racial lines (*Hansard*, Vol. 5, 1981: Cols 765–1193; *Hansard*, Vol. 31, 1982: Cols 692–761; *Hansard*, Vol. 34, 1982: Cols 355–429; *Hansard*, Vol. 37, 1983: Cols 178–280; *Hansard*, Vol. 83, 1985: Cols 893–989).

The main legislative action of the post 1979 Conservative administrations, the 1981 British Nationality Act, is a case in point. The Government argued that in introducing the Bill it was rationalising both existing nationality and immigration legislation, in order to create a British citizenship which automatically gives the right of abode in the UK. It did this by dividing the existing category of Citizen of the United Kingdom and Commonwealth into three categories; British citizens; British Dependent Territories citizens; British Overseas citizens. Although the Government argued that the

Act would make immigration control less arbitrary, public and Parliamentary responses criticised it for reinforcing racial discrimination (Layton-Henry, 1984: 157–9). Indeed the category of 'British Overseas citizens' effectively excludes British citizens of (mostly) Asian origin from the right of abode in the UK. In this sense it seems correct to argue that the 1981 Act 'enshrines the existing racially discriminatory provisions of immigration law under the new clothing of British citizenship and the right of abode' (Macdonald, 1983: 69).

A Government document prepared for the OECD conference on immigration policy states the broad policy objectives in traditional terms, but links them closely to other areas of concern:

> In recent decades, the basis of policy in the United Kingdom has been the need to control primary immigration–that is, new heads of households who are most likely to enter the job market. The United Kingdom is one of the most densely populated countries in Europe. In terms of housing, education, social services and, of course, jobs, the country could not support all those who would like to come here. Firm immigration control is therefore essential, in order to provide the conditions necessary for developing and maintaining good community relations. (OECD, 1986: 1)

In practice, therefore, the strategy pursued since 1979 has continued to legitimate the supposed link between 'firm controls' and 'good community relations'. The signs are that this amalgam will continue to guide the thinking of the mainstream of the Conservative Party.

At the same time the Government has steadfastly refused to strengthen the 1976 Race Relations Act or to adopt a more positive approach against discrimination and racism. Even after the Scarman Report of 1981 called for a co-ordinated and government-led policy against racial disadvantage, a call repeated a number of times since by Lord Scarman and others, the response of the various agencies of the state has been at best limited. Rather it has continued to emphasise the need for tight immigration controls because 'of the strain that the admission of a substantial number of immigrants can place on existing resources and services' (Leon Brittan, *Hansard*, Vol. 83, 1985: Col. 893).

The logic of this approach is to displace conflicts and strains in race relations on the black communities as a whole or specific section of them. This in term has allowed the common-sense ideas which see blacks as an 'enemy within' and a threat to social stability to take further root.

If the main rationalisation of the immigration laws and the race relations acts was the objective of producing an atmosphere for the development of good race relations and integration, it needs to be said that they failed to depoliticise the question of black immigration. The racialisation of British politics proceeded apace during the 1970s, and took on new forms in relation to specific issues or groups, e.g. education, the police, young blacks and urban policy (CCCS, 1982; Miles and Phizacklea, 1984; Jacobs, 1986). The restrictions imposed by the 1971 Immigration Act, and the successive Immigration Rules issued under this Act throughout the last fifteen years, have seemingly fulfilled the ostensible objective of post-1962 policies, which has been to control primary immigration and restrict secondary immigration, but the politicisation of race has continued during this time.

What explains this racialisation of political discourses in a context of firm immigration controls? A number of issues are involved, and not all of these can be analysed in this chapter, but at least two are worth noting. First, debates about immigration and race have taken place within a broader context of social, political and economic change which has influenced the ways in which such debates have developed. The rapid transformation of many inner city localities over the last two decades, particularly in relation to the economic and social infrastructure, has provided a fertile ground for the racialisation of issues such as employment, housing, education and law and order (Hall *et al.*, 1978; Phizacklea and Miles, 1980: 42–68; Solomos, 1986). This racialisation process has moved public and political debate beyond the question of immigration per se, with the focus moving towards the identification and resolution of specific social problems linked to race. But the link with the immigration question is maintained at another level, because it is the size of the black population, whether in the schools or the unemployed queue which is identified as the source of the problem (Macdonald, 1983; Castles *et al.*, 1984).

Second, the continuing racialisation of British politics in the context of firm immigration highlights the way in which political language is often a way of emphasising what one wants to believe and avoiding what one does not wish to face (Edelman, 1977; Katznelson, 1986). Thus, although calls for more controls on immigration are often laced with references to the number of immigrants or to the large numbers who could potentially arrive and swamp British culture, such statements are not necessarily based on the facts in any recognised sense. Rather references to statistics and reports are often highly selective and emphasise symbolic fears about the present or future. Good examples of this process are the debates which occurred during the mid 1970s about the Hawley Report on immigration from the Indian subcontinent (1976) and the Select Committee on Race Relations and Immigration report on *Immigration* (1978). In both cases the debates about these reports in Parliament, the media and in other contexts focused on the dangers of massive numbers of immigrants arriving and the possible social and political conse-quences; and this despite the fact that firm controls on immigration had been implemented during the 1960s (Freeman and Spencer, 1979). Perhaps a more recent phenomenon is the case of the visa controls introduced in 1986 for visitors from India, Pakistan, Bangladesh, Nigeria and Ghana on the basis of controlling the number of illegal immigrants from these countries. The fact that only 222 out of 452 000 visitors from the five countries absconded as illegal immigrants in 1985, did not prevent the symbolic use of visa controls as another means of 'holding the tide' of immigration (The *Guardian*, 2 September 1986).

The agitation of the extreme right wing groups and sections of the Conservative Party in favour of stricter immigration controls and repatriation came to focus in the late 1970s and 1980s as much on the supposed dangers of this 'alien wedge' as on the arrival of new immigrants. The symbolism of the language used by Enoch Powell in 1968–9 to warn of the dangers of immigration, was reworked by the late 1970s around the issue of the 'enemy within'; who was in many cases no longer an immigrant but born and bred in Brixton, Handsworth, Liverpool and other urban localities. The generation and amplification of the mugging issue in the early seventies, confrontations between the police and young blacks, and the identification of young blacks as an alienated group within the black communities and British society generally, helped to construct a new racialised discourse about black youth (Solomos, 1988). Increasingly this group was identified as drifting into either criminal activities or radical political activities which brought them into direct contact, and hence conflict, with the police. Just as in the 1950s and 1960s the numbers game mobilised a conception of the problem which focused on the need to keep black immigrants out, now the language of political debate seemed to shift towards the view that black youth were a kind of social time-bomb which could help undermine the social fabric of the immigration/race relations amalgam and possibly society as a whole.

Unrest and disorder in the inner cities

The experience of the 1981 and 1985 riots is an example of the power of immigration as a political symbol, even though there was no evidence of a causal relationship between the two processes. During both periods one of the central themes in public and Parliamentary debates about the riots was the question of race. A number of the popular papers and MPs focused on the role that young blacks played in the riots, and the linkage between the emergence of forms of violent protest and the growth of immigrant communities and alien values (Solomos, 1986). Indeed in the context of both the Parliamentary debates and the popular press Enoch Powell and other MPs and commentators constructed an interpretation of the riots which saw them as intimately linked to the size and concentration of the black population in certain localities. Powell proclaimed the 1981 riots as a vindication of his warnings about immigration since 1968 (*Hansard*, Vol. 8, 1981: Cols 1313–4). In 1985 he repeated this assertion and linked it to a renewed call for repatriation as the only effective solution to the problem (*Hansard*, Vol. 84, 1985: Cols 375–6). Similar arguments were made by other MPs and press commentators during both 1981 and 1985. The extreme implications of this analysis were rejected by both the Government and Opposition, along with other sections of political opinion. But there seems little doubt that the riots since 1981 represent an important watershed in the racialisation of British politics. They have helped to strengthen the common sense notion that black youth are a danger to the stability of domestic race relations.

Prospects for reform

The shift we have noted in the previous section from a preoccupation with immigration and the numbers game as such to the question of the enemy within and related images of social disorder is an important development. At least in relation to the disorders experienced in 1981 and 1985 it highlights the complex processes through which racialised political discourses are working in contemporary Britain. But we should emphasise that we are far from suggesting that immigration will become less important as a political issue. Rather we see the growing usage of political symbols which depict blacks as an enemy within as inextricably linked with the history of state responses which we have analysed in this chapter. Indeed the post-1979 Conservative administrations have continued to mobilise the immigration question as a political symbol, and to legitimate the maintenance of racially specific controls as a necessary response to the fears of ordinary people about too much immigration.

Since 1979, however, the Labour Party and the minority parties have shown some signs of questioning the basis of this approach (Fitzgerald and Layton-Henry, 1986). The Labour Party, which was responsible for the introduction of the 1968 Commonwealth Immigrants Act, has seemingly come round to the view that current immigration laws are racist, and it aims to introduce its own legislation when in power to ensure that controls are both non-racist and non-sexist. In a Parliamentary debate on immigration in July 1985 Gerald Kaufman affirmed that the intention of a future Labour administration would be to (a) maintain firm controls on immigration and (b) ensure that such controls were applied equally to all immigrants regardless of 'race' (*Hansard*, Vol. 83, 1985: Cols 909–10). He accused the Conservatives of trying to identify immigration with race, when recent history questioned this assumption:

> Viewed objectively, immigration should be neither a problem nor an issue in Britain. Substantial primary immigration ended at least a decade and a half ago, and there is no prospect of it starting again. In most years there is a net emigration from the United Kingdom. In 1983–4, 45 per cent of so-called immigrants are Britons returning to the United Kingdom. In that year only 15.5 per cent of immigrants came from the West Indies, Africa and the Indian subcontinent – the areas from which, according to the Government, there is the greatest pressure to migrate to the United Kingdom. (*Ibid.*, Col. 910)

This approach represents a marked shift from the actions of Labour Governments during 1964–70 and 1974–9, but it is difficult to say what is meant by non-racist immigration controls and how a future Labour administration could effectively break away from the logic of politics since 1962–which has been to construct black immigration into a problem. Certainly over the post-1981 period, in the aftermath of the riots, a strong black and anti-racist lobby has emerged within the Labour Party. This lobby is pressing the party into a firm commitment to implement the reforms (Fitzgerald and Layton-Henry, 1986: 110–14).

In the context of the current political climate, however, it is hard to see how a de-politicisation of the immigration/race question can come about. Growing urban unrest and violence create a space for the Powellite imagery of a racial civil war to take root in popular common sense, for the real fears of the white population to be deflected on to the enemy within. Promises of a fundamental break from its past practice by the Labour Party have to be set against the wider political background. What would be the response of Labour to a successful campaign around immigrant/race by the Conservatives? Already sections of the popular press are accusing Labour of promising to open the flood gates to future primary immigration from black Commonwealth countries, and in an electoral sense such accusations may become a burden. During 1974–9 the Labour Government failed to take immigration out of politics and in the 1979 election campaign suffered from the racialised language used by the Conservatives. Its response to these pressures showed up the ambiguities in Labour thinking since the mid-1960s. Whether its responses in the future will be significantly different remains to be seen, but given the entrenched nature of racist immigration controls it is clearly going to require major structural changes to make the promises of reform a reality.

The significance of politics

The above discussion has demonstrated that it is far too simplistic to see the state as a reactive instrument of either economic forces or popular pressures in relation to the control of immigration and the management of migrant labour. Rather, we have highlighted the social, economic, political and ideological contexts which have helped to shape state legislation in this field and to bring about the present articulation between racially exclusionary practices and social policies against discrimination.

In a broad sense the state interventions described above can be seen as making a contribution to the reproduction of the dominant social relations of contemporary Britain, particularly through the regulation of migrant workers and the reinforcement of racialised and ethnically-based social divisions. But such a generalisation does not capture the complexity of the role of the state in relation to immigration and other important issues on the political agenda of the period we have covered. Far from the state simply responding to pressures from the outside, we have shown throughout this chapter that its played a central role in defining both the form and the content of policies and wider political agendas. Indeed the state and its agencies have become the locus of struggles over the form of the political regulation of immigration and the management of domestic race relations.

Summary and conclusion

The central conclusion to emerge from this chapter returns us to the question of the role that political institutions play in the regulation of the entry and the incorporation of migrant labour. The story of post-1945 responses to immigration that we have covered in this chapter shows how popular responses and state policy-making have been shaped by specific contexts and political situations. The circumstances which bring about specific types of policy response are not given but are the product of struggles and contradictions, both within and outside state institutions. During the period covered in this chapter state responses to migration have by no means been uniform, although there are trends that can be delineated.

We still need to know more about the dynamics and the limits of state intervention in this field, the interplay between state policies and political mobilisation around racial issues. A more adequate understanding of these processes is required if we are to understand how the interplay between immigration and the state has produced a situation whereby racist immigration controls have become institutionalised. In this chapter we have concentrated on the broad contours of political debate and policy change since 1945, but in Chapters 9 and 10 we shall return to the dynamics of social change and racialised politics in the present.

Such an analysis inevitably takes us into debates about political practice, and beyond the confines of a narrow academic focus. In the context of virulent racism and calls for the repatriation of black citizens it is hardly possible to look at the history of immigration and race since 1945 without coming to terms with the practical impact of immigration controls on the everyday lives of black citizens.

But first we shall look at the other element of state intervention over the past two decades, namely, race relations legislation and anti-discrimination policies.

4 Race Relations Legislation and the Political Process

Introduction

We have seen in the previous two chapters that the genesis, legislative implementation and institutionalisation of controls on black immigration was a complex process. Similarly, the development of anti-discrimination legislation and policies aimed at promoting greater equality of opportunity for black British citizens has been a thoroughly contradictory process based as much on political expediency as on any commitment to justice and equality. The three major Race Relations Acts passed since 1965, for example, have been highly controversial and have aroused the opposition of those who see them as an attempt to give favourable treatment to blacks over whites in the search for jobs, homes, and other goods. At points this kind of opposition has boiled over into open calls for the dismantling of the major institutions of what is sometimes called the race relations industry (Flew, 1984; Palmer, 1986).

From another perspective the various legislative measures passed by successive governments since 1965 are seen as largely symbolic or inadequate. Fully two decades after the first Race Relations Act was passed in 1965 there seems to be little evidence of significant advances against entrenched forms of racial inequality. A recurrent criticism of the attitude of central government departments in this field is that they have not shown a clear commitment to or allocated adequate resources to racial equality programmes (Jenkins and Solomos, 1987; McCrudden, 1988).

This and the following chapter will explore the substantive

transformation of the politics of race, from the expansion of state policies dealing with racial discrimination and other aspects of racial inequality during the mid-1960s to the contemporary forms of state intervention. This chapter will analyse the national processes involved in this transformation, while Chapter 5 will concentrate on the development of racialised political debates and practice at the local level. This division is not meant to suggest that there is a clear break between national and local political processes. Indeed, it will be made clear throughout both chapters that there are many complex linkages between these levels and that it is to a certain extent impossible to understand one without some reference to the other. But for heuristic reasons it seems sensible to present the histories of state intervention at national and local levels as analytically distinct, albeit with important connections.

This chapter approaches the question of the political management of race by analysing the institutionalisation of the dual interventionist strategy adopted by both major political parties in the mid-1960s which was outlined in Chapter 3: namely the balance between controls on immigration and integrative measures aimed at improving race relations. It will analyse this process by (a) detailing the various legislative measures passed by successive Governments since 1965, and (b) analysing the most important political events in this field during the period from the early 1960s to the early 1980s. This will inevitably return us to the role of Enoch Powell in fashioning the racialisation of political debate from 1968 onwards, and the changing ideologies and practices of the Conservative and Labour parties. The account in this chapter of broad trends in state policies thus links up with the analysis in chapters 9 and 10 of the dynamics of racist, anti-racist and black political mobilisation. It provides the essential historical background to the development of the movements and groupings discussed in those chapters.

The context

The main objective of this chapter will be to explain the genesis, development and contradictions of political strategies on race relations, as pursued by both Conservative and Labour administrations since 1965. But it will also attempt to show what the substantive achievements of these strategies were, both at a practical and a

symbolic level. Thus apart from analysing the legislation implemented by the state over the past two and a half decades, it will look
at the interplay between the stated objectives and the actual outcomes
of the most important legislative measures.

By carefully analysing the interplay between stated objectives and
substantive outcomes the chapter will thus be able to analyse the
problems that past policies have helped to reproduce as well as those
that they have ameliorated. It will thus enable us to show the impact
of state intervention over the last two decades on the reproduction
and persistence of racial inequality, and to explore the possibilities
for alternative political strategies which can tackle racism and racial
inequality more effectively.

Much of the material used to illustrate these arguments will be
drawn from political debates, policy debates and media coverage of
the various legislative measures which successive governments have
passed on racial and related issues since 1965 when the first Race
Relations Act was passed. These measures are listed in Table 4.1,
which also lists the various immigration control measures passed
during this period, since in practice the two sets of legislation were
inextricably linked:

Table 4.1   *Legislation on immigration and race relations since 1965*

Year	Legislative measure
1965	Race Relations Act
1966	Local Government Act
1968	Commonwealth Immigrants Act
1968	Race Relations Act
1969	Immigration Appeals Act
1971	Immigration Act
1976	Race Relations Act
1981	British Nationality Act

The main justification for looking closely at these legislative measures
is that during the past two decades the debates and controversies that
have surrounded them have served to illustrate the changing terms of
political debate about the role of government in tackling racial
inequalities.

Additionally, however, we shall seek to link aspects of this account
to the dynamics of political conflicts and struggles about the politics
of race. This is an issue which we shall look at in more detail in

Chapters 8–10, but it would clearly be impossible to explain the genesis and development of state interventions without looking at the history of racist political mobilisation, black protest and changing racialised ideologies.

1965–75: the origins of anti-discrimination legislation

From the 1950s the question of what to do to counter racial discrimination emerged as a major dilemma in debates about immigration and race relations. Even in the early stages of black migration there was an awareness that in the longer term the question of racial discrimination was likely to become a volatile political issue. In the early stages of post-war black migration political debates about race were centred upon the question of immigration controls. However, an underlying concern, even at this stage, was the question of the future of racial relations in British society. The notion that the arrival of too many black migrants would lead to problems in relation to housing, employment and social services was already widely articulated (Patterson, 1969; Freeman, 1979).

In the context of the intense debate about immigration during the late 1950s, for example, the Labour Party set up a working party to look at the question of legislation to combat racial discrimination, and instructed it to make practical legislative proposals (*The Times*, 24 July 1958). Other discussions on this issue were encouraged through the efforts of politicians like Fenner Brockway and welfare groups which took a special interest in the position of the black communities either locally or nationally.

Two problems were usually seen as in need of urgent action. First, the negative response of the majority white population to the competition of black workers in the housing and labour markets. In the context of particular localities, such as London, Birmingham and the surrounding area, and Wolverhampton, such competition was seen as creating the conditions for future conflict. Second, the frustration of black workers who felt themselves excluded from equal participation in British society by the development of a colour bar in the labour and housing markets, along with related processes of discrimination.

Both these issues were perceived as potential sources of conflict which the government had to manage and control through direct intervention. In the early stages, however, it was not totally clear what the best mechanisms for state intervention actually were.

The genesis of race relations policies

The first attempts to deal with the potential for racial conflict and to tackle racial discrimination can be traced back to the 1960s, and took two basic forms. The first involved the setting up of welfare agencies to deal with the problems faced by black migrants and to help the white communities understand the migrants. The second stage of the policy response began with the passage of the 1965 and 1968 Race Relations Acts, and was premised on the notion that the state should attempt to ban discrimination on the basis of race, colour or ethnic origin through legal sanctions and public regulatory agencies charged with the task of promoting greater equality of opportunity (Rose *et al.*, 1969: 511–30).

This dual strategy was clearly articulated by the Labour Government's 1965 White Paper on *Immigration from the Commonwealth*, but it has its origins in the debates of the 1950s and the period leading up to the 1962 Commonwealth Immigrants Act. The notion that immigration was essentially an issue of race was consistent with the view that: (a) the growing number of black citizens resident in the UK was either actually or potentially the source of social problems and conflicts, and (b) that it was necessary for the state to introduce measures to promote the integration of immigrants into the wider society and its fundamental institutions.

The linking of immigration controls with integrative measures was a significant step, since it signalled a move towards the management of domestic race relations as well as legitimising the institutionalisation of firm controls at the point of entry. In the same year as the White Paper the Labour Government passed the first Race Relations Act, which enunciated the principle of ending discrimination against black immigrants, and their descendants, on the grounds of race. Although fairly limited in its scope the Act was important in establishing the concern of the state with racial discrimination and as an affirmation of the broad objective of using legislative action to achieve good race relations (Lester and Bindman, 1972 107–49).

Models of integration

Much has been written about the inherent contradictions involved in balancing racially specific controls on immigration with measures against discriminatory practices. Yet since the 1960s the two sides of state intervention were seen as inextricably linked. According to Roy Hattersley's famous formula, 'Integration without control is impossible, but control without integration is indefensible' (*Hansard*, Vol. 709, Cols 378–85). The rationale of this argument was never articulated clearly, but it was at least partly based on the idea that the fewer immigrants (particularly black ones) there were, the easier it would be to integrate them into the English way of life and its social cultural values.

During the tenure of Roy Jenkins as Home Secretary in the mid-1960s, this notion of integration was linked to the idea that unless the political institutions helped to deal with the social problems of the immigrants and of the areas in which they lived there was the prospect of growing racial tension and violence on the American model. In this context concern was particularly focused on the second generation of young blacks, who were perceived as a potentially volatile group (Solomos, 1988: 53–87).

Given this perspective the Race Relations Acts of 1965 and 1968 were based on the twin assumptions of: (a) setting up special bodies to deal with the problems faced by immigrants in relation to discrimination, social adjustment and welfare; (b) helping to educate the population as a whole about race relations, and hence minimising the risk of racialised conflict developing in Britain as it had done in the United States.

The basis of these assumptions lay, as we have argued above, in the notion that too many black migrants could result in racial conflict. Additionally, however, the numbers game was tied to the idea that the cultural differences between the immigrants and the host population were a potential source of conflict. During the period from 1962 onwards both the Conservative and Labour Parties have accepted the need for immigration restrictions to be balanced by measures to bring about integration in the areas of housing, education, employment and the social services.

Significantly, however, successive governments did not seek to use the mainstream Government Departments to tackle this issue. While the Home Office was directly responsible for the enforcement of strict immigration controls, the responsibility for enforcing the 1965 and 1968 Race Relations Acts was given to regulatory agencies and the judicial system. The 1965 Act set up the Race Relations Board, while the 1968 Act set up the Community Relations Commission and strengthened the powers of the Race Relations Board in dealing with complaints of discrimination (Abbott, 1971: chs 9 and 10). From 1965 to 1975 successive governments left the issue of tackling racial discrimination to these bodies, and there was little direction or support provided by central government itself.

The 1976 Race Relations Act

Critics of the 1965 and 1968 Race Relations Acts pointed out that these early attempts to tackle racial discrimination were limited both in their intention and their impact. By the early 1970s critics of the 1960s legislation were calling for a new and more effective strategy to tackle racial discrimination, particularly in areas such as employment (Abbott, 1971; Lester and Bindman, 1972). At the same time research on aspects of racial discrimination by a number of bodies showed that high levels of discrimination persisted, and this was taken to imply that the efforts of successive governments from 1965 onwards had produced little or no change (Smith, 1977). More critical studies took their cue from this evidence to argue that race relations legislation, particularly when linked to discriminatory immigration controls, could be no more than a gesture or symbolic political act which gave the impression that something was being done while in practice achieving very little (Moore, 1975; Sivanandan, 1982).

The debate about the effectiveness of the 1965 and 1968 Acts raged throughout the early seventies, and began to have an impact on the organisations charged with implementing the legislation. The Race Relations Board, for example, produced a critical analysis of the operation of race relations legislation which argued, among other things, that the 1968 Act was very limited in its effectiveness because of the concentration on individual forms of discrimination and the lack of resources for implementing the law fully. It also argued that racial discrimination was less a matter of 'active discrimination against individuals' than the reproduction of 'situations in which equality of opportunity is consciously or unconsciously denied'

(Race Relations Board, 1973). At the same time the Select Committee on Race Relations and Immigration launched a major investigation which produced a major report on *The Organisation of Race Relations Administration* in 1975.

Though this report looked at the situation from an administrative angle, it helped to put a number of arguments on the political agenda. The most important of these arguments were: (a) the need to go beyond the narrow definition of discrimination used in the 1965 and 1968 Acts, in order to include institutionalised or unintended forms of discrimination; (b) the need to strengthen the administrative structures and legal powers of the Race Relations Board in order to allow for a more effective implementation of anti-discrimination policies, including penalties for those found guilty of discrimination; and (c) the need for a more interventionist stance from central government departments, particularly the Home Office, to buttress the role of race relations institutions (Select Committee, 1975: vii).

Taken together these assumptions were seen to support the need for stronger action by government to promote equal opportunity because 'there is a growing lack of confidence in the effectiveness of Government action and, in the case of some groups such as young West Indians, this lack of confidence can turn into hostile resentment' (Select Committee, 1975: xvi–xix). In addition, they were seen as supporting the need for more efficient social policies on race in order to achieve the original aim announced by Roy Jenkins during the 1960s: namely, the achievement of a 'genuinely integrated society' where there was 'equal opportunity, accompanied by cultural diversity in an atmosphere of mutual tolerance'.

More fundamentally, perhaps, the weight of evidence that went into these reports had a major impact on the White Paper on *Racial Discrimination*, which was published in September 1975. This accepted the relative failure of past policies to achieve fundamental changes, the need for stronger legislation, and the need for a 'coherent and co-ordinated policy over a large field of influence involving many Government Departments, local authorities, the existing and future statutory bodies concerned with the subject and, indeed, many individuals in positions of responsibility and influence' (Home Office, 1975: 5). It also accepted the need for a broader governmental role to tackle those 'more complex situations of accumulated disadvantages and of the effects of past discrimination'. The rationale for this emphasis according to the White Paper was the recognition by the government that the majority of the black population was here to stay and that policies had to be based on recognition of this fundamental principle.

In this sense the White Paper was a departure from the policies pursued by successive administrations from the 1960s onwards. However, although the role of government and a political commitment to racial equality was prioritised there was no detailed analysis of how to link the legal and administrative framework with active political involvement by the Home Office and other government departments in the promotion of racial equality. More fundamentally, while this strategy was recognised as involving major expenditure implications, as well as a reassessment of priorities in existing programmes, no attempt was made to assess what these were, or to examine how the government's own contribution to the new strategy was going to be implemented.

In the ensuing legislative proposals therefore the emphasis was placed on changing the legislative and administrative framework, while the wider changes promised in the Select Committee report and the White Paper were put to one side. Against this background the 1976 Race Relations Act 'represented a strengthening and extension of existing anti-discrimination policy rather than a new and unfamiliar policy' (Nixon, 1982: 366).

The most important innovations were (a) an extension of the objectives of the law to cover not only intentional discrimination but racial disadvantage brought about by systemic racism; (b) a reorganisation of the Race Relations Board and the Community Relations Commission into a joint agency, the Commission for Racial Equality (CRE); and (c) a different procedure for the handling of individual complaints of discrimination, which in the case of employment cases were to be handled directly by the industrial tribunals rather than processed through the CRE (McCrudden, 1982: 336–48; Lustgarten, 1980).

Direct and indirect discrimination

The first innovation was intended to overcome the problems of proving the existence of institutional filter processes that were biased against minority workers. While *direct discrimination* was defined by the 1976 Act quite straightforwardly as arising 'where a person treats another person less favourably on racial grounds than he treats, or would treat, someone else', it also put on the statute book the category of *indirect discrimination*. This was defined as consisting of treatment which may be described as equal in a formal sense as between different racial groups, but discriminatory in its effect on one particular racial group. An example of what could be defined as indirect discrimination is the application of conditions and requirements for jobs which may mean that:

(a) the proportion of persons of a racial group who can comply with these is considerably smaller than the proportion of persons not of that racial group who can comply with them;
(b) they are to the detriment of the persons who cannot comply with them;
(c) that they are not justifiable irrespective of the colour, race, nationality or ethnic or national origins of the person to whom they are applied (Home Office, 1977: 4–5).

The introduction of the concept of indirect discrimination into race relations legislation was partly based on the American experience of affirmative action against institutionalised forms of racism, which was widely commented upon during the immediate period leading up to the 1976 Act (Abbott, 1971; Lester and Bindman, 1972). Indeed, according to one account both the American programmes based on the Civil Rights Act of 1964 and the post-1976 British concern with indirect discrimination are attempts 'to circumvent the problems of proof of intentional discrimination, to go beyond its individualised nature, and to provide a basis for intervening against the present effects of past and other types of institutional discrimination' (McCrudden, 1983: 56).

The Commission for Racial Equality

The second innovation, the setting up of the CRE, resulted from the experience of the organisational management of anti-discrimination policies during the period 1965–75. The setting up of an agency that combined roles previously held by the Community Relations Commission and the Race Relations Board was seen as paving the way for a more coherent implementation of the law and the promotion of equality of opportunity and good race relations.

The Commission was seen as having three main duties: (a) to work toward the elimination of discrimination; (b) to promote equality of opportunity and good race relations; and (c) to keep under review the working of the Act and draw up proposals for amending it. Under the first two headings the Commission was empowered to carry out formal investigations into organisations where it believed unlawful discrimination was taking place, to help individual complainants in cases of discrimination, and to issue codes of practice which contain guidance about the elimination of discrimination in the field of employment or for the promotion of equality of opportunity. In addition the Commission was to carry out promotional work aimed at bringing about changes in both the attitudes and behaviour of employers toward minorities.

Individual complaints

As mentioned above, the third major innovation introduced by the 1976 Act allowed individuals direct access to courts or industrial tribunals for redress in respect of complaints under the Act. Although the CRE could offer individuals assistance in carrying through their complaint, direct access to industrial tribunals was seen as providing a stronger basis for a legal strategy against discrimination in employment to complement the work of the Commission. This viewpoint was also supported by reference to the need to treat cases of race discrimination in the same manner as cases of sex discrimination or complaints of unfair dismissal.

From policy to practice

Given these stated objectives, and the government's promise of an effective race relations policy, it may seem surprising at first sight that in the decade since the 1976 Act came into force much of the discussion has focused on the disjuncture between its objectives and its actual impact. Even Lord Scarman's sober report on urban unrest during 1981 pointed out that policies had failed to make a major impact on the roots of racial disadvantage (Scarman, 1981: para 2.38).

Offe (1984: 144) has pointed out that 'the increasingly visible conflict between the promise and the experience, form and content, of state policies' can result in increased conflict and disenchantment.

Broadly speaking, this is what seems to have happened since the 1976 Act came into force. While the Act seemed to promise radical changes, the translation of broad objectives into practice has not been easy.

Detailed evidence about the workings of the 1976 Act has only recently begun to emerge, though it has been the focus of much critical comment from an early stage (Home Affairs Committee, 1981). It does seem, however, that the translation of the initiatives introduced by the Act into practice has at best been achieved in only a limited sense. Almost all the academic research that has been done on the effectiveness of the 1976 Act, has pointed to three ways in which policies have proved to be ineffective in tackling racial inequality. First, the machinery set up to implement the Act has not functioned effectively. Second, the policies have not produced the intended results. Third, policies have failed to meet the expectations of the black communities (Jenkins and Solomos, 1987).

For example, recent evidence indicates that both the formal investigations and the individual complaints procedure have had only a limited impact on discriminatory practices in areas such as employment or housing, and that the CRE has encountered severe problems in exercising its powers in such a way as challenge entrenched processes of discrimination (Brown and Gay, 1985; McCrudden, 1987). The Home Affairs Committee's investigation of the CRE in 1981 highlighted a number of organisational problems which hampered its formal investigations in the early stages of the Commission's work (Home Affairs Committee, 1981: xxiii–xxxiii). There is also clear evidence, however, that the ambiguous nature of the law has acted as a brake on its ability to carry out investigations successfully or speedily (Applebey and Ellis, 1984). By 1983 the formal investigation procedure was so unworkable that the CRE itself proposed a sharpening of its investigation powers in order to reduce delays (CRE, 1983 and 1985a), though its appeal has still to receive a positive response from the Government. The Commission has reported that by 1987 it had published 39 formal investigations, but it acknowledges that their impact on discriminatory processes has been limited (CRE, Annual Report for 1987).

The picture in relation to individual complaints is by no means clear, due to the lack of a critical analysis of the various stages of the complaints process, but research evidence suggests that there is a very low level of success in proving discrimination. The CRE can claim a certain amount of success in that most successful cases were supported by the Commission. But these successful cases can only amount to a small amount of reported cases of discrimination, let alone those cases that go unreported.

Proposals for reform

During the 1980s a number of bodies, including the CRE, have lobbied for a major reorganisation of the administration of race relations policies and for a stronger central government lead. Lord Scarman's report on urban unrest and numerous other reports have argued for a major radical programme of action to tackle the root causes of racial inequality (Benyon and Solomos, 1987).

The CRE itself has joined the voices calling for a more positive stance from the Government. The CRE's proposals for' change, which were first made in draft form in 1983 and have been on the table since 1985, recommended a number of basic changes to strengthen the implementation process, including: (a) a clarification of the meaning of both direct and indirect discrimination, to take account of the complex situation on the ground; (b) the setting up of specialist tribunals to deal with discrimination cases, which had the power to order changes to prevent a recurrence of discrimination; (c) a clarification of the procedures for formal investigations in order to cut out delaying tactics by employers or other bodies; (d) a redefinition of the law to allow for more effective positive actions to redress the effects of past and present discrimination; (e) a strengthening of the sanctions against those found to be unlawfully discriminating.

Such changes were seen by the CRE and by academic researchers as a way of overcoming some of the most well known limitations of the 1976 Act, and of reinforcing the political commitment of central government to racial equality. Additionally, they were seen as a way of showing the black communities that the CRE was able to distance itself from the Government and propose changes which were not necessarily popular with ministers and officials.

Such calls have remained unheeded throughout the 1980s. Yet, as the Commission has recently stated, levels of discrimination in employment, housing and other areas remain alarmingly high, and there is no sign that the Government is willing to strengthen the legislation so as to make it effective (CRE, Annual Report for 1987).

Failing a strong lead from central government the Commission has attempted to innovate within the terms of its powers. One of the major innovations introduced by the CRE during the early 1980s was the Code of Practice for the elimination of discrimination in employment, which came into force in April 1984. First published in draft form in early 1982 the Code went through a number of stages of discussion and redrafting before the government formally laid it before Parliament in April 1983. Since April 1984 the Code has been admissible in evidence to tribunals, and if they think a provision in it is relevant to the proceedings they can take it into account in determining the question (Home Office, 1977: 39).

The Commission itself considered that the Code 'will do much to advance the cause of racial equality at work' (CRE, Annual Report for 1983: 15), particularly when combined with the operation of formal investigations and the individual complaints process. Yet its own survey of employers' responses to the Code showed that many employers were still unaware of its existence (CRE, Annual Report for 1987: 8).

As the CRE itself seems to be aware, however, such changes only touch the tip of the iceberg. It recently stated that 'the Scale and persistence of discrimination are insupportable in any civilised society' (CRE, Annual Report for 1987: 8). The dilemma it faces, however, is that there seems little room for radical change in the present climate of political opinion.

Summary and conclusion

By the very nature of the political debates about race and immigration over the past two decades the development of race relations policies has formed part of a wider political process. The central element of that process has been the political and media debates about the impact of black immigration on various aspects of British society. This has meant that major policy initiatives have been largely the result of attempts by successive governments to meet the demands of those calling for action to tackle racial discrimination and to respond to those who oppose such intervention. The end result seems to be an unhappy compromise which pleases few and angers many for a variety of reasons.

Given this context it is difficult to be optimistic about the prospects of radical change within the constraints of the existing legislation. It is now over a decade since the 1976 Race Relations Act came into force, and there is little ground for arguing that it has achieved in practice the kind of radical changes which it promised. The failure of the Thatcher administrations to respond positively to calls for more powers for the Commission for Racial Equality and to remedy the weaknesses of the 1976 Act has led to increased cynicism about the willingness of the state to include the question of racial inequality as a central element of the policy agenda.

Moreover, over the past decade the new orthodoxies on social and economic policy advocated by the new right have attempted to undermine the case for any major intervention by the state, and the efficacy of legislative measures against racial inequality. While such ideas have not yet attracted the kind of support that the views of liberal market economists such as Thomas Sowell have in the United States (Sowell, 1981), there are signs that such ideas are gaining some currency in the work of the new right think tanks. Perhaps such ideas are more likely to find a hearing in the present political climate than the calls for stronger legislation and increased central government intervention in this field. The consequences of such a development remain to be seen.

5 Urban Politics and Racial Inequality

Introduction

During the controversy over her much discussed 'swamping' statement in 1978 Margaret Thatcher made it quite clear that she was on the side of those who saw black migrants as swamping British society. When in February 1979 she was asked if she had modified her view on this issue she forcefully restated her basic theme:

> Some people have felt swamped by immigrants. They've seen the whole character of their neighbourhood change . . . Of course people can feel that they are being swamped. Small minorities can be absorbed – they can be assets to the majority community – but once a minority in a neighbourhood gets very large, people Do feel swamped. They feel their whole way of life has been changed. (*The Observer*, 25 February 1979)

This statement highlights the important role that images of community and neighbourhood play in the political debates about race in British society, and the role that they can play as symbols for the changing terms of debate on this question. This has already been referred to in the course of the discussion of the politics of race and immigration in Chapter 3. In this chapter we shall analyse the development of political debates and policy change at the local level in more detail, concentrating particularly on the past two decades.

As has been made clear in previous chapters the politicisation of the public debate about race and immigration has been partly determined by local political processes. As we have already shown in Chapters 3 and 4 a number of local authorities, pressure groups and individuals had raised the question of the impact of immigration on

83

their specific localities. Moreover, through the 1950s and 1960s local political elites in areas such as London, Birmingham, Wolverhampton and other localities had to come to terms with the increasingly multi-racial composition of the local population.

This chapter will examine the history of the local politics of racism through (a) an analysis of the impact of local conditions and processes on the racialisation of the political agenda, and (b) a critical review of legislative and political interventions which have sought to structure race relations at the local level. The main focus of this chapter will, therefore, be on the dynamics of the incorporation of race into the local political agenda. This will allow us to link up with the questions raised at the end of Chapter 4 about the changing context of state intervention in this area and the prospects for transforming existing patterns of racial inequality in British society through political interventions at both the local and national political levels.

Concepts and models of local politics

Over the past decade a wide ranging theoretical debate about local politics and institutions has taken place, which has successfully sought to develop a more dynamic and critical perspective on various aspects of this subject (Dunleavy, 1980; Saunders, 1981; Gregory and Urry, 1985; Thrift and Williams, 1987). The main features of this debate have been (a) a concern to include wider questions about power and society in the study of urban politics, (b) attempts to develop a dynamic analysis of the processes of policy change and formation at the local level, and (c) a focus on the role of conflict and controversy in the shaping of local policy agendas.

In particular, a number of writers have argued that many of the crucial features of contemporary class and social relations in advanced capitalist societies cannot be fully understood without reference to the local and spatial context. Studies in both Britain and the United States have emphasised the massive impact of changes in the political economies, populations and spatial organisation of urban localities (Katznelson, 1982; Thrift and Williams, 1987).

Dearlove (1973) argues that far from being neutral arbiters between competing interests local authorities are actively engaged in resisting, obstructing and excluding certain groups from decision making. From this perspective the role of local authorities is intrinsically one of making political choices and the management of conflictual pressures and interests.

What is notable about this literature, however, from the perspective of this book is that, in Britain at least, issues of race and ethnicity have been largely left off the agenda. This is as true of orthodox political science as it is of radical class-based theories. A few writers have begun to acknowledge the significance of racial themes in urban politics, and attempted to integrate this issue as an important dimension of contemporary British politics. Stoker (1988: 242), for example, has argued that 'we need to address more systematically the structures of inequality and the history of powerlessness which can lead to the exclusion and non-mobilisation of the working class, women, ethnic minorities and other deprived groups within local politics.' There are also signs that the increasing awareness of gender and other non-class specific forms of social categorisation is resulting in an increasing interest in the local processes of racial categorisation and exclusion.

But these developments are still at a relatively early stage, and it is true to say that the local dimension of the politics of racism remains sadly neglected.

Local politics and race

Despite this neglect ever since the 1960s a steady stream of studies have looked at various aspects of racial relations and conflicts in particular cities or localities (Rex and Moore, 1967; Richmond, 1973; Lawrence, 1974; Katznelson, 1976). The wide variety of issues covered by these studies is a sign of the dynamic and volatile nature of this topic. These studies fall into three broad categories, at least for analytical purposes.

The first category is the body of work carried out over two decades by John Rex and his associates, that emanates from the tradition of political sociology (Rex and Moore, 1967; Rex and Tomlinson, 1979). The focus of this research, carried out during the early 1960s and the early 1970s, was on the sociological analysis of the position of black minorities in the housing and employment markets of Birmingham. One of the issues which the research did analyse, however, was the role of local and national political processes in structuring the incorporation of black minorities into the institutions of the welfare state and into the employment and housing markets.

For example, Rex and Moore analysed the interplay between race and housing in an inner urban area of Birmingham, Sparkbrook, that had a significant black population. Their central concern was to analyse the reasons for the concentration of Asian and West Indian migrants in this declining area. But a central part of their research focused on the role of the policies practised by Birmingham's Housing Department and their impact on the incorporation of migrant communities in the housing market. Indeed, it is this aspect of their research that has attracted continuous attention ever since (Flett, 1981; Henderson and Karn, 1987; Ward, 1984).

In a second research project, carried out in the early 1970s, Rex and Tomlinson analysed the position of the black underclass in the Handsworth area of the city (Rex and Tomlinson, 1979). Once again the central concern of this project was to analyse the social position of the black communities in Handsworth, but Rex and Tomlinson did analyse the role of local and national political processes in determining this position. Additionally, they looked in some detail at the political groups that developed within the Asian and West Indian communities in the area. They analysed the history of such groups and their interaction with local political institutions.

The second body of work emanates from political science, and has been concerned with a number of aspects of the political incorporation of ethnic minorities in the local political system. Important studies from this school have looked at the role of racial and ethnic politics in the political life of cities such as Nottingham, Birmingham and Bristol since the 1950s. The work of Nicholas Deakin, David Beetham, Ken Newton, and Ira Katznelson are the best known examples of this type of work (Deakin, 1972; Beetham, 1970; Newton, 1976; Katznelson, 1976). More recently important studies have been carried out by Gideon Ben-Tovim and his associates in Liverpool and Wolverhampton (Ben-Tovim *et al.*, 1986) and by Anthony Messina in Ealing (Messina, 1987).

The main themes in this body of work have been the impact of racial factors on both local and national politics, the role of the local media, the response of local authorities to the race question and the role of racial factors in electoral politics. As yet, however, no detailed historical or comparative studies of the interplay between race and politics at the local level have been carried out. This compares badly with the rich and diverse studies of this area of racialised politics in the United States political science tradition (Browning *et al.*, 1984). The final category is the body of research produced within urban politics and urban geography. This is more recent and has been influenced by the debates about urban politics and social change (Cashmore, 1987; Jacobs, 1986; Smith, 1987; Spencer *et al.*, 1986). The focus of this body of work has been on the role of social and economic change in the restructuring of racial relations in urban localities and the response of the local state and political institutions to these changes.

Policy and politics

Most studies of the local politics of race have, however, not been concerned with these broader questions about the dynamics of local political power and change, but with the policies and agendas which have been associated with particular local authorities, and with the specifics of the implementation of particular policies.

A good example of this trend can be found in the work of Ken Young and his associates over the past decade (Young and Connelly, 1981, 1984; Young, 1985). The main focus of this body of work has been on (a) the context and environment of policy change and (b) the implementation of policy change through particular initiatives and policies. In particular the emphasis has been on the assumptive worlds of policy makers, meaning the assumptions which are used to develop and implement policy change. According to this framework most of the changes in this field over the past decade have been unplanned and unintended, resulting from the diverse impact of pressures for change both at a local level and from the impact on local authorities of the urban unrest of 1981 and subsequently (Young, 1985: 287).

Young and Connelly (1981) looked particularly at two aspects of policy change in a number of local authorities. First, the environment of policy change, and the variety and local political actors that make up this environment. Second, the content of the policy changes which local authorities have actually adopted and the processes by which they have sought to implement change. From this study Young and Connelly constructed a model which distinguished between four different types of local authority responses to racial issues:

1. 'Pioneers': innovative authorities which created a new machinery of policy making and implementation on racial issues.
2. 'Learners': authorities that accepted the need for change, and learned from the experience of the 'pioneers'.
3. 'Waverers': authorities that issue formal statements but do little to put them in practice.
4. 'Resisters': authorities that do not accept the need for specific policies on racial issues (Young and Connelly, 1981: 6–7)

This model has influenced much of the debate about the local politics of race, and have helped to sharpen the interest of researchers in the analysis of the actual processes of policy making and diffusion in local multi-racial settings.

A somewhat different framework of analysis has been offered by Herman Ouseley, who has worked at various levels of local government during the past two decades and who has specialised on equal opportunity issues. In Ouseley's account of policy development in this field the central role is occupied by the actions of black communities, local black politicians and administrators and by the political debates surrounding the 1981 and 1985 riots (Ouseley, 1981 and 1984). From his own extensive experience of work in a variety of local government contexts he argues that the key to change in the practices of local authorities lies in the combination of pressure from within and without the institutions of local politics and policy making.

From this perspective in order to understand the changing role that local authorities are playing in relation to racial issues it is necessary to look at such factors as the role of black community groups, the voluntary sector, black political leadership, the role of Community Relations Councils as well as the shifts in local and central government politics (Ouseley, 1982).

The local context

During the 1960s the characteristic form of political intervention at the local level to deal with race issues involved a complex interaction between central government, local authorities and voluntary agencies. From as early as the 1950s, as we saw in Chapters 3 and 4, the emergent social policy response to black immigration involved a two pronged strategy aimed at: (a) providing newly arrived immigrants with special help in relation to housing, employment, social problems and cultural adjustment; and (b) helping the host community understand the immigrants and overcome its prejudices. At a local level this strategy built upon the work of special officers appointed in a number of cities to help immigrants cope with their special problems, and the work of local agencies which had helped to define the policy response to black immigrants in areas such as London, Nottingham and Birmingham. In some areas this led to the formation of voluntary committees which consisted of representatives of statutory and voluntary social services, interested groups and individuals and trade unions. These committees played a particularly important role in areas of the country where race and related issues had already become politicised and aroused the interest of local politicians, the press and voluntary agencies.

During the early 1960s the local political context of race was a central theme in debates about immigration, particularly in areas of the West Midlands and other localities. Additionally, as we showed in Chapter 4, the direct and indirect impact of racist political mobilisation in Birmingham and the Black Country played an important part during the early 1960s in pushing the racialisation of political debate to a new level. Indeed the election of Peter Griffiths in Smethwick in 1964 was an important symbolic event, since it helped to shape the terms of political debate on immigration and entrench the consensus that black migrants were a problem that had to be dealt with through the enforcement of strict immigration controls and ameliorative race relations policies.

Policy change and conflict

Over the last three decades the racialisation of local politics had undergone a number of transformations. The processes which have resulted in the racialisation of local politics are complex, and to some extent they have been determined by the specific histories of particular localities. Broadly speaking, however, they can be divided into several stages. These stages themselves correspond to the changing position of the black migrant communities in British society.

A number of local authorities had developed ad hoc policies on racial issues from the 1950s onwards. This was particularly the case in

London and Birmingham. In a number of areas special officers were appointed with the brief to help migrants cope with their special problems and promote good race relations (Ben-Tovim *et al.*, 1986; 65–94). In some areas this led to the formation of voluntary committees which consisted of representatives of statutory and voluntary social services, migrant organisations and interested groups and individuals and trade unions. These committees played a particularly important role in areas of the country where race and related issues had already become politicised and aroused the interest of local politicians, the press and voluntary agencies. From the late 1960s such committees began to receive the support of the Community Relations Commission and became known by the generic term of Community Relations Councils (Hill and Issacharoff, 1971; Gay and Young, 1988).

Perhaps the distinguished feature of the earliest stages of racialised politics at the local level was the use of race as a symbol of the changing nature of local social and economic conditions. The manifest concerns expressed in the local press and in the pronouncements of local politicians were concentrated on such issues as housing, employment and the social problems which were popularly perceived as linked to immigration.

At various stages since the mid-1960s a number of legislative measures have sought to give central govenment a degree of influence in shaping the response of local authorities to 'race' issues. The main measures are detailed in Table 5.1:

Table 5.1   *Legislative measures and the local politics of race*

Year	Legislative measure
1966	Local Government Act
1969	Local Government Grants (Social Need) Act
1976	Race Relations Act
1978	Inner Urban Areas Act

The two measures introduced during the 1960s seemed to have a rather limited impact on policy development within local authorities. Both Section 11 of the 1966 Local Government Act and the 1969 Local Government Grants (Social Need) Act had their origins in the intense debates about race and immigration which raged throughout the 1960s (Edwards and Batley, 1978). They were thus measures that were largely aimed at providing financial support from central government for those localities with particularly large black populations.

Section 11 of the 1966 Local Government Act was the result of the widespread debate during the mid-1960s about the impact of immigration on particular localities and was intended as a way of distributing central government money to local authorities in order to help meet the special needs of ethnic minority groups in relation to education and social welfare (*Hansard*, Vol. 729, 1966: Cols 1331–8). During the past two decades it has provided substantial sums to a number of local authorities, though there has been some controversy about the direct impact of these monies on the needs of minority communities.

The 1969 Local Government Grants (Social Need) Act implemented the Urban Programme, which had first been announced by the Government in May 1968. This was to some extent a direct response by the Labour Government to the 'rivers of blood' speech made by Enoch Powell in April 1968 (Edwards and Batley, 1978; Higgins *et al.*, 1983). It was meant to provide special help to areas where social deprivation was pervasive, including the special needs of ethnic minorities. Unlike Section 11 the Urban Programme was not presented as being concerned only with racial deprivation, but in practice many of the projects funded through it have had a strong emphasis on this issue.

These two initiatives were the first of a number of initiatives aimed at providing central government support to local initiatives aimed at tackling urban deprivation in multi-racial settings (Jacobs, 1986). The story of these policies would take us beyond the bounds of this volume, though two points need to be emphasised about their impact on the urban politics of racial inequality. First, the scale of these initiatives and the resources allocated to them did not in any way match the interventions of the federal government in the United States during this same period. Given the extent of the deprivation which they were supposed to tackle both Section 11 and the Urban Programme were largely symbolic measures rather than national programmes of action. Second, during the 1960s and early 1970s local authorities themselves showed little interest in developing policies in this field. Although some local authorities were beginning to give some recognition to the existence of racial inequality, this rarely went beyond limited support for the work of Community

Relations Councils and allocation of grants to some local community groups (Ouseley, 1981).

The 1976 Race Relations Act

By the mid-1970s the general picture was one of a limited or non-existent response by most local authorities to the question of racial inequality. This was why during the passage of the 1976 Race Relations Act through Parliament, a Labour back-bencher, Fred Willey, argued forcefully that an amendment should be included about the role of local authorities in the promotion of better race relations. Although Willey's amendment was initially opposed by the Government it was eventually included as section 71 of the Race Relations Act, and it consisted of the following general injunction:

> Without prejudice to their obligation to comply with any other provision of this Act, it shall be the duty of every local authority to make appropriate arrangements with a view to securing that their functions are carried out with regard to the need: (a) to eliminate unlawful racial discrimination; and (b) to promote equality of opportunity, and good relations, between persons of different racial groups. (Race Relations Act, 1976)

Thus Section 71 of the Act placed a particular duty on local authorities to eliminate unlawful racial discrimination and promote equality of opportunity between persons of different racial groups. This statutory provision did not seem to have an immediate effect on the policies or practices of the majority of local authorities, although a few did take up the opportunity offered by the Act to consolidate their efforts in this field (Young and Connelly, 1981). Additionally, the CRE attempted from an early stage in its existence to encourage local authorities to develop better practices and learn from the experiences of the more innovative ones.

Whatever the limits of Section 71 in the late 1970s, in the aftermath of the urban unrest in Bristol, London and Liverpool during 1980–1 a growing number of local authorities started to develop policies on racial discrimination. As Ouseley (1984) has noted, whatever the impact of the urban unrest in other fields, it does seem to have acted as a mechanism for encouraging local authorities to respond to the demands of their local black communities for action to tackle racial discrimination in employment, service delivery and housing. At the same time although the impact of Section 71 remains unclear, it seems to have provided the basis of promoting policy change within the existing structure of local government (Young and Connelly, 1981; Young: 1987).

Urban left politics and racial inequality

Since the early 1980s public attention has been focused on the experiences of a number of local authorities which have introduced radical policy changes in relation to racial inequality. The most notable cases have been the Greater London Council before it was abolished, the Inner London Education Authority and the London boroughs of Lambeth, Brent, Hackney and Haringey. Nationally, a number of other local authorities have adopted comprehensive policy statements on racial equality and equal opportunity generally.

In all these cases a combination of factors seems to have prompted rapid policy change. First, bolstered by the urban unrest that has been much in evidence during the 1980s local black politicians and groups have sought to include racial inequality on the local political agenda. Second, a number of left local authorities sought to use the issue of equal opportunity as a mechanism for widening their basis of support among ethnic minorities and other constituencies (Stoker, 1988: 207–8). Third, the failure of central government to respond to calls for radical reform was seen as a sign that relatively little change could be expected as a result of the actions of central government.

Three main policy changes

The result of these pressures was reflected in three main policy changes. The first addressed the central question of 'who gets what?', and the emphasis has been on establishing equality of treatment and equality of outcome in the allocation process. Ethnic records have been introduced to monitor channels of access and allocation. For example, in relation to housing, authorities such as Hackney and Haringey have sought to monitor mobility within the local housing stock and the quality of distribution, and to change procedures that facilitated discretion and contributed to discriminatory outcomes.

The second policy change has addressed the question of the employment of black staff within local authorities. This has resulted in a number of authorities linking the question of allocative equality with representation of black and ethnic minority staff in local government departments. Racially discriminatory outcomes, it was argued, were not solely the function of organisation procedures but also related to the under-representation or exclusion of black and ethnic minority staff. Consequently, targets have been established to increase the employment of black and ethnic minority staff.

Finally, a number of local authorities have introduced promotional measures that are intended to improve communications with, and awareness of, the difficulties faced by black and ethnic minorities. These include such measures as translation of policy documents into ethnic languages, race awareness and equal opportunity training, and more effective controls against racial harassment.

From policy to practice

Once again, however, the experience of local authorities seems to mirror that of central government initiatives, since there has been a gap between the promise embodied in policy statements and the actual achievements of policies.

During the early 1980s authorities such as Lambeth and Hackney did make some progress in changing their employment practices and service delivery to reflect the multi-racial composition of their local populations. Initiatives in specific policy areas such as social services and housing have also been put into practice. In Hackney's case the combination of pressure from the local black communities and a formal investigation by the Commission for Racial Equality forced the council to rethink its housing policy and introduce major changes. During the early 1980s local authorities were also the site of important debates about the delivery of social services and education.

Yet after the flurry of policy activity and change during the early 1980s the last few years have been a period of conflict, negative media publicity about racial equality policies and in some cases resistance to change by the local white population. The debates about multi-racial education in Brent, Bradford, Dewsbury and most recently Manchester, the media coverage of the activities of the loony left in a number of local authorities in London, and the attack on anti-racism launched by sections of the political right have tended to push even the most radical local authorities on the defensive. Indeed in some cases the public attention given to anti-racism has tended to take attention away from the persistence of racial inequality and direct critical attention at those local authorities attempting to allocate resources to minority groups.

Most importantly, perhaps, the increasing fiscal constraints imposed by central government and pressure on the resources available to local authorities have left little room for the maintenance of the initiatives already introduced or for new developments.

Urban political change and racial equality

Prospects for the future

During the early 1980s, at the height of local authority intervention in the area of racial equality, much hope was placed in the role of local authorities as an agent of change, particularly in the context of the neglect of racial equality by the Thatcher administrations. Indeed one study of the local politics of race argued that the local political scene has 'provided important sites of struggle, particularly for local organisations committed to racial equality' (Ben-Tovim *et al.*, 1986: 169). Yet in recent years the experience of a number of local authorities seems to indicate that any gains in this area were fragile and vulnerable.

During the late 1980s there have been signs that even previously radical local authorities are now adopting a lower profile on issues concerned with racial equality. This seems to be partly the result of the increasingly negative public attention given to the policies and programmes pursued by a number of local authorities in London. Additionally, the Labour Party has increasingly sought to distance itself from being directly identified with the actions of the urban left in these local authorities and to encourage them to give a lower profile to issues which are seen as either controversial or minority causes.

Perhaps one of the most widely publicised features of this retreat is the increasing attention given by the popular media to the activities of local authorities that have traditionally been seen as at the forefront of race equality initiatives. It is perhaps a sign of the nature of the present political climate that increasingly it is not racism which is presented as the central problem but anti-racism.

During the 1980s anti-racism has come to occupy a central position in debates about the local politics of race in British society. It has become a catch-all phrase to which various meanings are attributed. It has also become the target of much critical debate and attack in a number of policy arenas.

Indeed over the past few years there has been a noticeable trend to either dismiss the relevance of anti-racism or for the neo-right and the media to articulate an anti-anti-racist position, which sees the anti-racists as a bigger political threat than the racists.

The local political scene has proved to be one of the most volatile and controversial in this context. In certain arenas, such as education and social welfare, the issue of anti-racism has become a source of conflict and resistance. In educational politics the recent experience of Labour LEAs attempting to implement programmes of change in educational provision proves how explosive this issue can be. The massive media coverage given to the cases of Ray Honeyford in Bradford and Maureen McGoldrick in Brent, are perhaps the most important examples of this process, although there have been numerous other less publicised cases over the past few years (Murray, 1986). More recently the controversy about the policies pursued by Manchester Council in the field of anti-racist education in Burnage High School has highlighted the problematic nature of policy developments in this field even further (*Manchester Evening News*, 25 April 1988; *Guardian*, 3 May 1988).

The dynamics of this phenomenon are an important aspect of the changing political scene on racial issues in British society, but they take us beyond the confines of this chapter. We shall return to the wider dimensions of the emergence of anti-anti-racism in Chapter 7.

Thatcherism and local government

Perhaps the most important constraint on the role that local authorities will be able to play in the promotion of racial equality is that within the overall political programme of Thatcherism there seems to be little room for positive initiatives on racial equality or to the political autonomy of local government.

On the first point, the language which Thatcher has used to talk about the impact of the black presence on urban localities has tended to lend support to the fears of the majority white community. In the context of the controversies over actions of local authorities on such issues as multi-racial education the interventions of the Thatcher Government have helped to emphasise that Mrs Thatcher's swamping statement of 1978 was by no means an isolated utterance but an affirmation of a more deep seated commitment to the values of the white majority in British society. Her role in the controversies about Ray Honeyford and the dispute between local white parents and the local education authority in Kirklees emphasise this point.

On the second point the massive changes which the Thatcher Governments have introduced in relation to local government emphasise the limits which central government can impose on the autonomy of local authorities. According to a recent study of the politics of change in local government in an environment of economic retrenchment and political uncertainty it is likely that local authorities will be (a) less willing to experiment with innovation in areas which are controversial, and (b) less responsive to demands for more resources from previously excluded groups. In such a situation it becomes likely that women's, race relations and equal opportunity committees, their units and advisers, can find themselves isolated and marginalised (Stoker, 1988: 200). There is increasing evidence that this process of marginalisation has already started, and the consequence of this can be seen in the disputed nature of race equality and anti-racist initiatives.

The increasing incorporation of black politicians and community groups within the local political system may have some impact as to how far black interests will be ignored or put on the back burner. Already there is evidence that black politicians are beginning to exercise a degree of influence in a number of local authorities. The extent and permanence of this influence remain to be seen.

Summary and conclusion

The main question we have addressed in this chapter is simply stated: What has been the impact of local political processes on the politics of racism in contemporary Britain? It seems impossible, however, to generalise and say that there has been a uniform pattern of policy response in this field throughout the past three decades, since local political and policy responses have been conditioned by both national and local determinants which have produced important variations in both the form and content of local state interventions. While at a broad level the wider social, political and economic context has imposed constraints on the extent of policy change, it is impossible to ignore the role of local politicians, professionals and bureaucrats in defining policy objectives and priorities.

Perhaps the most important conclusion to emerge from this and the previous chapter is that throughout the past two decades policy change in this field, whether at a national or local level, has been a complex process of responsive actions to pressures from both within and outside the main political institutions. The actual impact of these policies on the extent of racism and discrimination in British society has been fairly limited, and during the 1980s there has been increasing resistance and opposition to anti-racist policies at the local level.

The politics of race may remain a central feature of the local political scene in many localities over the next decade. But in making any assessment about the possibilities for bringing about greater racial equality through local initiatives it is important to bear in mind the fundamental changes which local politics has undergone over the past decade and the changes to come.

6 Policing, Law and Order and Urban Unrest

Introduction

Some reference has already been made in the previous two chapters to the impact of two processes on the politics of racialisation during the 1970s and 1980s. First, the evident racialisation of policing, particularly in inner city areas, during this period. Second, the impact of the riots during 1980–1 and 1985 on the politics of race, at both the national and local levels. Even from these general references it should be clear that no account of the politics of race in contemporary Britain can ignore the role that urban unrest has played in public debate about racial issues during the 1980s.

In this chapter we want to look in more detail at the political and ideological context of the interplay between policing, law and order and urban unrest during the early 1980s, although some reference will also have to be made to the late 1970s. This will in turn lay the foundations for the account of racism, anti-racism and social change which follows in the rest of this book. This chapter will concentrate on events during the early 1980s, while more recent examples of urban unrest will be discussed in Chapter 9.

The politics of urban unrest

Urban unrest has become a recurrent feature of the political scene in Britain since 1980. Major outbreaks of unrest were recorded in 1980, 1981 and 1985 and smaller scale disturbances occurred in every other year. There is little doubt that these outbreaks of unrest have helped to transform the nature of public and policy debates about racial issues in a number of fundamental ways.

99

Ever since the violent confrontations on the streets of Bristol on 2 April 1980, the ideological and policy responses to such events have taken a number of forms. First, there has been a vigorous discussion about the causes of violent protest, particularly in inner city multi-racial areas. Second, a more limited debate has taken place about the dynamics of riot participation, and the individual and social factors which may lead to some groups participating in riots or more limited confrontations with the police. Third, attempts have been made to show what kind of reforms and policy changes may be necessary to deal with violent protests and to prevent them becoming a regular feature of urban localities.

All these questions are important and need to receive more detailed investigation. The core concern of this chapter, however, is the question of the interrelationship between the first and third set of responses, namely between the symbolic political language which has sought to explain violent protests and the language of reform and policy change. This is an issue which has received only limited attention so far, particularly in relation to the role of the police (Benyon, 1984; Benyon and Solomos, 1987), the media (Murdock, 1984; Burgess, 1985), government agencies (Parkinson and Duffy, 1984) and youth policies (Solomos, 1988).

This chapter will explore the symbolic political language used in generating explanations of and responses to the riots during the early 1980s. This was an important period in the racialisation of the British state both at a national and a local level, and was a turning point in the politicisation of law and order. The focus of this chapter will be on the political and policy dimensions of these processes. This will involve an analysis of the Scarman Report and its impact on policy, as well as wider policy issues. Before moving on to the events of 1980–1, however, it is necessary to say something about the period of the late 1970s.

Race, policing and law and order

As we have seen in earlier chapters the perception of black migrants as a source of social problems and of instability was a common theme in both political and ideological responses to immigration. From the

1950s onwards the police were intimately involved in the construction of this imagery, and in certain areas of London and other urban conurbations debates about crime and related problems gradually became inflected with racial symbols.

Clear manifestations of conflict between sections of the black communities and the police became a regular phenomenon from the late 1960s onwards, but the roots of this conflict can be traced back to the 1950s. Differential treatment of black migrants by the police is by no means a recent phenomenon. There is also a wealth of evidence of manifest racial prejudice within the police force dating back to the early stages of migration. In the 1950s some of the main areas of concern were the involvement of some black men in prostitution and in drugs. Yet it is important to note that despite concern over these issues, the police in the 1950s and 1960s were of the opinion that there was no causal relationship between immigrants and crime, or between the concentration of black migrants in certain areas and problems of public order.

Increased public attention on black crime came about later on, and was connected with the criminalisation of young black people from the late 1960s onwards. During the 1960s political opinion about race and immigration began to shift from a preoccupation with the arrival of migrants per se to the question of the future of those migrants and their children who were settled in Britain and were likely to remain so. As evidence of continued discrimination against young black people emerged, fears were expressed that this group could become increasingly disaffected and drift into the kind of ghetto subcultures that had emerged in the United States.

The politicisation of the form of street crime that came to be known as mugging during the early 1970s, along with reports of confrontations between young black people and the police, helped to generate popular images of young blacks as criminals and as a threat to public order (Solomos, 1988). These images were amplified further during the late 1970s, when small-scale confrontations between the police and young blacks became a regular phenomenon. The clashes between the police and young blacks at the Notting Hill Carnival of 1976, and at subsequent Carnivals, were merely the most publicised of a series of confrontations which attracted the attention of the media and of policy makers to the question of the potential for violent urban unrest in Britain's inner city areas.

Conflict, disorder and urban unrest: 1980–1

The events of the late 1970s, however, have tended to be pushed into the background by the weight of public attention given to the more large-scale disturbances that have occurred with regularity throughout the 1980s. These events have attracted widespread attention from the media, the police, central and local government, voluntary agencies and black political and community groups on a scale never witnessed before in the post-1945 politics of race in Britain.

The modalities of ideological and policy response to these events since 1980 can be delineated along chronological and thematic lines. The advantage of the first approach is that it is clearly important to know the sequential development of such responses between Bristol in 1980 and Brixton in 1985. In other words we need to know what happened, who participated in the actual events, the responses of various governmental and non-governmental agencies, and the prospects for the future. This reconstruction of events will occupy part of this chapter. But the mere cataloguing of the facts is not enough to tell us how the events were experienced politically, their mythological construction, and the competing symbols which they gave rise to. It is also important to analyse the language used to construct beliefs about the significance of the events, since it is 'language about political events and developments that people experience' (Edelman, 1985: 10). This will be the central concern of this chapter.

During 1980 and 1981 three main examples of urban unrest were recorded. First, in April 1980 violent confrontations took place in the St. Paul's district of Bristol between groups of predominantly black residents and the police. Second, during April 1981 violent confrontations between the police and crowds of mostly black youth took place in the Brixton area of London. Finally, in July 1981 widespread outbreaks of urban unrest were reported in the Southall area of London, in the Toxteth area of Liverpool, and in Brixton and other localities in London. During both 1980 and 1981 other smaller scale disturbances also took place and attracted some attention in the media and within government (Benyon, 1984).

The scale of the confrontations varied considerably, but in combination the sequence of riots after April 1980 forced the questions of urban protest onto the political agenda. Government departments, local authorities, the police, and other agencies were forced to make sense of the events and to respond to them.

The Brixton events of April 10–13, 1981 led the government to set up the Scarman Inquiry, which, although much more limited than the various American inquiries in the 1960s, sought to explain what happened and also what should be done by government and other agencies in the future (Scarman, 1981; Benyon, 1984). The more widespread events during July 1981 led to a flurry of responses at both central and local government levels, and real and symbolic interventions which sought to prevent the further spread of disorder and violence. It is not surprising, for example, that after years of inaction many local authorities actively sought to develop equal opportunity strategies, that promises were made to reform police training to take account of multi-racialism, that initiatives to tackle the roots of racial disadvantage and discrimination were promised (Joshua and Wallace, 1983).

All of these responses are examples of the 'symbolic reassurance' which was noted by American analysts (Lipsky and Olson, 1977), but they took different issues as the core variables. There were at least four basic explanatory frameworks used, which emphasised in turn race, violence and disorder, the breakdown of law and order, social deprivation and youth unemployment and political marginality as the core issues. We shall now look at how these issues influenced the terms of political debate about the riots during the 1980–2 period.

Race and disorder

The racialisation of the 1980–1 events was evident from the very first confrontation in Bristol on 2 April 1980, although in a somewhat convoluted manner. Under the headline 'Riot Mob Stone Police' the *Daily Mail* talked of 'mobs of black youths' roaming the streets (3 April 1980). This was a theme repeated in the coverage of the *Sun*, *Daily Star* and *Daily Express*. The *Financial Times*, however, covered the same events under the headline: 'Bristol: a multiracial riot against the police' (5 April 1980). The *Guardian* was even more ambiguous, with the headline: 'The Bristol confrontation: racial but not racist' (5 April 1980).

The tension between the racial and non-racial elements in media coverage of the Bristol events reflected, according to Joshua and Wallace, a wider divergence in political responses to violent protest: between modes of explanations which saw race and law and order as the essential variables and those which saw the riots as the outcome of inner city decay and unemployment (Joshua and Wallace, 1983: ch. 2). This tension was partly the result of official resistance to the idea that Britain was experiencing race riots on the American model, and the wish to defuse the situation by separating out the actions of groups of youth from wider social, economic and political grieveances. The very fact that the events occurred in Bristol, a city with a popular image of good race relations was taken as evidence that they were not a race riot. A local paper reported that both William Whitelaw and Tony Benn were agreed that the events could not be described as a race riot (*Evening Post*, 3 April 1980).

Reactions to Bristol are worth remembering, precisely because they highlight the changing symbolism attached to race as an explanatory factor in urban violence during the 1980s. Bristol represented a dilemma even for those who had warned of the possibility of urban violence, since such predictions were premised on areas such as Brixton, Handsworth, Moss Side, and Toxteth rather than St. Paul's. Its very unexpectedness made it all the more difficult to locate the role of race or racism as causal factors. But the linkage between black youth and street violence was already established in popular media images.

This can be seen partly by the reactions to small-scale street confrontations between Bristol 1980 and the next major outbreak, in Brixton on 10–13 April 1981. During this intervening period a number of smaller confrontations took place with the police. The most important took place on 3 March 1980, during a demonstration held to protest the death of 13 young West Indians in a fire in Deptford, South London. The *Daily Express* covered the events under the headline 'Rampage of a Mob' (3 March 1980), while the *Daily Mail* saw them as, 'When the Black Tide Met the Thin Blue Line' (3 March 1980). Racialisation of the confrontation between the mostly-black marchers and the police was achieved around the themes of the 'mob' and 'young blacks'. As the *Daily Mirror* saw it:

A peaceful protest by 10 000 of London's West Indians was ruined by the hooliganism of 200 young blacks. (March 4, 1981)

The ambiguity of the coverage of the events in Bristol was replaced by the emphasis on the involvement of small groups of young blacks in street confrontations with the police, and the role of black militants and outside agitators in fostering violence for their own objectives. Whatever the symbolic importance of Bristol and the Deptford march, however, there is no doubt that the period between April and July 1981 constituted the crucial phase in the racialisation of discourses about violent protest. Events in Brixton (10–13 April) and nationwide (3–28 July) led to a number of accounts of the events which saw them through the prism of race. The most stark usage of racial symbols to explain the violence was articulated by Enoch Powell and a small but vociferous group of Conservative MPs and journalists. Powell had already intervened in a somewhat muted form during the Bristol events, but he made series of interventions during 1981 which articulated his view of why the riots could not be understood without reference to race and immigration. In a confrontation with William Whitelaw in Parliament he concluded by saying that in view of the 'prospective future increase in the relevant population' future outbreaks were inevitable, and that 'Britain has seen nothing yet' (*Hansard*, 1981, Vol. 3: Col. 25). By July 1981 he had warmed up to this theme and argued his case in a number of articles in the popular press, as well as in his parliamentary speeches. During a vigorous speech in the House he disagreed with Roy Hattersley that the three main causes of the July riots were poverty, unemployment and deprivation. Pouring scorn on this analysis he offered his own causal factor and constructed the linkage with race without actually uttering the word:

> Are we seriously saying that so long as there is poverty, unemployment and deprivation our cities will be torn to pieces, that the police in them will be the objects of attack and that we shall destroy our own environment? Of course not. Everyone knows that, although those conditions do exist, there is a factor, the factor which the people concerned perfectly well know, understand and apprehend, and that unless it can be dealt with – unless the fateful inevitability, the inexorable doubling and trebling of that element of a population can be avoided – their worst fears will be fulfilled. (*Hansard*, 1981, Vol. 8: Col. 1313)

He repeated his argument in a series of graphic warnings in the popular press over this period. In addition a number of right-wing

Conservative MPs, newspaper columnists and commentators took up Powellite themes and embellished them with different symbols, as did the extreme neo-fascist groupings.

If Powellite imagery was the most stark usage of race as the main explanation for the riots, it was by no means the only one, whether it be in the official reports about the riots, in press and television coverage or in the general public policy debate. In all of these categories such as race, racial discrimination or black youth played a central role either implicitly or explicitly. During both the Brixton riot of April 1981 and the nationwide riots of July 1981 the press was full of images, both pictorial and written, that emphasised that race was somehow a central variable or even the main one. The strength of these images is particularly clear during July 1981 when headlines proclaimed the hatred that blacks had for the police, their alienation or detachment from the mainstream values of British society, and the growth of racial tension in certain important localities. Among the early reports on the riots the *Daily Mail's* headline proclaimed simply: 'Black War on the Police' (6 July 1981). This was perhaps the most extreme, but the *Sun* was only marginally less direct when it talked of 'The Cities that Live in Fear' while the *Daily Mirror* proclaimed the words of Merseyside's Chief Constable, Kenneth Oxford, when it argued: 'This was not a race war. It was blacks versus the police.'

A number of lead articles in both the popular and the serious press over the period from 6 July to 25 July devoted much attention to the race issue, which they saw as important in various degrees. In addition, Enoch Powell's statements and those of other politicians in favour of repatriation were widely reported, though usually with a disclaimer which distanced the paper from such extreme views. Ronald Butt, writing in the *Daily Mail*, argued that the culprits in the riots were for the most part black and that this meant that one could not blame white society for the kinds of attitudes that led young blacks to stage disturbances. Rather the blame lay with the attitudes of young blacks and with those agitators who directed such attitudes to their own ends (10 July 1981).

The ambivalence about whether the events in Bristol had been a race riot had been replaced by July 1981 by the imagery that since a sizeable number of riot participants were black the riots were racial or at least the outcome of bad relations between the police and young blacks. But racism as such was only rarely talked about, since the riots were not seen as linked to real grievances but only to the perceptions that young blacks had of their position in society, and to the wider processes which were undermining the role of law.

Law and order

The second symbol that was prominent in debates during 1980 – 1 was Law and Order. This was by no means an accident, since throughout the 1970s a powerful body of media, political, policy and academic opinion had been constructed around the theme of how Britain was drifting into a violent society, and how the basis of consent was being shifted by the pressures of forces undermining the moral fabric of British society (Hall *et al.*, 1978). An article by Peregrine Worsthorne during this period underlined this fear:

> The spectre haunting most ordinary people is neither that of a totalitarian state nor Big Brother but of other ordinary people being allowed to run wild. What they are worried about is crime, violence, disorder in the schools, promiscuity, idleness, pornography, football hooliganism, vandalism and urban terrorism. (Worsthorne, 1978:151)

The riots, however, were instrumental in popularising Worsthorne's image of 'ordinary people being allowed to run wild' beyond the readership of neo-conservative tracts and readers of the *Daily Telephraph*. By forcing the debate on law and order onto the streets they helped give actuality to the warnings which had been expounded by a number of commentators for over a decade that lawlessness and corrosive violence were undermining traditional British values and institutions.

A glimpse of the impact of the 1980 – 1 riots at this level can be achieved through two important debates in Parliament. The first took place in the midst of the July riots, and had as its theme 'Civil Disturbances'. The importance of the debate is indicated by the fact that more than 60 MPs showed a wish to participate in it. The tone of the debate was set by William Whitelaw's introductory statement which spoke of the need to (a) 'remove the scourge of criminal violence from out streets', and (b) the urgency of developing 'policies designed to promote the mutual tolerance and understanding upon which the whole future of a free democratic society depends' (*Hansard*, Vol. 8, 1981: Col. 1405). The scourge of criminal violence was, Whitelaw argued, a danger to the whole framework of consent and legality on which the political institutions of British society were based. In reply Roy Hattersley supported the call for the immediate suppression of street violence, but warned that the roots of such riots could not be dealt with until all people felt they had a stake in our society (*ibid.*, Cols 1407–9).

The second debate took place on 26 November 1981 and had as its theme 'Law and Order'. The importance of the riots in pushing the law and order issue, and specifically policing, onto the main political agenda was emphasised by the Liberal Leader, David Steel, who argued that urgent action to prevent a drift into lawlessness from both a moral and political perspective (*Hansard*, Vol. 13, 1981: Cols 1009–11). A subsequent debate on the same issue in March 1982 was also full of references to the experience of 1981, the impact of street violence, crime, decaying urban conditions, the breakdown of consent between the police and many local communities, and the spectre of more violence to come if changes at the level of policing tactics and social policy were not swiftly introduced (*Hansard*, Vol. 20, 1982: Cols 1107–81).

The psychological and symbolic impact of the riots was also grasped by Lord Scarman, whose report on Brixton contained the following graphic description:

During the week-end of 10–12 April (Friday, Saturday and Sunday) the British people watched with horror and incredulity an instant audio-visual presentation on their television sets of scenes of violence and disorder in their capital city, the like of which had not previously been seen in this century in Britain. In the centre of Brixton, a few hundred young people most, but not all of them, black – attacked the police on the streets with stones, bricks, iron bars and petrol bombs, demonstrating to millions of their fellow citizens the fragile basis of the Queen's peace. These young people, by their criminal behaviour – for such, whatever their grievances or frustrations, it was – brought about a temporary collapse of law and order in the centre of an inner suburb of London. (Scarman, 1981: para. 1.2)

It is perhaps all too easy to forget this sense of shock and the fear that more violence was to come which pervaded much of the discussion of the riots during and after 1981. But even a brief glance at both the popular and quality press during April 1981 and July 1981 reveals the deep sense of shock at the street violence which was popularly perceived as not having occurred on the same scale during this century. On the 13th of April *The Times* reported that looters and mobs of young people had virtually taken over the Brixton area from the police. The *Guardian* saw it somewhat differently, but it still talked of 'The Battle of Brixton'. The *Daily Mail* talked of an 'army of rioting black youths' taking to the street, the *Daily Star* talked of 'Flames of Hate'. The *Daily Mirror* took a longer term view when it warned that the Brixton events were 'The Shape of Things to Come' and that the next riots could come in Birmingham, Manchester or many other inner city localities. Under a picture of groups of youths facing and throwing stones and missiles at the police it ran the following headline:

> THE BATTLE RAGES: Youths, white and black, hurl their barrage of missiles at point blank range as police attempt to take cover behind their shields.

Similar, and more detailed reports are to be found in most of the papers during 14 and 15 April, and intermittently throughout April and into May.

The messages which such reporting contained were complex and quite often contradictory. But the centrality of the law and order theme, the fear that disorderly street violence was becoming an established fact of the English way of life and the linkages constructed with black youth as the main group involved highlight the symbolic evocation of the re-establishment of order as the main concern of official political language during this period. Under the headline 'Order Before Research' a *Daily Telegraph* editorial asserted:

> Mob violence must be stopped. Existing laws should be used to the full to punish the offenders and guarantee safety in our cities. If the Public Order Act . . . cannot cope with the threat of disorder now, then new riot legislation must be enacted. (6 July 1981)

The need to support the police was accepted by both the Labour and Conservative speakers in the Parliamentary Debate on the riots, and was established as a benchmark for the official response to the riots long before the Scarman Report was published in November 1981.

Any substantive disagreement centred around the issue of what role social deprivation and unemployment had in bringing young people to protest violently on the streets.

A particularly interesting sub-theme within the law and order arguments was the emergence of the outside agitator and the middle men who were seen by some sections of the press as directing the violence. Under the headline 'Search for the Masked Men' the *Daily Mail* reported on 7 July:

> Masked figures on motor cycles were seen issuing instructions to groups of rioters on the second night of violence in the predominantly black district (of Toxteth). They appeared to be giving tactical orders to sections of the 500 strong mob of mainly white youths. As the battle developed, groups armed with petrol bombs and stones were moved quickly from street to street.

During July 1981 a whole sub-mythology grew up around this imagery of outside forces directing the actions of mobs on the street, and the purposes which they had in mind. As we shall see later this was precisely an image that was taken up and reworked in 1985 to become one of the main symbols used to analyse the causes of the riots in Handsworth, Brixton and Tottenham.

Social causes

Intermingled with the discourses about race and law and order but somewhat autonomous were constant references to unemployment, particularly among the young, and various forms of social disadvantage and poverty. The attack by Enoch Powell on the arguments articulated by Roy Hattersley was but one example of the clash between explanations of the riots on the basis of social deprivation arguments and other political discourses. Throughout 1980 and 1981 debates about the riots in the media, Parliament and in various official reports hinged around the interrelationship between racial, law and order and social factors. The importance of this debate can be explained, partly, by the political capital which the opposition could make from linking the social and economic malaise of the country at large with violent street disturbances. Hence throughout this period numerous government ministers strenuously denied that unemployment and social deprivation were the most important roots of urban unrest.

The tone of this debate and the ambiguities contained in 'social' explanations of the riots highlight the complex dilemmas which were faced by the political establishment during 1980–1. These dilemmas became even greater when the Scarman Report was published in November 1981, to be followed by a vigorous public debate about how the report could be implemented, what other policy initiatives were necessasry, and what immediate measures could prevent a recurrence of the July 1981 events in 1982.

Although the Scarman Report is often taken to be the central text which argues for a link between social conditions and disorder, the terms of the debate were by no means set by Scarman. During both April and July 1981 vigorous exchanges took place in both the press and in Parliament about the role that deteriorating social conditions and unemployment may have played in bringing about the riots. During the 16 July Parliamentary Debate on 'Civil Disturbances' Roy Hattersley's formulation of this linkage provided a useful summary of the 'social conditions' argument. After some preliminary remarks about the Labour Party's support for the police, he went on to outline his opposition to the view of the riots as essentially anti-police outbursts:

> I repeat that I do not believe that the principal cause of last week's riots was the conduct of the police. It was the conditions of deprivation and despair in the decaying areas of our old cities – areas in which the Brixton and Toxteth riots took place, and areas from which the skinhead invaders of Southall come. (*Hansard*, Vol. 8, 1981: Col. 1408)

He went on to outline the four common features shared by such areas, namely:

(1) inadequate housing and inadequate government spending on improvements;
(2) a lack of social, cultural and welfare amenities;
(3) inadequate provision of remedial education for deprived families; and
(4) high levels of unemployment, particularly youth unemployment.

Much of the subsequent controversy about this analysis, apart from Powell's retort which is discussed above, centred on the question of youth unemployment. Hattersley had suggested that the riots are a direct product of high levels of youth unemployment, and a furious debate ensued in both Parliament and the media about this assertion. Though the Scarman Report will be discussed later in the chapter, it is worth noting that a similar debate took place in the aftermath of its publication, linking up many of the reports arguments with the Hattersley version of the social conditions argument.

What is interesting about the debate surrounding this symbol, however, are the different emphases which were put on the four common features which Hattersley identified in his parliamentary speech. While challenging any causal link between unemployment and violent protest, both William Whitelaw and Margaret Thatcher accepted that social conditions in many inner city areas were bad. What they disputed, however, was the jump from such conditions to violent confrontations on the streets between youth and the police. During the Brixton riots the Prime Minister replied angrily to Labour suggestions that unemployment was a primary cause of the riots:

> If you consider that unemployment was the only cause – or the main cause – of the riots I would disagree with you. Nothing that has happened to unemployment would justify these riots. (As quoted in the *Financial Times* 15 April 1981)

A number of exchanges along the same lines took place during July 1981, about both unemployment and urban poverty. The existence of unemployment as such was not denied, though its impact was disputed, but the formula which established a link between high levels of young unemployed and urban disorder remained a hotly debated issue.

Alienation and powerlessness

The final symbolic cue used to make sense of the 1980–1 protests is more difficult to categorise, but its basic meaning can be captured by the term 'political marginality'. While a number of discussions of the roots of urban unrest in the USA have noted the salience of political marginality in determining participation in violent protests (Skolnick, 1969; Fogelson, 1971; Edelman, 1971), this issue has received relatively little attention in Britain. Nevertheless, during the 1980–1 events and their aftermath the political context was discussed from a number of perspectives.

The Scarman Report, for example, located part of the explanation for the riots in the feeling of alienation and powerlessness which were experienced by young blacks living in depressed inner city areas. A successful policy for tackling the roots of urban disorder was seen as one which sought to involve all the community in dealing with the problems of each area so that they could come to feel that they have a stake in its future (Scarman, 1981: para 6.42).

A good number of examples of the political marginality argument can also be found in the media coverage during 1980–1. After the Bristol riot, for example, the *Observer* reported the events by quoting a 'lanky Rastafarian with dangling dreadlocks' who argued:

> Discrimination accumulates; chickens come home to roost. They wanted to strike fear in people's hearts with law and order. You have no say in your life. People may give you some grant, some urban aid, but they are not really interested in getting to the root of the situation. (6 April 1980)

While such a viewpoint was rarely heard, throughout this period the question of politics and power did enter into some aspects of the public debate about the causes of urban violence. Precisely because it raised questions about power, however, the issue of political marginality was difficult to handle and touched upon the thorny problem of how far the riots were in fact a form of political action.

The ambiguity and tension which the 1980–1 riots created meant that though the statements of lanky Rastafarians could be repeated and to some extent taken on board, they were not accorded the detailed coverage in the mass media that the other symbols were given. Where such arguments did not fit in with the overarching themes of race, violence and disorder and social deprivation they were either sidelined or pushed into the sub-clauses of official reports. The Scarman Report, for example, contained the following policy proposal:

> I . . . recommend that local communities must be fully and effectively involved in planning, in the provision of local services,

and in the management and financing of specific projects. (Scarman, 1981: para 8.44)

Such a move towards greater political integration was seen by Lord Scarman as essential if the gap between inner city residents and the forces of law and order was to be bridged and constructive co-operation developed.

But the concern with overcoming political marginality remained on the sidelines of the main public debate because it questioned the perception of the rioters as driven by irrational, uncivilised and criminal instincts. According to Martin Kettle:

> The attempt to depict the riots as irrational was very important. It denied legitimacy to the rioters, their actions and their views. It made them events without cause, and events that therefore posed no direct threat to any existing assumption. (Kettle, 1982: 404)

This did not, however, stop the question of political marginality and the need to reform existing policies from being raised at all, as can be seen subsequently by the numerous attempts after 1981 to introduce measures both locally and nationally which were meant to address some of the grievances of the rioters and to ensure that further disturbances did not occur. It is to this issue that we now turn.

The impact on policy: Scarman and beyond

As argued above the 1980–1 riots resulted in a wide variety of responsive measures, emanating from both central and local government, as well as other agencies. The very multiplicity of ideological constructions of the riots is an indication of the complexity of the responses which resulted in policies and programmes of action. There are, however, three analytically distinct and important political and policy responses which need to be analysed: (a) the Scarman Report; (b) policing and law and order; (c) economic and social policies.

In the aftermath of the April 1981 riots in Brixton the Home Secretary, William Whitelaw, used his powers under the 1964 Police Act to appoint Lord Scarman to inquire into the events, produce a report and make recommendations. This brief was subsequently widened to cover the occurrence of other disturbances during July

1981. Lord Scarman's inquiry was not on the same scale as the famous Kerner Report on the US riots, but since the publication of his report in November 1981 his views and prescriptions have played an important role in fashioning political debate about the riots. It is therefore important to look into the basic analysis which the Scarman Report puts forward in order to understand how the political agenda of riot response has developed since 1980.

The starting point of Lord Scarman's explanation of the riots is important here. He began his analysis by distinguishing between the background factors which had created the potential for urban disorder in areas such as Brixton and the precipitating action or event which sparked off the riots. Scarman identified two views that were commonly held as to the causation of the disorders. The first explained them in terms of oppressive policing, and in particular the harassment of young blacks. The second explained them as a protest against society by deprived people who saw violent attacks upon the forces of law and order as a way of calling attention to their grievances. For Scarman both views were a simplification of a complex reality, or at least not the whole truth. He linked the social and policing aspects of the complex reality of areas like Brixton in an analytic model which emphasised the following issues:

(i)   the problems which are faced in policing and maintaining order in deprived, inner-city, multi-racial localities;
(ii) the social, economic, and related problems which are faced by all residents of such areas; and
(iii) the social and economic disadvantages which are suffered particularly by black residents, especially young blacks (Scarman, 1981: paras 2.1 to 2.38).

He saw the existence of all these features in certain deprived areas as 'creating a predisposition towards violent protest', which could be sparked off by incidents such as confrontations between local residents and the police or by rumours about the actions of the police or other authority figures.

From this account Lord Scarman drew the conclusion that once the roots of a predisposition towards violent protest had taken it was difficult to reverse the situation. Talking about the position of young blacks, he noted that because they felt neither socially nor economically secure many of them had drifted into situations where more or less regular confrontations with the police were the norm of their daily experience. Noting that despite the evidence of academic and government reports, which had pointed to widespread discrimination against young blacks, very little had been done to remedy the situation, Scarman concluded that: (a) many young blacks believed that violence was an effective means of protest against their conditions; and (b) that far from the riots being a meaningless event, they were 'essentially an outburst of anger and resentment by young black people against the police' (*ibid.*, paras 3.110 and 2.38). What is important to note here is that aside from Lord Scarman's condemnation of the criminal acts committed during the riots, the report was a strong argument in favour of a historical and social explanation of the riots.

Another line of argument which was embodied in the Scarman Report related to the social and family structures of the black communities in the inner cities, particularly the West Indian family. Explaining the drift towards violence and crime it painted the following picture of the young black in Brixton:

> Without close parental support, with no job to go to, and with few recreational facilities available, the young black person makes his life on the streets and in the seedy commercially run clubs of Brixton. There he meets criminals, who appear to have no difficulty in obtaining the benefits of a materialist society. (*Ibid.*, para. 2.23)

Though the report went on to point out that 'many young black people do not of course resort to crime', it can nevertheless be said that it used the image of the rootless black youngster as a visible symbol of the despair and injustice suffered in areas such as Brixton. This despair had to be remedied through the actions of the Government and local government departments, which were seen as the agencies that could help the minority communities overcome their special problems.

Given the close link which the Scarman Report established between questions of policing and the wider social context the programme of action which it outlined contained proposals not only about the reform of the police and the introduction of new methods of policing and riot control, but about employment policy, social policy and policies on racial discrimination. In a telling phrase Lord Scarman argued:

The social conditions in Brixton do not provide an excuse for disorder. But the disorder cannot be fully understood unless they are seen in the context of complex political, social and economic factors which together create a predisposition towards violent protest. (*Ibid.*, para. 8.7)

Although some of these issues went beyond the main remit of his Inquiry he drew the conclusion from this basic finding that only a national Government-led initiative to deal with problems of policing, unemployment, poor housing and racial disadvantage could get to the roots of the unrest.

Parliamentary and media responses to the Report varied widely, although it was widely seen as making an important contribution to the debate about how to respond to the riots and prevent the outbreak of violence in the future. But what became clear after the immediate debate on the Report in late 1981 and early 1982, was that the Government was not going to implement all the recommendations uniformly. Some aspects of its proposals for reforming the police and rethinking police tactics were implemented during 1982 and 1983 (Reiner, 1985), but evidence of the urgent action which it called for in other areas remained scarce (Benyon, 1984; Benyon and Solomos, 1987).

This returns us to the point we made earlier about the other major forces which contributed to the development of political responses to the riots: namely the media, Parliament, political parties and popular common sense debate. The Scarman Report formed a part – and a vital one – of this process of political debate, but its role cannot be understood in isolation. This can be seen if we look more closely at the issues of policing and economic and social problems.

Although the Scarman Report considered issues of policing in some detail and influenced the course of subsequent Government responses in this field, it should be clear from Chapter 5 that the construction of a law and order response drew on a wider set of pressures and influences.

Indeed in the aftermath of the Scarman Report's publication police opinion was divided on the question of whether its proposals for reforming the police and the adoption of new methods of policing could be implemented, or whether such changes could insure against further violence and unrest. Sim (1982) has argued that the police were particularly worried by Scarman's recommendations that they should (a) tackle racial prejudice and harassment, (b) improve their methods of policing inner city multiracial areas, and (c) develop new methods of managing urban disorder. He sees the police and sections of the media and right-wing Parliamentarians as launching a counter offensive to counteract criticisms of the police handling of the riots or their handling of the black community in general.

Certainly even before the publication of the Scarman Report the police and sections of the media were engaged in constructing a rather different explanation of the riots and of the participants in such events.

During July 1981 a number of accounts of the events focused on the issue of the family background of riot participants and the decline of firm parental control over children. Kenneth Oxford, the Chief Constable for Merseyside, made a number of statements which argued that the main responsibility for the riots lay with parents who either could not control their children or who did not care. The *Daily Telegraph* reported Mr Oxford as saying:

> What in the name of goodness are these young people doing on the streets indulging in this behaviour and at that time of night? Is there no discipline that can be brought to bear on these young people? Are the parents not interested in the futures of these young people? (8 July 1981)

According to this model the cause of the riots lay not in the conflict between young people and the police but in the failure of families to control the actions of their children. Such arguments are articulated with regularity throughout the period of the riots. Both the Prime Minister and the Home Secretary supported such arguments. *The Times* reported the Prime Minister as saying that if the parents could not control the actions of their children what can the Government do to stop them from engaging in 'hooliganism' and a 'spree of naked greed' (10 July 1981). At the same time the Home Secretary was reported as saying that the Government was looking at plans to involve parents in 'the consequences of offences committed by their children' (*The Times*, 10 July 1981).

Such arguments were not necessarily linked to race, but as we saw earlier Lord Scarman himself partly explained the drift of black youngsters into crime and violence by reference to the weak family units of the West Indian communities. And during 1981 much media coverage was given to the supposed pathology of the West Indian family and the isolation of young blacks from both their families and society as a whole. Moreover, it has been shown in earlier chapters how the history of political responses to black immigration is deeply infused with the notion that blacks were intrinsically a problem, either in social or cultural terms. Thus even when such arguments were not racialised per se, popular common sense helped to link the notion of weak family structure to the West Indian communities; and it was a short step from this to explaining the riots as an outcome of pathological family structures.

Arguments around the question of the family were linked to other issues: e.g. the crisis of youth, the growth of violence in society generally, the phenomenon of youth hooliganism, the drift of young people into crime. Whether such images were based on factual evidence or not they succeeded in becoming part of the public debate about the 1980–1 riots and became even more important during 1985. By becoming part of public debate they helped to construct a model of the riots which saw them as the outcome of causes which were outside of the control of either the Government or the police. They thus helped to deflect attention away from the broader social context of Lord Scarman's report and towards specific social problems which undermined law and order.

In terms of economic and social policies the impact of the 1980–1 riots was equally ambiguous and contradictory. Part of this ambiguity, as we have shown above, resulted from the Government's strenuous efforts to deny any link between its policies and the outbreak of violence and disorder. This denial was particularly important, since at the time the Thatcher administration was going through a bad period in terms of popular opinion on issues such as unemployment, social services and housing (Leys, 1983; Thompson, 1986). While Lord Scarman was careful not to enter the political dispute between the Government and the Labour Party on issues such as unemployment and housing, his call for more direct action to deal with these problems, along with racial disadvantage, posed a challenge to the political legitimacy of the policies which the Government had followed from, 1979 onwards. It also posed a delicate problem for the Home Secretary himself, since Lord Scarman had been appointed by him to carry out his Inquiry. Having spent the whole summer denying any link between its policies and the riots, the Government had to tread wearily in responding to the economic and social policy proposals of the Scarman Report when it was published in November 1981.

The parliamentary debate on the Report shows the Home Secretary adopting a two pronged strategy in his response. First, he accepted many of the recommendations of the Report, particularly in relation to the role of the police. Additionally, he accepted the need to tackle racial disadvantage and other social issues. Second, he emphasised the Government's view that, whatever broader measures were taken to deal with racial and social inequalities, the immediate priority was to restore and maintain order on the streets. When the Home Secretary talked of the need for the Government to give a lead in tackling racial disadvantage he therefore saw this as an issue for the longer term. On the other hand, he was much more specific about the reform of the police and the development of new tactics and equipment for the management of urban disorder (*Hansard*, Vol. 14, 1981: Cols 1001–8).

Summary and conclusion

In this chapter we have looked at the impact of the outbreaks of urban unrest in Britain during 1980 and 1981 on the terms of political and policy debates about race and related issues. We have shown that the main themes in public debates about the disturbances helped to emphasise the role of racial factors and thus to racialise the events. Because the people involved in the disturbances tended to be predominantly young, predominantly male, and predominantly black attention was particularly focused on the role of young blacks and on the difficulties faced by the police in maintaining law and order in multi-racial localities.

This focus on the interconnections between the social position of young blacks and urban unrest did not produce uniform policy conclusions. The proposals made by Lord Scarman in his report on the Brixton disturbances, for example, differed markedly from the policy conclusions of the law and order lobby. There were also marked differences between the approach of the Labour Party, which tended to emphasise social deprivation as the central issue, and the Conservative Party, which saw the events as yet another example of the growth of violence and disorder in British society.

The implications of these different responses to the 1980–1

disturbances for policy remained to be worked out, but already in the period from 1981 onwards the emphasis of the Thatcher administration was on (a) the need to strengthen the police and (b) to train them more fully in the managment of riot situations. The assumption seemed to be that the main objective of the government should be to contain social protest by strengthening the forces of law and order. We shall return to the consequences of this approach in Chapter 9, which includes a discussion of the outbreaks of urban unrest in the period since 1985.

7 Racism, Nationalism and Ideology

Introduction

The previous five chapters have provided both a chronological and thematic analysis of racialised politics in the period from 1945 to the 1980s. The concerns of this and the following two chapters are somewhat different, though they are closely linked to the themes we have covered already at a more general level. The main objective of these chapters is to analyse in more detail something we have only touched upon in previous chapters: namely, the role of racial ideologies, political action and social movements in the racialisation of contemporary British politics.

This chapter will look at how the racialisation of British political culture has been achieved through the social construction of ideological notions of the nation, culture and politics. This is a relatively neglected issue, despite the importance of racialised discourse in the political language of the new-right and the usages of racial symbols in the construction of national identity in contemporary Britain.

By analysing the changing meanings attached to race and nation, particularly in the political discourses of the old and the new-right, we shall be able to explore the interaction between racist politics and broader ideologies about the British way of life and national consciousness (Seidel, 1986; van Dijk, 1988). Additionally, this exploration should allow us to show how the symbolic political languages which attempt to define who is British and who is not represent a powerful and volatile political force in contemporary Britain.

Chapters 8 and 9 will then take the analysis a step further by looking in more detail than has been possible so far at (a) the

122

development of black political consciousness and forms of group mobilisation, anti-racism and forms of social protest, and (b) the politics of racism in the context of social change. Both these issues have been raised in previous chapters, but we have been unable to explore the dynamics in any depth. For the purposes of this volume this account of the interactions between racialised ideologies and political action in contemporary Britain serves to complete the analysis of the theory and practice of racism.

Given the wealth of empirical material which can be included in these chapters we have opted to be selective rather than exhaustive. For example, the analysis of the National Front and other extreme right wing groups is limited to some of the broader features. A number of case studies of such groups exist, and we have no wish to duplicate the analysis which they offer (Billig, 1978; Fielding, 1981; Taylor, 1982). A similar point can be made about black political organisations and pressure groups. They also have a long and dynamic history of struggles and achievements. On both these issues it would have been possible to write separate books. Our concern here, however, is to provide an outline of the complex ways in which notions of race and national identity have been articulated to give support to political movements and pressure groups.

The changing forms of racial ideology

The impact of post-1945 debates about black immigration on the definition of national identity and 'Britishness' has been discussed in some detail in Chapters 3 and 4, but there are a number of dimensions of this issue which remain to be analysed.

In particular there is the question of (a) the changing forms of racial ideology during the 1970s and 1980s, (b) the transformation of ideologies of race and nation, and (c) the emergence of what is sometimes called a new racism. We have hinted at these processes in previous chapters, but in this section we want to make a more detailed analysis of their development.

Changing terms of racial discourse

In Chapter 4 we looked at the rise of 'Powellism' as a process of political mobilisation which helped to redefine the terms of political discourse about racial relations in British society during the late 1960s and early 1970s. The responses of the Labour Government during 1968–70 and the Conservative Government from 1970 to 1974 in their different ways showed how powerful a political symbol this mobilisation was. Both administrations responded to the appeal of Powell's ideas about immigration and race by attempting to depoliticise these issues (Freeman, 1979; Layton-Henry, 1984). The two most important manifestations of this process were the acceptance by both the Labour Party and the Conservative Party of (a) the need for tight restrictions on immigration and (b) the necessity to allay the fears of those attracted to Powell's ideas.

In this sense the period of the late 1960s and early 1970s has been quite rightly characterised as one in which Powellite ideas helped to racialise British political life. Quite apart from the impact of Powell's intervention at the political level, however, it is important to acknowledge a less evident aspect of his role: namely, his influence on the political language used to discuss race-immigration issues. His emphasis on the social and cultural transformations brought about by immigration helped to create or recreate in popular political debate understandings of Englishness and Britishness which relied explicitly or implicitly on notions of shared history, customs and kinship which excluded black minorities from the polity (Powell, 1969; Powell, 1972).

From the late 1960s through to the 1980s Powell's interventions have continually returned to two themes: First, the growth of the black population, and the prospect that by the end of the century a large proportion of Britain's population was likely to be made up of black immigrants and their descendants. From the 1960s onwards this concern with the size of the black population has become part of the wider political common sense about immigration. Second, Powell's speeches have emphasised that the scale of black migration represented a threat to the national character of such a magnitude that the whole social and cultural fabric of British society was likely to be undermined by the presence of migrants from a different cultural, racial and religious background.

It is this second theme that has increasingly occupied a central role in Powell's politics during the 1970s and 1980s. A good example of this emphasis in Powellite discourse can be found in his interventions during the urban unrest of 1981 and 1985, when he continually emphasises the threat to the nation posed by the danger of a civil war on the streets of Britain's inner cities and the growth of multi-racialism.

More recently, he has reiterated some of the themes from his 1968 'Rivers of Blood' speech in a series of articles which coincided with the twentieth anniversary of this speech. As we have already emphasised, for Powell the source of the main threat to the British nation is the volatile mixture of different nationalities and cultures that black migration has created in many inner city areas, rather than any external enemies. It is to this issue that he returned repeatedly in 1988, on the twentieth anniversary of his 'Rivers of Blood' speech. For example, in a speech given in Birmingham he chose to speak on the theme of 'Englishness' and the threats posed to its revival in the current period. He identified a number of factors which represented a threat national identity, and among these he emphasised the danger posed to the distinctiveness of English culture by the presence 'of those who not only visibly do not share with them a common identity but are to be encouraged to maintain and intensify their differences' (*The Independent*, 23 April 1988). In Powell's terms this was a danger not so much because of the number of immigrants and their descendants, though this was an issue, but because the nation itself had lost its identity to such an extent that it had failed to respond to the dangers it faced from the presence within its major cities of minorities whom he perceives as outside of the primordial ties of nation and culture.

By the 1980s therefore the language that Powell uses to describe the politics of race in contemporary Britain is as much to do with a definition of 'Englishness' or 'Britishness' as it is with characteristics of the minority communities themselves. He makes no claims to knowing all the sources which 'since neolithic times, or earlier, have contributed to the gene pool of the English people' (*ibid.*), but he warns of 'The spectre of a Britain that has lost its claim to be a nation':

> The spectacle which I cannot help seeing . . . is that of a Britain which has lost, quite suddenly, in the space of less than a generation, all consciousness and conviction of being a nation: the web which binds it to its past has been torn asunder, and what has made the spectacle the more impressive has been the indifference, not to say levity, with which the change has been greeted'. (*The Guardian*, 9 November 1981).

From this perspective the loss of Britain's national identity is caused not just by immigration, but by the failure of the nation to recognise the importance of this process for the unity of the national culture. This kind of argument links up with earlier themes in Powell's interventions on this issue, although the presentation of his argument is less dependent on immigration as a political symbol and more reliant on a definition of the cultural basis of 'Englishness' (Seidel, 1986; Gilroy, 1987).

Such arguments are by no means limited to Powell. During the 1980s Powellite arguments about national identity and culture have indeed been given more respectability by the growing influence of the arguments of the new right, whose proponents have adopted race as one of the main components of their political discourse.

Conceptions of race and nation

As in other areas of political life the new right has begun to exercise more influence in the past decade in public debates about racial questions. Through channels such as the Centre for Policy Studies, the Social Affairs Unit and the *Salisbury Review* a number of new-right commentators have attempted to define what they see as a critique of established dogmas and policies in areas such as multi-racial education, race and housing and anti-racism generally (Flew, 1984; Palmer, 1986). These writings are a clear example of how ideologies about race are not static, but constantly changing.

The political language of the new right still resonates with old Powellite themes, such as immigration, and stereotypes of the black muggers, aliens and black criminals. But over the past decade, as with Powell's political language, we have seen two main shifts in the concerns of the new-right. First, there has been a move away from the language of nativism and anti-immigration. By the late 1970s the concern with the social position of young blacks signalled the new preoccupation with the dangers of the political and social alienation of sections of the black communities for the polity as a whole (Keith, 1987; Solomos, 1988). The image of inner city areas becoming black enclaves where British law and order could not be easily enforced is one of the recurrent themes in new right writings in this field. The very presence of black communities is presented as a potential threat to the way of life and culture of white citizens.

Second, new right racial discourses increasingly present black people as an enemy within, that is undermining the moral and social fabric of society. In both popular and elite discourses about immigration and race black communities as a whole, or particular groups such as young blacks, are presented as involved in activities which are a threat to social order and political stability.

Such ideological constructions do not necessarily have to rely on notions of racial superiority in the narrow sense. In practice the most resonant themes in contemporary racial discourses are not concerned with absolute notions of racial superiority, but with the threats which black communities are seen to represent to the cultural, political and religious homogeneity of white British society.

Common images of black people include assumptions about differences between the culture, attitudes and values of black people as compared to the white majority. Additionally the attempts by black groups to assert their rights and claims to social justice have often been presented in the media as a sign of the failure of the minority communities to adapt to British society, and not as a sign that racial injustice is deeply embedded.

This type of argument has been summarised by van Dijk (1988) as amounting to the claim that the demands of black minorities are not legitimate, that they are in fact the product of attempts to claim special privileges and thus a threat to the majority. Because such claims are presented as coming from groups which are outside of the traditions and culture of British political life they are more easily portrayed as a challenge to the values of the majority communities, and by a twist of logic as unjust.

As we saw in Chapter 6 the emergence of urban unrest during the 1980s, and the widely publicised involvement of young blacks in these events, has also provided an important cue in the use of racial symbols by sections of the popular media and the extreme right. The media coverage of the 1985 riots in particular did much to reinforce the popular image of young blacks as involved in anti-social acts such as crime, and to allow the extreme right to present them as a threat to social and political stability.

The notion that the seeds of racial conflict were sown by the failure of successive governments to tackle immigration has been a major theme in the interventions by Enoch Powell since the 1960s. The outbreak of urban unrest, however, allowed Powell to expand his notion of the threats posed by immigration to include within it the notion that the whole nation and society was under threat from actual rather than impending civil war, and that the origins of this situation could be traced back to the imposition of alien cultures into British society. This is the theme which has proved to be particularly attractive to the new-right in the political climate of the 1980s, as we shall show in more detail in Chapter 9.

New-right ideologies and national identity

What has become increasingly clear in recent years is that racial discourses are rarely concerned only with the role of minority communities and cultures. They are also typically an attempt to define the characteristics of the dominant national culture, and the ways in which these differ from those of racial and ethnic minorities. It is precisely on this issue that the ideologists of the new-right have begun to concentrate over the past decade, though it has to be said that this is by no means a new phenomenon.

Over the centuries, for example, the meanings attached to 'English-ness' and 'Britishness' have constantly changed. Or as one account puts it: 'Englishness has had to be made and re-made in and through history' (Colls and Dodd, 1986: i). The symbols used in this process have included ideas about shared language, customs, religion, colour, family and numerous other assumed attributes of the national culture.

Within the context of more contemporary debates about race and immigration it is noticeable that a recurrent issue is the definition of the historical and cultural attributes of the British way of life. While the position of black minority communities in the inner cities may be the immediate point of reference in discussions of crime and disorder, the overarching concern is about the threat posed to the majority culture by the developmenht of multi-racial communities.

One example of this process is the attention given to young Afro-Caribbeans. During the 1980s this group became in many ways the centre of much political debate, particularly in the aftermath of outbreaks of urban unrest (Solomos, 1988), But although the immediate source of concern was the outbreak of violent unrest on the streets of major cities, the underlying concern of new right commentators was the argument that the permanent settlement of black communities, a phenomenon which young blacks symbolically represented, was a threat to the unit of British society.

John Casey, writing in 1982 in the *Salisbury Review*, expressed such views succinctly when he argued that black migration had broken down the social order which had been established during the Victorian period, and was therefore a threat to the way of life of the majority population. From this he drew the conclusion that the source of the problem was a failure to understand the role of national identity in the development of British society:

> There is no way of understanding British and English history that does not take seriously the sentiments of patriotism that go with a continuity of institutions, shared experience, language, customs, kinship. There is no way of understanding English patriotism that averts its eyes from the fact that it has as its centre a feeling for persons of one's own kind. (Casey, 1982: 25)

This 'feeling for persons of one's own kind' thus becomes a way for Casey to argue that any opposition to the settlement of black migrants in Britain is not necessarily based on racial antipathy but is a natural response to outsiders.

The famous swamping statement made by Margaret Thatcher on television in February 1978 is another example of how this image of the threat of black immigration can be utilised politically to mobilise political support without resorting directly to racialist language. Referring to trends in immigration Mrs Thatcher argued that the present rate of immigration would, by the end of the century, mean that there would be four million people from the New Commonwealth or Pakistan in Britain. She drew the following conclusion from this:

> That is an awful lot, and I think it means that people are really rather afraid that this country might be swamped by people of a different culture. The British character has done so much for democracy, for law, and done so much throughout the world that if there is any fear that it might be swamped, then people are going to be rather hostile to those coming in.

In the same interview she sought to explain the support achieved by the National Front during the 1970s as the result of the failure to deal with immigration through the mainstream political institutions. She went on:

We are a British nation with British characteristics. Every nation can take some minorities, and in many ways they add to the richness and variety of this country. But the moment a minority threatens to become a big one, people get frightened. (*The Guardian*, 31 January 1978)

The use of notions such as 'British nation' and 'British character' helps in this context to establish Thatcher's concern for protecting the interests of the nation against threats from within and from without. And in the context of the political climate of the late 1970s there is evidence that this helped the Conservative Party to draw support from National Front sympathisers, who saw the Party as a more likely channel for translating their views into policy (Layton-Henry, 1986).

Taken together, these processes have helped to redefine the terms of political discource about race in British politics. What is interesting, however, is that unlike the simmering controversy aroused by Powell's speeches during the late 1960s and 1970s, new-right arguments about race and nation have achieved a certain respectability in both popular and elite political discourses. This does not mean that the more extreme arguments of the new-right have not aroused anger and opposition. But within the political climate of Thatcherism the ideas of the new-right on culture, nation and identity represent a potent political force, whose political impact has yet to be fully understood.

Neo-fascist politics

One of the most important features of the politics of racism during the past two decades was the emergence, and decline, during the early 1970s of the National Front, and other minor neo-fascist groups, as a more or less credible political force (Walker, 1977; Billig and Bell, 1980; Husbands, 1983). Indeed, during the early 1970s there was serious concern that the National Front could become an established political force in the way the French National Front has during the 1980s.

The history and political impact of the National Front has attracted widespread attention, and there have been numerous studies of the rise and decline of the National Front, the social context of support for neo-fascist and racist political groups, the role of racialised ideologies and the prospects for the future mobilisation of racist beliefs and ideologies by political parties and movements. These studies date mostly from the 1970s, which represents the high point of the impact of the National Front on both local and national political life.

The National Front was founded in 1967, as a unified organisation of groups supporting neo-fascist and anti-immigration viewpoints (Walker, 1977). One of the primary impulses behind the formation of the Front seems to have been the relative neglect of immigration race-related issues by the mainstream political parties. This was seen as providing an opening for a party openly committed to the defence of racial purity and to clear anti-immigration stance to capture support from both main political parties.

As a union of the right wing British National Party and the League of Empire Loyalists, the Front inherited the ideological baggage of anti-semitism and resistance to Britain's post-war decolonisation, two prominent themes among far right political groups in the 1960s. In its political rhetoric it made clear its links with the politics of anti-semitism, and there is evidence that both its leadership and membership were committed to a nationalist ideology based on a notion of racial purity (Thurlow, 1975; Edgar, 1977).

Research on the social basis of support for the National Front and racist political groups has brought out two important features. First, Phizacklea's and Miles's study of working class racism argued that it was important to look at the social and economic context in order to understand the attraction of sections of the white working class to the politics of the National Front. Drawing upon research in London they argued that one of the most important factors in the growth of support for racist political groups was the wider context of economic and social restructuring in many inner city working class areas (Phizacklea and Miles, 1980).

Husbands's study of support for the National Front in particular localities, such as the East End area of London, argued that it is important to look particularly at the influence of such issues as the presence of black communities, changes in the national and local politics of race and the restructuring of local political economies in order to understand the level and solidity of Front support in some areas and its relative weakness in others (Husbands, 1983).

These studies emphasise the need to locate the support for racism within a wider social, economic and geographical context. A similar theme has been taken up by Cashmore (1987) in his detailed analysis of the social basis of racism in Birmingham and its surrounding area during the 1980s. But it is important not to lose sight of the role of politics and ideology in the mobilisation of this support.

It is interesting to remember, for example, that during the 1970s both the Conservative Party and the Labour Party lost voters to the National Front. Throughout the 1970s, the National Front's membership level of electoral support ebbed and flowed with the tide of political debate and public controversy over racial questions. Its membership peaked at 14 000 to 20 000 during the period from 1972 to 1974, at the height of the moral panic about the arrival of Ugandan Asians. In 1973 it achieved a vote of 16.2 per cent in the West Bromwich by-election. It also achieved respectable results during the local elections of 1976 and the local elections in London during 1977 (Taylor, 1982).

This level of suppport and political mobilisation was not maintained, however, and fell dramatically in the aftermath of Mrs Thatcher's swamping statement in 1978 and the attempt by the Conservative Party to draw the support of Front sympathisers. From 1977 to 1979 the activities of the Front also became the focus for anti-racist political mobilisation, orchestrated by the Anti-Nazi League and Rock Against Racism. This counter mobilisation helped to counter its claim to be a defender of the national interest and helped to increase awareness of the political dangers which its growth as a major political force was likely to lead to.

From its foundation, however, it was the issue of black immigration which occupied a central role in its political rhetoric and in its propaganda. Despite periodic attempts by the National Front's leadership to broaden the movement's appeal and political platform, immigration and race remained the single most salient issue among Front members and sympathisers during the 1970s and it was the ability of the Front to utilise this issue at both a local and a national level that allowed it to mobilise electoral support and attract members.

In neo-fascist political discourses about race common sense images resonate with references to racial purity, cultural superiority or difference and the defence of the nation from the threat posed by immigration and racial mixing. The alien, the stranger, or the subhuman are the themes struck repeatedly.

Since 1979 there has been a decline in the electoral performance of the National Front and other overtly racist political groups. The National Front in Britain has not had the same political impact as the National Front in France. This has been interpreted from a number of perspectives: (a) as representing a marginalisation of the racist political message that the Front was propounding; (b) as the outcome of the incorporation of the Front's ideas within mainstream political institutions; (c) as the result of factional strife and conflict within the racist groups themselves. Certainly since 1979 the National Front and other extreme right organisations have splintered in a number of directions, and have failed to make any significant interventions in electoral politics.

Whatever the reasons for the decline in electoral support for the Front and other neo-fascist political groups their influence in other arenas of British political life has persisted and they continue to mobilise effectively in a number of localities. Their role, however, cannot be seen in isolation from other forms of political mobilisation around the symbols of race and nation. This can be illustrated in relation to the question of racial attacks.

The politics of racial attacks

Racially motivated attacks have a long history, but it is during the late 1970s and 1980s that increasing public attention has been given to the phenomenon of racially motivated attacks on black people. The context within which such attacks take place is complex, and far right groups are not always involved, but the impact that they have had on the everyday lives of many black people in Britain during the 1980s is clear. One report lists the following as relatively typical cases of this phenomenon:

As a boy sleeps, a pig's head, its eyes, ears, nostrils and mouth stuffed with lighted cigarettes, is hurled through the window of his bedroom. A family do not leave their home after 7 in the evening; they stay in one large room, having barricaded their ground floor. A family are held prisoner in their own flat by a security cage bolted to their front door by white neighbours. A youth is slashed with a knife by an older white boy as he walks along a school corridor between classes. A family home is burned out and a pregnant woman and her three children killed. A ticket collector is stabbed in the eye with a metal stake and killed simply because he refused to take racial abuse from some white passengers. (Gordon, 1986: v)

A number of surveys by the Home Office, the Commission for Racial Equality and local authorities have confirmed the widespread nature of these types of attacks, as well as everyday forms of racial harassment (Home Office, 1981; GLC, 1984; CRE, 1987a and 1987b).

The involvement of far right racialist groups in some of these cases has been clearly shown. What seems to have happened is that as the National Front found itself electorally isolated in the period after 1979 sections of its membership, along with supporters of other far right groups, turned to more direct forms of attack on black communities.

But it also seems clear that the overall political climate has contributed to the growth of this phenomenon. Given the prevalence of racialised political discourses, and the emphasis of the new-right on the need to reassert the importance of patriotism and nationalism in British political culture, it is perhaps not surprising that it is during the 1980s that the issue of racial attacks has become such a major issue.

This may explain the low key nature of the response to racial attacks both by the Government and the police for most of the past decade. This contrasts sharply with the oft expressed views of the police and government on the criminal activities of young blacks, and the amplification of images of black crime in the popular media on an almost daily basis. By contrast the policy response to racial attacks and related phenomena has been at best muted and at worst non-existent.

Racialised politics and the 'enemy within'

Perhaps the most important theme in contemporary political discourse about race in British society, even after successive attempts to develop anti-discrimination policies, is the image of blacks as a whole or particular groups of them as a threat to the unity and order of British society. Cohen (1988) notes that one way in which this tendency is expressed in contemporary political discourse is in attempts to attribute the persistence of racial inequality not to racism but to the presence of black minorities and the problems that result from this presence.

Such images are by no means unique to the post-1945 period, or to Britain. Edelman (1971), writing about the United States, has shown how in situations of conflict and protest one of the ways in which dominant groups or political institutions defend themselves is to rationalise threats as the product of outsiders and enemies who are outside of the social and moral values of the society as a whole. Referring to the political debates about the race riots of the 1960s he argued that one of the ways in which the dominant elites of American society attempted to reduce the political impact of the events was to portray them as the work of enemies of American society and its values.

In contemporary British political life, however, we have seen a somewhat different variant of this process in the context of racial relations. In the language of the new-right black people are increasingly portrayed not as an enemy without but as an enemy within: as a threat to the cultural and political values of the nation. They are increasingly presented in the media and other channels of communication as a threat to the way of life of the majority white community and as a group which is difficult to integrate into the mainstream of British society.

Two of the ways in which this process has influenced recent political debates about race are to be found in new-right discourses about the naturalness of racial antipathy and the increasingly vociferous attacks on anti-racism which are to be heard in the popular media and in public political debate.

Naturalisation of racism

Barker (1981) notes that one important aspect of contemporary racial ideologies in Britain is the tendency to obscure or deny the meaning and implications of the deployment of race categories. This fits in with the wider tendency (a) to deny the importance of racism in British society, and (b) to deny that hostility to the presence of black communities in Britain is a form of racism. According to this line of argument it is only natural that, given the choice, people should prefer to live with their own kind and not become a multi-racial society. Such a wish is not seen as a manifestation of racialist attitudes, but as a natural response to the presence of people of a different cultural and racial background.

Thus when in 1978 Margaret Thatcher expressed the view that 'the moment a minority threatens to become a big one, people get frightened', she was giving voice to an argument that has since become part of the accepted common sense of new right writings on racial questions. A more recent expression of this kind of argument can be found in the arguments developed in the *Salisbury Review*. Mishan (1988), for example, argues that opposition to the emergence of a multi-racial society is not necessarily an 'irrational or super-stitious reaction':

> Opposition to the creation of a multi-racial society may well spring primarily from a deep concern about the future of one's country, one arising form a belief that its transformation over a short period form a relatively homogeneous population to one of a particular racial mix may, on balance, have adverse effects on its institutions and character or, at any rate, may be more likely to do harm than good. (p. 18)

For Mishan, and other new-right commentators on racial issues, opposition to immigration and support for the repatriation of black communities already settled in this country is thus a natural response to the new racial mix in British society, and not a sign of racism.

Some of the policy implications of new-right political discourses are not fundamentally different from those of Powellite discourse. John Casey, for exmple, writing in the *Salisbury Review* in 1982 argued that the only feasible solution to the problems caused by the presence of black communities was the voluntary repatriation 'of a proportion of the immigrant and immigrant-descended population' or the retrospective withdrawal of the rights of black migrants to citizenship and the creation of a status analogous to the position of guest-workers in Europe (Casey, 1982: 27).

Even those of the new-right who do not go along with such a scenario accept that the social problems which they see as caused by black migrants require constructive measures to encourage repatri-ation or to ensure the integration of those who want to remain in Britain. What is interesting, however, is that increasingly such arguments are presented not as extreme solutions but as a rational political response to what the new-right presents as an intractable problem. Within the logic of the politics of the new-right any attempt to create a multi-cultural society can only lead to social conflict and present a threat to the values and culture of the majority.

Anti anti-racism

Today some of the most strident voices in the mass media and in academic discourse are raised not against racism but against one of the favourite targets of the new-right, namely 'anti-racism'. Sections of the media are almost daily concerned with aspects of the work of either local authorities or of agencies such as the Commission for Racial Equality in this field. Additionally it has become an important focus of concern for the various right wing think tanks, who see anti-racism as an intrusion on individual freedom and a threat to the interests of the white majority.

According to van Dijk (1988) the strategy of such attacks on anti-racism is to defend the assumed virtues of British tolerance and decency against the attacks of enemies within:

> Within a more embracing framework of defending white British culture and its values, the targets of such press campaigns were obvious: assumed positive discrimination, ethnic projects, cultural pluralism, multicultural education, and in general each initiative based on the recognition that Britain is no longer white. (p. 184)

Over the past few years these are precisely the targets which sections of the popular media and new-right pressure groups have singled out for particular attention. There has been a whole series of controversies over the actions of local authorities which have sought to take a positive stance on racial equality and on anti-racism. Increasingly what the new-right calls the ideology of anti-racism has become the subject of virulent attack, and indeed the whole notion of racism has been dismissed in some circles as an invention of the loony left and the race relations industry.

Russell Lewis's *Anti-Racism: A Mania Exposed* represents one of the most strident attacks on the work of what he sees as the anti-racist fanatics. It was published amid much publicity, with a preface by Enoch Powell, and has been taken up by the new-right as a fundamental critique of anti-racist politics. Starting out from a denial of the importance of racism in contemporary British society Lewis argues that the source of contemporary problems was the failure of successive governments to control immigration, and the creation of the race relations industry by successive Labour and Conservative administrations. Indeed for Lewis the main harm to race relations results not from racism but from the lunatic outrages done in the name of anti-racism and the failure of the black minorities to respect the way of life and customs of the white majority.

Arguments such as these are still a minority position. But they represent an important phase in the politics of racism in post-1945 Britain. In attacking the activities of the anti-racists they have helped to shift public attention away from the processes of racial discrimination and racism, and focus it on the activities of the black communities themselves and the anti-racists who are seen as having a vested interest in claiming that Britain is a racist society.

One consequence of these attacks on anti-racism is that they help to legitimise the relative inaction of the three Conservative administrations since 1979 in the field of public policy to tackle racial inequality, and allow open discussion of issues which have tended to be talked about at the margins of political life over the past two decades. In a commentary on Lewis's book, William Deedes, a former Conservative minister, argued that it proved that Britain needed to have less guilt over race and more open discussion about the impact of minority communities on the majority values (*Daily Telegraph*, 30 June 1988).

But interestingly the debate over this issue has also led to attempts by those on the left and in the Labour Party to rethink the politics of racial equality. The controversy over the events at Burnage High School in Manchester has led to a debate among sections of the left about the role and future of anti-racist initiatives (*New Statesman*, 9 May 1988; *New Socialist*, 27 July 1988). In the medium term therefore it is likely that there will be a fundamental rethinking of these questions from both the left and the right.

Nationalism and the interests of the majority

It is perhaps no accident that the prevalent theme in political debate over the past few years has been the issue of anti-racism. Such a pre-occupation fits in with the mobilisation of national symbols and the attack on enemies within which Thatcherism as a political philosophy has done much to foster. As Mrs Thatcher's swamping statement of 1978 made clear a recurrent theme in her political discourse during the past decade had been her commitment to defending the interests of the white British majority against the claims of minority communities.

The emphasis in her political rhetoric on the shared history, customs and values of Britishness has been one way in which she has attempted to draw together a social basis for her political project. This was emphasised to some extent in the aftermath of the Falklands war, and the mobilisation of nationalism against the 'Argies'. But within the context of domestic British politics it is emphasised continuously by Mrs Thatcher's expressed sympathy for the fears of the majority about the impact of immigration and race on their localities, their schools and their cultural heritage.

Summary and conclusion

Much of the substance of this chapter has been concerned with unravelling and exploring the role of ideology and political language in contemporary process of racialisation. But the various forms of racist mobilisation, at the level of both theory and practice, analysed in this chapter also provide a basis for understanding how policy issues as diverse as urban change, law and order, unemployment and youth policy are racialised and constantly transformed.

The transformations in racist ideologies that we have witnessed in the past decade point to the need for a deeper understanding of the logic of racist ideologies and mobilisations, particularly by those interested in challenging the roots of racism as well as its everyday manifestations. The prevalence of racialised ideologies about Englishness and national identity shows perhaps how far we have to go before we achieve a situation of racial justice and equality, but it also highlights the importance of understanding the complex forms of racial thought in contemporary British society.

8 Black Politics and the Struggle for Equality

Introduction

In previous chapters, we have seen that the politicisation of race and related issues in the post-1945 period was a complex process, which involved interventions by successive governments, political parties, pressure groups, politicians and other political actors. The sequence of events that we have witnessed since 1945 have been the product of political mobilisation of one sort or another, rather than the inevitable consequence of processes beyond political control.

It is also clear, however, that black and ethnic minority groups have played an active role in the political debates about questions of race and immigration over the past four decades. Both at a national and local level black political groups, or anti-racist alliances between black and white groups, have attempted to mobilise either in order to counteract the activities of racist groups or to promote measures aimed at bringing about racial justice and equality (Pearson, 1981; Sivanandan, 1982; Anwar, 1986; Carter, 1986). Such mobilisations have proved to be as controversial as the activities of extreme right wing groups, and in some localities the actions of black political activists have attracted widespread media attention. Recent examples of such controversies are the debates about the politics of anti-racism and the long drawn out debate during the 1980s on black sections within the Labour Party.

Indeed, one of the ironies of the late 1980s is that in the media and in popular political discourse it is the anti-racists who are often seen to be doing more harm to good race relations than extreme right wing racist groupings. Recently, for example, the editor of the *Sunday Telegraph*, Peregrine Worsthorne, argued forcefully that the Notting Hill Carnival was not threatened by white racists or the police, but by

140

black racists who were keen to use the occasion for their political ends (28 August 1988). Within the logic of this argument the greatest threat to the development of racial harmony lies in the politicisation of racial issues by black activists and politicians and by race relations professionals.

This approach helps to marginalise the issue of white racism, and at the same time to invoke the threat of black racism. It thus fits in with the common sense view, articulated most recently in the language of the new-right, of black communities as a threat to the political and social unity of British society.

In this chapter we will examine in greater detail the nature and impact of black political mobilisation, and responses to it. The focus will be on delineating the basic forms of black mobilisation, the interplay between race and class, the role of anti-racist political alliances, minority political participation and the impact of racial factors on local political processes. In the final part of the chapter we shall reflect on the prospects for black political mobilisation, particularly in the context of the social changes that are taking place within the various black communities.

Political participation and exclusion

Before moving on to the central concerns of this chapter, however, it is necessary to introduce some general arguments about political participation and processes of political mobilisation. Political participation and action are an essential element in the development of political systems and institutions. Historically the development of political systems in different societies has involved the integration of disparate groups into the polity and the development of channels of political participation and inclusion.

In liberal democratic societies such as Britain the most obvious means for enabling, as well as constraining, participation are elections, parties, trade unions and pressure groups. Such processes and institutions tend to reinforce identification with the rules, procedures and values of the polity, they enable the articulation of demands, to facilitate consent and they strengthen acceptance of the legitimacy of the political system (Edelman, 1977; Alford and Friedland, 1985).

What is clear, however, is that not all groups enjoy the same opportunity to participate politically through channels which are defined as legitimate (Piven and Cloward, 1977; Bowles and Gintis, 1987). According to Katznelson and Weir groups in society may be (a) incorporated fully and equally and may possess the capacity to affect the contours of policy change, (b) incorporated fully and equally but have relatively little influence on the political system, (c) incorporated in a partial and structurally subordinate way, but possess the capacity to influence policy outcomes at some moments, or (d) may be structurally subordinate and without resources to affect what the state does (Katznelson and Weir, 1985: 204).

Thus once individuals or groups gain access to channels of political participation they do not necessarily gain equal access to agenda setting and decision making. Some groups and individuals have far greater power to place issues on the agenda. Indeed it has been argued that certain types of problems and many groups of people are systematically excluded from participation: there is a mobilisation of bias whereby some issues are organised into politics while others are organised out.

Prevailing social and political values, as well as institutional practices, can also limit the political agenda. A good example of this is the way in which, with the shift in political values to the right since 1979, calls for political intervention to promote greater racial equality and positive action have been marginalised politically. Because such calls do not fit in with the development of an enterprise culture, the three Thatcher administrations since 1979 have systematically refused to make any major initiatives to strengthen race relations legislation or to allocate more resources to those bodies charged with promoting greater racial equality.

The context of black political participation

As we argued above, racist political mobilisations, whether in the form of Powellism or the actions of extreme right groups, have tended to attract most attention over the past three decades or so. Yet, it is clear that during the same period black and anti-racist political mobilisations have played an important political role in shaping the politics of race in contemporary Britain.

What explains this relative neglect of this important facet of the politics of race and racism in contemporary Britain? It seems to stem partly from the noticeable failure of political scientists to study the growth and development of this form of political action. Until the mid-1970s the common assumption seemed to be that there was little, if any, political mobilisation by the ethnic minority communities at the political level. This assumption seemed to be supported by national studies of electoral behaviour and local political studies such as Newton's study of Birmingham, which found no significant evidence of political mobilisation (Newton, 1976).

Another factor which worked against the serious study of black politics was the sensitivity of research on political issues. During the 1970s and 1980s research on either the national or local politics of race proved to be a highly controversial issue and there was a marked reluctance by social scientists to carry out research in the context of opposition from local black community groups and activists (Jenkins, 1971; Rex and Tomlinson, 1979; Mullard, 1985).

The combination of these two processes helped to produce a situation where the political participation of Afro-Caribbean and Asian communities was little understood or analysed, with the exception of a few studies during the late 1960s and early 1970s which looked at the experience of specific cities or of ethnic minority organisations.

From the mid 1970s onwards, however, the issue of black political participation attracted the attention of a number of researchers and political commentators. Although this interest was as yet not clearly focused it helped to clarify some aspects of emergent forms of black political organisation, of electoral participation and of the response of political parties and institutions to black political action (Fitzgerald, 1984; Anwar, 1986).

One of the main concerns of a number of studies has been the question of the future development of black politics, particularly as the black communities become more established and incorporated into political processes. These studies have suggested three possible patterns for the future political incorportion of minority black communities within the British political system:

(1) First, it has been argued that with the passing of time it is possible that black migrants and their descendants will become incorporated fully, if unequally, within the political institutions of British political life, including political parties, pressure groups and trades unions.

(2) Second, it has been argued that migrant communities could be incorporated into the political system through their own ethnically or regionally based organisations. Such organisations would seek to advance the interests of particular ethnic groups by political means.

(3) Third, it has been argued that in response to institutionalised racism and the politicisation of racial issues in British society black communities, whatever their ethnic origins, could develop a common political identity as an excluded black minority.

There is little agreement as yet about the most likely course of political incorporation which the various black minorities are likely to follow, or to the degree of choice they have in this process. But it seems to be generally agreed by both Marxists and pluralists that black political participation is likely to follow one of the above three patterns.

For example, a study by Phizacklea and Miles, which was based on fieldwork in London during the late 1970s and utilised a Marxist framework, concluded that in Britain what seemed to be happening involved a combination of class based and ethnically based political mobilisation. Because of their class composition minority black communities showed a strong interest in traditional forms of working class participation in the British political system, expressed through their support for the Labour Party and involvement in trades unions. But because of the pervasiveness of racial exclusionism at all levels of British society, according to Phizacklea and Miles, minority communities were also forced to organise autonomously on ethnic or racial lines to defend their interests (Phizacklea and Miles, 1980).

In broad terms this is also the argument developed by Layton-Henry (1984), though his account lays more stress on the incorporation of minority politics within political parties and electoral processes.

It has to be said, however, that as yet there are few research based studies of the patterns of political incorporation or autonomous political mobilisation among the various minority communities. It is very difficult therefore to draw firm conclusions about the future of black politics in British society without such detailed accounts, but in the rest of this chapter we shall attempt to outline some of the main aspects of black political involvement over the past four decades and look briefly at prospects for the future. In the course of this account we shall return to the themes that have been outlined in this section.

Origins of black political mobilisation

During the 1940s and 1950s the position of the newly arrived black communities can be seen in terms of the pattern of political exclusion and marginalisation from the political system which we have described above. Black organisations or groups during this period had little or no resources to affect what the state did. This does not mean that there was an absence of political involvement or organisation within the newly arrived minority communities. Throughout this period there is evidence of a lively interest in both the mainstream of British politics and in community based associations and groupings (Sivanandan, 1982; Ramdin, 1987; Gilroy, 1987).

In the 1960s, however, a number of black groups and individuals began to challenge this exclusion and to invoke fundamental issues of citizenship and equality. Afro-Caribbean and Asian migrants launched a series of local and national organisations that sought in various ways to challenge the exclusion of blacks from equal participation in British society. Such organisations included the already established Indian Workers' Association, the West Indian Standing Conference and other ethnically based groups (Pearson, 1981; Jacobs, 1986; Carter, 1986).

The organisation that received widespread public attention during the 1960s, however, was the Campaign Against Racial Discrimination (CARD). This organisation was formed in 1964–5 by a coalition black political groups, white liberals and campaigners against racism. It had as its main objectives the struggle to eliminate racial discrimination in British society, opposition to racially discriminatory legislation, and the co-ordination of the work of local and national organisations fighting racial discrimination (Heineman, 1972; 20–35). Although it collapsed after a brief and highly controversial power struggle within the organisation during 1967, it did play a role in public debates about the development of policies to tackle racial discrimination and it also served as a catalyst for a wide-ranging debate about the need for an autonomous black political organisation to tackle the roots of racial inequality at all levels of British society.

Forms of black political organisation

From the early 1970s there has been a noticeable growth in the levels
of political involvement and mobilisation among the Afro-Caribbean
and Asian communities. A growing literature of sensitive studies of
the black experience in Britain has shown that in practice there is a
complex and rich diversity of political and cultural expression at the
local level within many black communities. This diversity can be seen
at the level of electoral politics, community mobilisation, political
party involvement and more recently at the level of parliamentary
politics.

Electoral politics

During the 1970s the political participation of the various black
communities attracted the attention of both political parties and
researchers. A study carried out by the Community Relations
Commission of the importance of the black vote in certain constituencies during the general elections of 1974 helped to arouse media
and public interest in this issue.

In the period leading up to the 1979 general election Mrs
Thatcher's swamping statement helped to politicise the race issue
further, particularly in relation to the question of party allegiances.
Despite the attempt by the Conservative Party to draw support
among the white electorate away from the National Front, this did
not prevent the party from attempting to draw the support of sections
of the black communities in some constituencies. This was particularly the case in relation to Asian voters.

During the late 1970s and early 1980s all the major political parties
showed some interest in attempting to draw support from the black
communities, particularly in important inner city constituencies
where the black vote could make a difference to the outcome.

In practice, both Asian and Afro-Caribbean voters have tended to
express a preference for the Labour Party in both national and local
elections over the years. This trend goes back to the 1950s, though we
have clear evidence only for the period since the 1970s. In the general
elections of 1974 and 1979 there was strong evidence of support for
the Labour Party among both Asian and Afro-Caribbean voters.
This was the case for both working class and professional black
voters, though there was some variation according to class position.

This trend was repeated, but with some change, both in 1983 and 1987. The distribution of Asian and Afro-Caribbean voting intentions in the 1983 and 1987 general elections is shown in Table 8.1, which is based on surveys of voting intentions carried out by the Harris Research Centre.

Table 8.1 *Voting intentions of Asians and Afro-Caribbeans 1983 and 1987*

Party	Asians		Afro-Caribbeans	
	1983	1987	1983	1987
Conservative	9	23	7	6
Labour	81	67	88	86
Alliance	9	10	5	7

Source   The Guardian, 19 June 1987.

This trend was broadly corroborated by exit polls taken after the 1987 election, though the evidence is less clear from this source (Layton-Henry, 1988). In broad outline the evidence from such sources shows a depth of support for the Labour Party among both major minority communities, though increasingly less so among Asian voters. But what is also clear is that as compared to the majority white electorate, in England at least, the black electorate is overwhelmingly likely to support the Labour Party.

There are, however, other issues that need to be taken into account. Some evidence exists of a lower turnout at elections among some sections of the Afro-Caribbean communities, particularly the young. Such groups are more likely to be disillusioned with the ability of politicians to bring about changes in major issues that concern them. Additionally, it may be important to look at the issue of generational differences in voting behaviour. The trend of sections of the Asian electorate towards the Conservative Party may not be uniform, and there is a need to look into the class and generational patterns behind this transformation (Crewe, 1983; Layton-Henry and Studlar, 1985; Anwar, 1986).

Interestingly, although during both the 1983 and 1987 General Elections there was much speculation about a major move towards the Conservative Party by middle class Asians and Afro-Caribbeans the scale of the change does not support such generalisations. Layton-Henry (1988) argues that the trend towards class-based voting may be more limited than some studies have suggested:

In the future, one would expect that class voting will increase among members of the black electorate but there are a number of reasons why this is likely to be rather slow. These include Mrs Thatcher's determination to bring New Commonwealth immigration to an end, her lack of sympathy for anti-discrimination measures and her willingness to allow the Labour Party to be identified with what she regards as unpopular minorities. (p. 22)

Whether the shift towards more class-based voting behaviour among the Afro-Caribbean and Asian communities is likely to become more pronounced over the next decade is the subject of much academic debate, and it has aroused the interest of the major political parties. But before we can begin to analyse this issue in more detail there is a need to look more deeply into the question of the sociology of the black electorate and its different component parts.

Community politics

During the past four decades a variety of community-based organisations and groups have been formed within the various minority communities. Indeed, one of the features of both Afro-Caribbean and Asian self-organisation has been the array of communal, religious, political and issue oriented groups that have arisen over the years. Such organisations have frequently been of a local or community-based character, and have involved a variety of different forms of autonomous organisation in a number of different contexts, rather than unified ethnic movements.

Few detailed studies of the history and political ideologies of such groups have been carried out. During the 1960s and 1970s some studies of Asian political and cultural organisations were carried out, particularly in relation to their political involvement and ideological commitments. A more limited number of studies of Afro-Caribbean organisations and groups were also carried out during this time. Such studies were, however, limited both in scope and in geographical context.

Part of the reason for the neglect of this dimension of black political action may have been the assumption that such organisations and groups were not very influential at the political level. Goulbourne (1987), however, argues forcefully that without looking at the role played by such groups it is impossible to understand the growing political impact of minority politics on the major political parties and mainstream institutions. He sees this influence as particularly important in placing such issues as the education of black children, police relations with black children, police relations with black people, black unemployment and racial attacks on the political agenda at both local and central government levels.

Other studies of black community organisations have helped to show how active self-organisation is an everyday feature of the political life of various black communities. Cheetham (1988) notes the most important feature of ethnic associations in Britain seems to be their 'extraordinary vitality, energy, and commitment'. She concludes from her study of a sample of ethnic associations that two issues were held to be important by most of the groups she studied. First, the question of culture, language and ethnic identity, including the politics of the country of origin of the associations' members. Second, the issue of how to bring about greater equality and integration into British society, without losing minority traditions and values (pp. 150–1).

The importance of the role played by community-based and ethnic associations in the political life of the various ethnic minority organisations is only now being fully appreciated. This is likely to lead to more detailed studies of the processes of political mobilisation and community organisation, both in relation to issue-centred politics and electoral and party politics. One example of this trend is the attention which has been given to the growth of political mobilisation among ethnically- and religiously-based community groups in recent years. The two most important examples in this context are the Muslim and Sikh communities, which have developed high levels of political organisation and community-based mobilisation on issues related to British politics and the politics of their countries of origin.

The Labour Party and black sections

As we have already seen, from the very earliest stages of post-war black migration one of the themes in the discussion of the political allegiances of black migrants was their tendency to give their support in elections to the Labour Party. Yet it is clear that the Labour Party itself made little serious attempt until the late 1970s to incorporate its black supporters fully in its own organisations or to tackle the institutionalised racism in its own organisational structures.

During the late 1970s, however, both black and white Labour Party members began to press for more action on issues concerned with racial inequality and racism. In 1975 the Labour Party Race Action Group was established as a pressure group within the Party, and along with other individuals it helped to increase awareness of the politics of racism within the Labour Party. From the late 1970s internal debates the policy change within the Labour Party helped to bring issues such as racial inequality, along with other previously neglected issues, onto the political agenda of the party at both a national and a local level.

These pressures were given greater force during the early 1980s, in the aftermath of the political attention given to the outbreaks of urban unrest. In many local Labour Party constituencies, as well as at a national level, race-related issues became the focus of intense policy debate. The early 1980s were a period of innovation as a number of left wing Labour local authorities took the initiative in developing race equality policies, in promoting anti-racist initiatives and in tackling institutionalised racism within their own institutions.

It was in the context of these changes that black Labour Party politicians and activists began to demand both greater attention to racial issues and more black representation in local and national political institutions. Such demands for increased black representation were seen as a way of (a) including black politicians in the institutions of political power, (b) helping to put black issues on the political agenda, and (c) giving a voice to the demands of those excluded from equal political participation.

Increasingly, the focus for these demands became the issue of the formation of black sections within the Labour Party, which are seen as a way of increasing the influence of black Labour Party members on policy making and attracting more black people to become involved in political activity. Resolutions calling for the recognition of black sections were debated at the annual conferences of 1983 and 1984, and at subsequent conferences. The leadership of the party came out against the idea of black sections, largely on the grounds that it could be seen as divisive and as a form of apartheid. There seems also to have been an underlying fear among the leadership of the party that the black sections of the movement could become a political liability if they were led by radical left-wing black groups.

Marc Wordsworth, a leading figure in the black sections campaign, expressed the thinking behind the campaign for black sections when he warned that:

> If the Party did not begin actively to take the issue of black representation seriously, it must face the possibility of increased abstentions, a tide of black independents and perhaps a tendency, particularly amongst black youth, to redress their grievances through extra-parliamentary action (*The Times*, 16 April 1984).

Within the terms of this argument the recognition of black sections within the Labour Party will help to institutionalise black representation and allow black members a channel for mobilising for changes in the political programme of the party both locally and nationally.

According to Diane Abbott, a leading figure in the black sections movement, who was elected to Parliament in 1987, a number of factors helped to make the black sections issue a central theme. First, the longstanding institutionalised racism in the Labour Party and the increasingly glaring contradiction between the Labour Party reliance on the black vote and the fact that the structures of the Labour Party were almost all white. Second, the way in the late 1970s, that the Left in the Labour Party had used constitutional means, like mandatory selection, as a way of organising against the status quo. Finally, there was 'the emergence in the Labour Party of a different generation of black activists, who took for granted that they should organise themselves as black people' (*Marxism Today*, September 1985: 31).

Despite the failure of the black sections movement to achieve formal recognition from the party it has survived in the form of the Labour Party Black Section. A number of active groups exist in various localities. These groups continue to campaign for formal recognition and to meet regularly at both a local and a national level. During 1988 they produced a detailed Black Agenda which seeks to put forward proposals on such issues as inner city policy, education, policing and housing (Labour Party Black Section, 1988). The agenda itself has proved to be controversial and it is unlikely at this stage to influence the policies being pursued by the Labour Party, particularly given the identification of the document with a number of controversial issues. But in the longer term the likelihood is that black pressure for increased political incorporation into political institutions will be difficult for the Labour Party to resist as black representation becomes more established.

Representation in Parliament

The final aspect of black political involvement that needs to be mentioned in this context is the election in 1987 of four black MPs representing the Labour Party. Bernie Grant was elected for Tottenham, Diane Abbott for Hackney North and Stoke Newington, Paul Boateng for Brent South, and Keith Vaz for Leicester East. Their election meant that black people were represented in Parliament for the first time in sixty years, and because of this it was popularly represented as a major change in British political life.

Part of the reason for the interest in the election of the four black MPs in 1987 can be found in the controversy surrounding their selection, which was popularly presented as the outcome of pressure from the black sections movement and sections of the left of the Labour Party. Certainly one of the most controversial aspects of the rise of black political power at both local and national level has been the election of black politicians, particularly those seen as representing left-wing or black power views. Many black politicians have been represented in the media and in popular political discourse as representatives of black power or of the extreme left.

When in the period leading up to the 1987 general election the Labour Party selected a number of black candidates in winnable seats there were clear signs of unease about the possible impact of black representation in Parliament. The *Sun* warned in the lead-up to the election that the election of black MPs would not help the majority of the black population since they were 'all holders of loony left ideas which have shocked the nation' (14 February 1987). At a broader level the selection of black candidates became embroiled in the wider controversies about the influence of the loony left on Labour Party politics and on the activities of left wing local authorities such as Lambeth and Brent. The controversy over the selection and de-selection of Sharon Atkin as the candidate for Nottingham East in the lead-up to the 1987 general election was a clear example of how these issues coalesced in popular political debate.

In the aftermath of their election much attention has been focused on the parliamentary performance of the four black MPs and their impact on debates in Parliament and in committee. It is certainly too early to make a reasoned judgement on the role of black MPs or whether they will be able to use their position to influence debates in and out of Parliament on race and related issues, as well as on wider policy questions. But already there are signs that their position in Parliament has given rise to quite unique pressures and has rendered their position very difficult both as constituency MPs and as black politicians.

Anti-racist politics and political alliances

One of the recurrent themes in debates about the development of black political action is the question of political alliances between black and anti-racist political groups. The search for such alliances is based on two main assumptions. First, it is argued that the relatively small size of the minority population means that black demands would have a greater chance for success if they received the support of sections of the majority white population. The second assumption is that racism in British society is as much a problem for the white majority as it is for the black minorities, and that racialist political groups can best be dealt with on the basis of an alliance between black and white anti-racist groups.

One example of a national attempt to develop an alliance of anti-racist political groups was the Anti-Nazi League, which was founded in 1977. The League was particularly active in the period from 1977 to 1979, and it concentrated its interventions on political action to counter the propaganda of the National Front and other extreme right groups. It drew its support from members of the Labour Party, the Socialist Workers Party and from other left organisations that had become concerned about the growing popularity of racist political groups. One of these organisations was Rock Against Racism, which had been active since 1976 in mobilisations aimed at turning young people against the National Front and other racist organisations, and which helped to draw many supporters to the ANL (Widgery, 1986; Gilroy, 1987).

The ANL used a variety of initiatives to organise against the National Front, and emphasised in particular two modes of action. First, direct extra-parliamentary initiatives such as rallies and demonstrations which helped to publicise its arguments on racism and on the political dangers which the extreme right represented. The ANL in particular chose to emphasise the links between the ideology of the National Front and Nazi ideology in order to mobilise opposition to it, and to dwell on the links between the Front and underground fascist groups. This helped to mobilise opposition to the Front in the period leading up to the 1979 election.

Second, during 1978 and 1979 it organised a series of successful musical events in association with Rock Against Racism, which were aimed at attracting to the anti-racist cause the young people who were seen as particularly vulnerable to National Front propaganda.

The speed of the rise of the ANL was matched by the rapidity of its decline as a political force from 1979 onwards. Although it continued to exist for some time afterwards its high point was over and had little impact on public political debate.

This does not mean that attempts to organise anti-racist political alliances have not persisted through the 1980s. Ben-Tovim *et al.* (1986) have argued, on the basis of research in Liverpool and Wolverhampton, that locally-based anti-racist alliances have been an important channel for the promotion of black political demands and for the development of mobilisations against racist organisations. From this they conclude that at the local level at least the role of anti-racist political alliances remains an important aspect of the politics of racism in contemporary Britain.

The politics of race and class

The interplay of race and class in the formation of black political action has been one of the most resonant themes in studies of this question. As we saw in Chapter 1 the theoretical debate about how race and class interact is far from being resolved, and indeed it is still one of the themes of heated debate among social scientists. Underlying these theoretical controversies, however, are more practical questions about the relationship between autonomous black political mobilisation and class-based politics.

This theme is central, for example, in the controversy surrounding the electoral behaviour of the black communities and the formation of black sections within the Labour Party. Similar questions have been raised about the development of black politics in the United States, particularly in the debate between Marxists and black nationalists (Marable, 1981).

In Chapter 1 we looked at some of the ways in which a number of scholars have attempted to overcome the dichotomy between race and class relations. At that stage we did not attempt to provide a full answer to the problems we raised. After the above discussion, however, we are in a better position to look more deeply into this issue.

In broad outline there are two questions we have to confront in rethinking the terms of political debate about race and class.

First, there is the question of what we mean by class. The role of political mobilisation in determining the formation of class consciousness, national consciousness and other identities has been the focus of a lively debate over the years. One of the sharpest formulations of this problem is to be found in a study of the politics of schooling in the United States Ira Katznelson and Margaret Weir, who argue that:

> It is important to think of the formation of a class as a conditional process. Whether people who share objective traits in the material organisation of society will form a class in action cannot be predicted from the profiles of the social structure, nor can the rhetorical and practical bases of their action be deduced from such profiles. (1985: 62)

Within the terms of this perspective what is important in the development of political mobilisation is not the objective position of political actors in the social structure but their actual experiences and responses to the social, economic and political processes of the societies in which they live.

Second, and following on from the above, there is a need to understand the connection between race as a political category and wider social processes and conflicts.

In contemporary Britain the main problem with trying to see black politics from a pure class perspective is that it is impossible to see contemporary forms of black political mobilisation as separate from the everyday experiences of discrimination and exclusion which have operated over four decades. The distinctive experiences of Afro-Caribbeans, Asians and other minority groups need therefore to be understood, and this necessarily takes us beyond a dogmatic conception of class formation. At the same time it is important to remember that their distinctive historical experiences are joined by a common thread: either a full or partial denial of citizenship or the rights that accompany it.

Politics, social movements and reform

The central question which underlies all accounts of black political mobilisation is: What impact can black communities have on the political agenda? Another related question is: What are the prospects that an effective challenge to racism can be mounted within the current political environment?

These questions have certainly become a common reference point in debates about such specific policy issues as education and policing, which have been areas of active concern among the various black communities for some time.

What is also clear, however, is that there is by no means a uniform answer to these questions. Responses range from deep scepticism as to the possibility of blacks exercising a major influence on the mainstream political agenda, to a degree of optimism about the ability of black politicians to transform political institutions.

Perhaps the most noticeable political development in recent years, however, has been the attempt by black politicians to gain access to positions of political patronage and power at both a national and a local political level. The assumption behind this strategy is that it is only through their integration into the mainstream channels of political power and patronage that black communities can move beyond political exclusion and powerlessness to a situation where they are incorporated equally into the political system and have the resources to bring about policy changes in their interest.

Such an optimistic view of the possibilities for black advancement through the political system is not shared by all commentators. The relative failure of the mainstream political institutions to tackle the root causes of racial inequality and racism in British society has led some commentators to look beyond the channels of formal politics for a way out of the present problems.

Gilroy (1987), for example, concludes his account of urban social change and the role of black community struggles by arguing that:

> In the representation of the recent riots, it is possible to glimpse a struggle, a sequence of antagonisms which has moved beyond the grasp of orthodox class analysis. Unable to control the social relations in which they find themselves, people have shrunk the

world to the size of their communities and begun to act politically on that basis. (p. 245)

While it is difficult from this rather general and cryptic statement to fathom a clear political strategy, Gilroy seems to be suggesting (a) that the view which sees black communities becoming increasingly incorporated into existing class-based political institutions is inadequate, and that (b) excluded groups are likely to develop forms of political involvement at the micro rather than the macro level.

This line of argument stands in direct contrast to the attempts by other black radicals to prioritise the need to see more direct black involvement in national and local political institutions. This tension is also reflected in the ongoing debate about the formation of black sections within the Labour Party and the wider debate about increasing black representation in the mainstream political institutions.

At the present time, even the election of four black MPs and the election of a sizeable number of black councillors in many local authorities is unlikely to have much effect on the allocation of resources and political influence. This seems to be implicitly recognised by the so-called Black Agenda issued by the Black Sections movement during 1988 (Howe and Upshal, 1988).

Black demands for full citizenship will not easily be achieved in the present political climate. The urban unrest that has occurred sporadically throughout the 1980s may be better managed in the future, but the underlying conflicts which produced it are not thereby going to disappear. Ordinary patterns of dispute resolution have so far proved to be incapable of managing conflict with this content, meaning and intensity, and the prospects for the future are not hopeful.

Yet it is important to note that this situation is not likely to result in any wholesale withdrawal from all means of political activity. This is perhaps the best hope in the long term struggle of the black communities for equality and full citizenship.

Reflecting on the history of attempts to form a national body to fight for black interests at the political level Hall (1985b) has argued that one reason for the failure of such attempts is the distance between such organisations and the 'actual day-to-day experience of repression and exploitation which the black community has gone through'.

Summary and conclusion

This chapter has looked at the role of black and anti-racist political mobilisation in the context of the racialisation of British political life since 1945. It has shown that, far from being helpless victims, black communities have actively attempted to challenge racialism and injustice. Indeed the experience of the past few years would seem to indicate that the political participation and involvement of both the Asian and Afro-Caribbean communities is likely to increase over the next decade.

Anti-racist political mobilisations have also played an important role at various stages over the past four decades, and have attracted widespread sympathy and support from outside the black communities. Local and national attempts to create alliances against racism have been inherently contradictory and have proved to be unstable, but the experience of groups such as the Anti-Nazi League and Rock Against Racism, along with various locally-based initiatives, seems to indicate that the potential for political mobilisation against racism is there.

The prospects for the 1990s are already becoming a focus of debate. Concern seems to be particularly focused on young blacks and other disaffected groups within the black communities. Rose (1985) has warned, for example, that the main question in the 1990s is likely to be whether public policy succeeds in bringing about greater social integration or a situation where 'a small, politically alienated and active group will identify themselves as blacks rather than Britons' (p. 59). From a rather different perspective, Gilroy (1987) has put forward the argument that the immediate prospect of change from the present situation is to be found among 'those groups who find the premises of their collective existence threatened' (Gilroy, 1987: 246).

Perhaps the most important lesson we can learn from the experience of the past decade is that it is far too simplistic to search for one model of either black or anti-racist political mobilisation. Rather, it is important to recognise the volatile and to some extent unpredictable nature of political struggles over race, whether such struggles have a racist or an anti-racist political objective. Once this is done it becomes clear that the active involvement of black and ethnic minority communities is an integral element of any realistic strategy for challenging the existing political agenda about race in British society.

9 Protest, Racism and Social Change

Introduction

In previous chapters we have seen that black and ethnic minority groups have by no means been passive political actors during the past four decades, and that they have been an active political force over such issues as immigration policy, race relations policies, social policies and policing. In Chapter 6 we looked at some aspects of the experience of urban unrest in the late 1970s and early 1980s, and explored the ideological and policy responses to this phenomenon.

In this chapter, we will advance the analysis a step further by examining the role of racialised politics within the broader economic, social and political changes in contemporary British society. In the context of this chapter we shall also look at the experience of urban unrest in 1985 and in the late 1980s, and the political repercussions of these events in the context of the politics of Thatcherism. This will allow us to explore the question of how far these developments help to explain the new forms of racialised politics that have emerged in British society in recent years.

Power, legitimacy and political disorder

Perhaps the most important lesson of the 1980–1 riots was the way they emphasised the role of political protest as a channel for challenging racial injustice, after decades of ameliorative reforms. But in the aftermath of the riots many of the issues that were raised and the reforms that were promised did not become a central item on the political agenda of the Thatcher administration. Part of the reason for this may have been the hope that the events of 1980–1 were an aberration outside of the normal pattern of British politics and that urban disorders on a similar scale were not likley to recur.

Between 1982 and 1985 the differential nature of the Government's response to the riots became clear and a matter of comment in both the media and in academic research. Writing in 1985 John Clare, the BBC's Community Affairs Correspondent, noted that although the Government had carried out many changes in relation to the police after 1981 it had done 'remarkably little' in relation to political, social and economic issues (Clare, 1985). Indeed, during this period many of the conditioning factors which had commanded attention during 1981 had steadily worsened. This is particularly the case when one looks at issues such as unemployment, housing and welfare provision Government policies, far from remedying the employment situation, for example, had helped to produce levels of unemployment in inner city areas which were up to two or three times higher than during the 1980–1 disorders (Cross and Smith, 1987). Perhaps even more disastrously the Government had steadfastly refused to strengthen either the legislation on race relations or to take administrative measures to tackle racial inequality. After the 1981 riots the Government seemed to believe that it had the situation under control, and that future violent disorders were unlikely.

Any complacency about the likelihood of more urban violence on the scale of July 1981 was, however, short-lived. During the period form September to October 1985 serious outbreaks of violence took place in the Handsworth area of Birmingham, in the Tottenham and Brixton areas of London and in Liverpool. Other smaller scale disturbances occurred in 1986 and 1987 (Benyon and Solomos, 1987).

The scale and the location of the 1985 riots seem to have surprised even some of the most astute commentators. Handsworth, for example, was widely perceived as a success story in terms of police–community relations, and therefore the outbreak of violence in this area was seen as an aberration. Similarly the spread of violence in London to areas such as the Broadwater Farm Estate in Tottenham was seen as a break from previous experience, which had centred on areas such as Brixton. In this sense the interpretation of the 1985 riots proved to be as difficult as the 1980–1 riots.

What is clear is that the dominant political language used during the 1985 events sought to establish the senselessness of violent protest by arguing that the lessons of 1980–1 had been learned and that solutions were being applied to the main problems. Responding to the Handsworth events Douglas Hurd was moved to argue with some force that such events were senseless and reflected more on those who participated in them than on the society in which they took place:

> The sound which law abiding people in Handsworth heard on Monday night, the echoes of which I picked up on Tuesday, was not a cry for help but a cry for loot. (*Financial Times*, 13 September 1985)

The Chief Constable for the West Midlands, Geoffrey Dear took this argument further by pointing out that the day before the riots a successful carnival had taken place, with the support of local community leaders. He drew the conclusion from this that the riot 'came like a bolt out of the blue' (*The Guardian*, 21 November 1985). Such language focused attention on the individuals or groups who were breaking the law, committing criminal acts, and threatening the interests of the law-abiding majority.

It also helped to rework some of the main themes that were evident in the aftermath of 1980–1 around the central role of law and order in relation to (a) race and social disadvantage, (b) urban decline and unemployment, (c) crime, drugs and hooliganism, and (d) internal enemies and political disorder.

Let us take the example of the political debate about race and urban unrest in the aftermath of the 1985 riots. There are many continuities between 1980–1 and 1985 in relation to the race issue. But responses in 1985 can be said to be different at least in terms of degree, and probably in relation to the extent to which the riots were seen as a race phenomenon by a wider body of opinion. The ambiguities and sub-clauses to be found in much of the press coverage during 1980–1 had at least acted as a countervailing tendency against the more extreme forms of discourse which blamed the riots completely on blacks. During the 1985 riots and their immediate aftermath, however, the imagery of race was used by sections of the press without the sense of ambiguity which could still be found in 1980–1. The silence over race was breached in 1980–1, but in a more limited way than in 1985.

An example of this greater openness about racial issues is the way new-right commentators used the urban unrest in 1985 to question the possibility that a multi-racial society could develop without conflict. Peregrine Worsthorne, for example, argued that the ferocity of confrontations in Handsworth, Brixton and Tottenham posed a major question mark over the possibility of assimilating the coloured population into mainstream British values (*Sunday Telegraph*, 29 September 1985). To be sure there was still a strong response opposing Enoch Powell's call for repatriation, from all shades of political opinion, but the racialisation of public debate about the riots went even further than 1980-1. Consider for example the following headlines the day after the outbreak of violence in Handsworth, 11 September:

'Bloodlust' (*Daily Mail*)

'Hate of Black Bomber' (*Sun*)

'War on the Streets' (*Mirror*)

'Torch of Hate' (*Star*)

'England, 1985' (*Daily Express*).

All five headlines were next to a picture of a black petrol bomber, who was variously described as 'stalking the streets of Handsworth' or as a 'prowling West Indian'. These images fitted with the official view that this 'was not a social phenomenon but crime' which was also reported by the press on the same day. They established a linkage between race, crime and disorder much more firmly than the riots of 1980-1 had done.

In this context it was the externality of West Indians and Asians which was highlighted rather than the racist institutions and processes which worked against blacks at all levels of society. The usage of race during the 1985 riots took on new meanings, which had little if anything to do with the impact of racism as such, since the emphasis was on the cultural characteristics of the minority communities themselves. After Handsworth part of the press response was to blame the riot on rivalry between West Indians and Asians, and even after the arguments were criticised by local residents and community leaders they were used to explain what happened. In addition, the questions of whether the cultures and values of the black communities, their family structures, and their political attitudes bred violence were constantly raised.

The actual facts of who was arrested during the riots, whether black or white, were hardly debated since it was assumed that they were mostly black and mostly unemployed and involved with crime. The imagery of the black bomber used in Handsworth was extended to the notion that there were groups of alienated and criminalised young blacks who saw the riots as a chance to engage in an orgy of looting. The Dear Report on Handsworth captures this image and links it to the social condition of young blacks:

> The majority of rioters who took part in these unhappy events were young, black and of Afro-Caribbean origin. Let there be no doubt, these young criminals are not in any way representative of the vast majority of the Afro-Caribbean community whose life has con- tributed to the life and culture of the West Midlands over many years and whose hopes and aspirations are at one with those of every other law abiding citizen. We share a common sorrow. It is the duty of us all to ensure that an entire cultural group is not tainted by the actions of a criminal minority. (Dear, 1985: 69)

This black criminal minority was constructed not only into the leading force behind the riots, but sometimes as the only force. Indeed through September and October 1985, and during the following months, the imagery of race continued to dominate debate both about the causes and the policy outcomes of the riots.

As pointed out above the social causes argument was another major plank of public debate about the 1980–1 riots, particularly in relation to the highly politicised issue of unemployment. During 1985 this issue was raised once again, though by then the extent of mass unemployment and urban de-industrialisation and decay was more stark than it had been in 1981. Images of urban decay, tinderbox cities, and ghetto streets linked up with the images of race inequality and black ghettoes to produce an analysis more complex but contradictory set of arguments.

An interesting mixture of the various images was provided by a story in the *Daily Telegraph* under the headline: 'Broadwater Farm: Like the Divis Flats with Reggae' (8 October 1985). The *Mirror* described the estate as 'Living Hell', and quoted one resident as saying that 'You've no idea how awful daily life is' (8 October 1985). Such images were reworkings of arguments already used about Toxteth in 1981 and Brixton in 1981, but they were used more widely than in 1980–1. Even the *Daily Mail*, which deployed the clearest use of 'race' and 'outside agitator' type arguments, ran a major story on

Broadwater Farm under the headline: 'Burnt-out hulks litter this concrete jungle . . . despair hangs heavy' (8 October 1985). A number of stories using such imagery were run by both the quality and popular press during this period, but similar arguments are to be found in Parliamentary Debates (*Hansard*, Vol. 84, 1985: Cols 30–46 and Cols 368–88), and even in official reports produced by the police on the riots in Birmingham and London.

The following editorial from the *Mirror*, printed in the aftermath of the Brixton riot illustrates the point:

THE FIRE DOWN BELOW
The fires in Brixton have been damped down but the spark that ignited them is still glowing in every inner-city area with a large black population. That spark will not be extinguished easily or painlessly.

There is no excuse for what happened on Saturday and there can be no mercy for those who committed crimes . . .

But bad conditions make bad people of some who would otherwise be good. If they had pleasant housing, secure jobs and favourable prospects, they would be far less likely to behave as they did on Saturday. (1 October 1985)

The imagery of a fire down below and the policy implication that as well as tackling the criminal acts the government should be doing something about housing, employment and leisure facilities challenged the notion that the riots were a mere cry for loot but only to a limited extent. It did so largely by including the causes for the crimes under a broader social explanation of the roots of disorder.

The cities of inner despair were conceived as the breeding ground for disorderly protest, and however hard the government tried to break the causal link between the two it was forced to take on board the need to restore order not only through the police but through promises of help for the inner cities. Much as in 1980–1 the social causes argument cannot be seen separately from the broader debate about the future of the British economy and society more generally. The Government's record on unemployment was a heavily politicised issue, and just as in 1981 it vehemently denied any responsibility for the riots through its pursuit of free-market policies. But the Government did find a way of accepting a link between the riots and social problems without bringing its main policies into the debate:

namely by linking the growth of violent disorder to crime and drugs.
debate: namely by linking the growth of violent disorder to crime and
drugs.

Race, crime and disorder

The emphasis on crime and the criminal acts of the rioters in the
official responses to the 1985 riots took a general and a specific form.
The general form relied on the argument that the riots were not a
form of protesting against the unbearable social conditions of inner
city areas or the actions of the police, but a criminal act or a cry for
loot. This was an argument put most succinctly by Geoffrey Dear,
Chief Constable of the West Midlands (Dear, 1985) and by Douglas
Hurd, the Home Secretary, in relation to Handsworth. But it
recurred as a theme in official and press responses to the other riots.
The specific form was built upon the notion that the outbreak of
violence in Handsworth and Brixton, in particular, was brought
about by drug barons who saw the police attempting to curb their
activities and control their territory. Numerous examples of this line
of argument can be found in Dear's report on Handsworth, and in a
number of major press stories published during the riots.

The attack on crimnal acts and the emphasis on order, resonated
through a long debate in Parliament on 23 October 1985, on 'Urban
Disturbances'. Rejecting the Labour Party's call for an independent
inquiry into the causes of the riots the Government succeeded in
pushing through the following resolution:

> That this House recognises the crucial importance of the
> maintenance of public order; applauds the courage and dedication
> of the police and responsible community leaders in restoring order;
> and welcomes Her Majesty's Government's commitment to early
> effective action in the light of the recent urban disturbances.
> (*Hansard*, Vol. 84, 1985: Col. 388)

A measure of how the law and order argument was used can also be
found in the numerous calls made by Douglas Hurd for people to
rally round the police in order to defend the rule of law, and the
acceptance by virtually all the media that, in the short term at least,
the restoration of police authority on the streets of fear was the first
priority.

Taking the specific argument about the role of drugs and drug barons in stimulating the riots, this seems to have served two purposes. First, it distanced the riots from the social, economic, political and other grievances which had been linked to them, by locating the cause outside of the social problems of inner city dwellers and in the simple greed of the drug barons to accumulate. Second, just as Dear's image of a few hundred young black criminals was used to explain what happened in Handsworth, the problem of drugs was used to explain what happened at a national level. The issue of drugs provided an everyday image, already a national issue through saturation media coverage and public debate, around which the police, the Home Office and other institutions could de-socialise the riots.

What is clear, therefore, is that the public pronouncements branding the riots as criminal acts and a cry for loot were only one element of a wider ideological construction of the events around the theme of a 'drift towards crime'. While the branding of the riots as criminal seemed to depoliticise them, it is quite clear that a more complex analysis of why crime and disorder were a growing phenomenon exercised an influence on police and other official ideologies.

The theme of outside agitators had been widely used to explain the 1980–1 riots, but 1985 saw a massive explosion of this imagery and its use to explain the causes of the attacks on the police. The masked men of 1980–1 were to some extent unmasked. Take for example the treatment by the press of Bernie Grant, and other black and white local Labour Party leaders. They were labelled by Douglas Hurd as the 'High Priests of Race Hate', and then followed lurid press stories which attempted to show how 'GLC leftists', 'Black activists' or 'plain reds' were behind a campaign to undermine the police, to stimulate urban violence and to bring about a collapse of law and order. Such stories served a double function. First, they unmasked the forces behind the riots and gave credibility to claims that even if they were not pre-planned they had been sparked off by agitation from leftists and other folk devils. Second, they helped to decontextualise the riots from the issue of racism and the social position of inner city black communities by laying the blame for race hate squarely on the door of the extreme left and the black activists. Indeed according to Ronald Butt, a regular columnist for *The Times* and other papers on race issues during 1980–1 and 1985, race had become a new weapon in the class war.

If blaming assorted types of Reds for the outbreak of street violence had taken on new forms in 1985, the traditional outside agitators theme of masked men and foreign agents did not exactly disappear. A classic of its own kind is the following story from the *Daily Express* about the death of PC Blakelock on Broadwater Farm:

Moscow-trained hit squad gave orders as mob hacked PC Blackelock to death.

The thugs who murdered policeman Keith Blakelock in the Tottenham riots acted on orders of crazed left-wing extremists. Street-fighting experts trained in Moscow and Libya were behind Britain's worst violence.

The chilling plot emerged last night as detectives hunted a hand-picked death squad believed to have been sent into North London hell-bent on bloodshed.

They include men and women from Commonwealth countries like Jamaica, Barbados and Nigeria, who have been trained in Russia and Libya in street revolutionary tactics. (8 October 1985)

A number of similar stories resonated through the pages of the popular press, even when there was no evidence supplied or when the links seemed to be a matter of assertion. Looking for the men behind the riots turned out to be less a matter of the individual leftists who were named in such stories but of the construction of symbolic clues about the threat posed to Britain by outside agents, men and women from Commonwealth countries. In fact what is interesting about the *Daily Express* story, apart form the classic headline, is the way it highlights the supposed use of immigrants by Russia and Libya to undermine order and stability.

The symbolic political value of such metaphors has been noted in studies of riot response in the USA, where the 'outside agitators' argument was used to deflect attention away from social, economic and policing issues (Edelman, 1971; Lipsky and Olson, 1977). The experience of 1980–1 and 1985 in Britain suggests that such an analysis needs to be contextualised against a broader historical perspective, since the 'outside agitators' line of arguments do not seem to have any relation to the facts of the riots as such. They seem to form part of a wider use of symbolic political language to help make sense of the crisis facing British society. Ambiguous political situations such as riots help engender anxieties about the role of external threats to order, but they do not create such beliefs. But when they are contextualised against the background of wider political debates about race and immigration in posts-1945 Britain it becomes easier to see the interconnections between images of outside agitators and the popular stereotypes of blacks as alien.

'Symbolic locations' and urban change

The notion that the growth of street violence was the product of a combination of social problems leading to the emergence of a criminal element and hooliganism was one of the main themes in accounts of the 1980–1 riots, as pointed out above. But in the responses to the 1985 riots we see not only a common sense use of such ideas but a more sophisticated use of such an explanation by sections of the police. Some reference to this development has been made in relation to Dear's report on Handsworth. A more developed version was offered in the aftermath of the 1985 riots by Sir Kenneth Newman, Chief Constable of the Metropolitan Police. During the period 1982–5 he had already made a series of influential speeches on the issue of disorder and the growth of violence in British society. In a paper delivered in 1983 he had warned that in many inner city areas the police were under threat and unable to maintain order:

In many multi-ethnic areas police encounter not merely apathy and unhelpfulness when making enquiries or engaging in order maintenance, but outright hostility and obstruction. (Newman, 1983: 28)

He warned that such a situation could result in a cycle of increasing crime, law-breaking, police inability to maintain order and the reinforcement of urban decay. He argued that increasingly policing was not an isolated service but part of a wider set of agencies which helped to maintain social stability and order and prevent a drift towards crime and lawlessness. He saw such agencies as particularly important in the areas of education, health and social services, housing and environment, and employment.

In the aftermath of the 1985 riots Newman extended his analysis by arguing that crime and the fear of crime helped to reinforce attitudes towards the police and society which allowed violent protests to break out and challenge the legitimacy of the established order

(Newman, 1986a and 1986b). Crime, according to Newman, provided not so much a causal explanation for riots, but one element in a broader crisis of social policy and control. He saw this as particularly important in areas of a multi-ethnic nature where cultural and political hostility towards the police was growing.

Policing the inner cities

The policy responses after the 1985 riots, and subsequent events, show some of the same characteristics as those during 1980–1, but as we have argued above the emphasis on the criminality of the riot participants favoured explanations that linked disorder to the athological characteristics of inner city residents which pushed them towards lawlessness and crime. This in turn produced a sharper contrast than in 1980–1 between (a) responses which emphasised the need to strengthen and buttress the role of the police, and (b) responses which called for greater emphasis on the rejuvenation of the social and economic fabric of the inner cities. As Douglas Hurd argued after the 1985 Handsworth disturbances, 'this is not a case history for sociologists to pore over, but a case for the police' (*The Guardian*, 23 September 1985).

The above quote from the Home Secretary, which can be backed up by numerous others from Government Ministers and MPs, reflects the most important shift in political language between 1981 and 1985: namely, the emphasis given to the interpretation of the riots as a criminal enterprise more suited to investigation by the police than by social analysts or judicial experts such as Lord Scarman. The question of policing and law and order had been central in 1981 as well, but it had been balanced to some extent by an emphasis (e.g. in the Scarman Report and the interventions of opposition parties) on the wider social policy context.

In 1985, however, the Government specifically rejected calls for another Scarman type inquiry, arguing that since the riots were a criminal enterprise it was useless to search for social explanations or to have yet another report advising it about what to do. Implicitly the Government was saying that it knew what the problems were, and how they could be tackled.

While some senior policemen, like Newman, wanted to stress the link between the police and other areas of social policy, the official

Government response attempted to decontextualise the riots and see them as the actions of a small minority who were either criminalised or influenced by extreme political ideas. The dominant approach of the Government attempted to emphasise two main arguments:

(a) that the riots were 'a lust for blood', an 'orgy of thieving', 'a cry for loot and not a cry for help'; and

(b) that the riots reflected not a failure to carry out the 'urgent programme of action' recommended by Lord Scarman in 1981, but were the outcome of a spiralling wave of crime and disorder in inner city areas.

The logic of this approach, articulated by Douglas Hurd most clearly, was that the riots were both unjustifiable and a criminal activity. In a widely reported speech to police chiefs at the time of the disorders Hurd made this point clear:

Handsworth needs more jobs and better housing. But riots only destroy. They create nothing except a climate in which necessary development is even more difficult. Poor housing and other social ills provide no kind of reason for riot, arson and killing. One interviewer asked me whether the riot was not a cry for help by the rioters. The sound which law-abiding people heard at Handsworth was not a cry for help but a cry for loot. That is why the first priority, once public order is secure, must be a thorough and relentless investigation into the crimes which were committed. (*Daily Telegraph*, 14 September 1985)

Such arguments resonated through the media and in the various parliamentary debates during September and October. They became part of the symbolic political language through which the riots were understood by policy makers and by popular opinion.

The ascription to the rioters of wickedness and pure naked greed did not go unchallenged, as the analysis in the previous section has shown. Indeed Lord Scarman and numerous other commentators have sought to implicitly or explicitly challenge such simplifications. American experience, however, shows that the official espousal of explanations which see riots as irrational outbursts of criminal activity cannot be easily countered by oppositional forces, however well founded and empirically sound are their arguments (Edelman,

1971; Lipsky and Olson, 1977). This certainly seems to be one of the dangers in the aftermath of the 1985 riots, particularly if one looks at the nature of the response to the social and economic issues which underlay the riots.

Social and economic policies

The preoccupation with law and order responses did not preclude initiatives on other issues, most notably inner city and employment policies. The Parliamentary Debates during September–December 1985 are full of promises form the Government and the Opposition that they were both interested in transforming the social conditions of inner city areas (*Hansard*, Vol. 84, 1985: Cols 348–88; *Hansard*, Vol. 88, 1985: Cols 929–1004). The media showed similar concerns, and a number of feature articles analysed the problems of the inner cities, the ghettoes, and the lives of people living in such areas. A feature article in the *Mirror* on the Broadwater Farm Estate described it as a 'Living Hell', and went on to summarise what it saw as the feelings of the local people:

> If you don't live in desolate apartments where no one seems to care – and even the police have declared a no-go area, you have no idea how awful your daily life can be. (8 October 1985)

When combined with no jobs, inadequate social facilities, and no real help from either central or local government, the *Miror* went on, such areas can become another world, a world where disillusion and violence are everyday facts of life.

During late 1985 and early 1986 the Government announced a number of initiatives on the inner city and employment, and it presented these as part of an effort to rejuvenate depressed areas on a sound basis. Examples of such actions include the introduction of more government finance to encourage black business enterprise, promises to regenerate inner city localities, the setting up of task forces to generate jobs in problem areas, and attempts to integrate black youngsters into the training schemes run by the Manpower Services Commission. Additionally, having done little if anything to implement the Scarman Report's recommendations on positive action the Government belatedly promised to look at what new initiatives it could take to tackle racial discrimination in employment and other areas.

The evidence that has emerged since then, however, points to a major discrepancy between the Government's promises of action and the allocation of resources to implement them. This discrepancy again became evident in the aftermath of the inner city initiatives launched by the Government after the June 1987 General Election. It is perhaps too early to reach a conclusion on this point, but a repeat of the period of inaction between 1982 and 1985 cannot be ruled out within the current political context. Indeed a number of researchers and commentators have argued that this is the most likely course of development (see the papers in Benyon and Solomos, 1987). A number of local authorities have attempted to take more positive action to deal with the issues raised by the 1985 riots, but such local initiatives are often severely limited by the actions of national government, the police and broader economic and political pressures. We shall return to this issue in Chapter 10, which will look specifically at the possibilities for reform and the limits which are faced both nationally and locally.

Summary and conclusion

Between 1981 and 1985 there was much discussion whether the lessons of 1980–1 had been learned, whether the political response to the riots had been adequate, and whether forms of collective violence had become a permanent feature of British political life. In the aftermath of the 1985 unrest a similar debate has taken place, with profound concern being expressed about whether the initiatives promised after the 1985 riots will prevent the recurrence of such confrontations in the near future. The array of inner city initiatives, expressions of government concern, and promises of more effective actions to tackle unemployment are in many ways responses to this overriding concern about how to manage and depoliticise the impact of the riots.

The actual impact of these initiatives on the lives of inner city residents will, in all likelihood, be minimal within the current reality of economic and social restructuring, increasing arbitrariness of police powers, and emphasis on market forces. This is not to say that the political objectives of these forms of state intervention have not been achieved. Precisely because it is the symbolic political language about the riots which most people experience, promises of reform seem to reassure popular opinion that something is being done and thus help ensure the political viability of unsuccessful policies (Edelman, 1977). But the limits of symbolic action which does little to change the underlying problems are clear enough today when we see constant complaints from black groups and other inner city residents that promises without actual change are not enough.

This is an inherent contradiction since it is clearly impossible to separate the analysis of the riots from the wider social and economic changes in contemporary Britain. Nor is it possible to ignore the deep political and ideological shifts which have taken place, particularly the development of nationalist and neo-racist ideologies at both the academic and the popular level (Troyna and Williams, 1986; Gilroy, 1987). Such transformations inevitably overdetermine the possibilities of implementing reforms of existing inequalities, however limited these reforms may be. But it seems clear that this pattern, if reproduced over the next period, will result in a situation where the symbolic value of violent protest will become an even more important form of action for oppressed and marginalised social groupings. The reforms necessary to tackle the core issues may well be beyond the limits of the current political realities. It is to this question of the limits and possibilities of political action that we now turn, in order to provide a rounded analysis of the political dynamics of racism in contemporary Britain. We shall, however, return to some of the themes of this chapter in the discussion of racism and social change in Chapter 10, where we shall also examine the period since 1945 in more detail.

The main argument developed in this chapter can be easily summarised: namely, that we cannot understand the dynamics of racialised politics in contemporary Britain without at the same time looking at the dynamics of the social, political and economic changes through which we are going. Thus in addition to looking at the role of central and local government, any analysis of the role of race in contemporary British politics must also address itself to the question of social protest and the changing socio-economic processes which are fundamentally transforming many urban localities.

10 Conclusion: Prospects for the Future

This book has analysed the trajectory of racialised political debate and policy change over the past four decades. It has shown that the racialisation of British political life did not come about in a linear fashion; it was the outcome of complex political, social and economic processes that interacted in specific ways at particular points of time.

In the course of this analysis we discussed the main dimensions of racialised politics in contemporary Britain. Additionally, we outlined a number of questions about the likely futures of race relations and the evolution of political ideologies in this field. For example: What is the relationship between racial ideologies and politics? How far has the social and economic context influenced the racialisation of political life? What are the prospects for any fundamental reforms which de-racialise political discourses and tackle the roots of racial inequality?

In this concluding chapter we shall examine these and related questions and pull together the analytical arguments of previous chapters. We shall not provide a summary of the previous chapters, since their basic themes should be clear enough. What we shall attempt to do is to pull together some of the arguments that have resonated throughout the book, and reflect tentatively on future prospects. For the purposes of clarity the arguments will be organised around five themes which have run through the book as a whole. The changing forms of racialised politics and ideology in contemporary Britain provide the starting point for the chapter. We then move on to examine the interrelationship between racism and social and economic change. The third theme is the question of the limits of reforms which have sought to remedy racial inequalities and injustice. From this we move on to offer some reflections on the political consequences of urban unrest and disorder. Finally, we shall

175

look at the implications of the arguments developed in this book for the analysis of race and racism in Britain and other advanced capitalist societies.

Racism, politics and ideology

How have political and ideological discourses about race become an entrenched element of political life in contemporary Britain? This is one of the central questions that we have addressed in this book, both at a theoretical and at an empirical level. By its very nature it is a question of immense complexity, and there are a number of issues that we have touched upon here that need more detailed analysis. But we have explored enough aspects of this question to allow us to offer some broad reflections on the changing forms of political and ideological discourses about race in British society.

Zubaida (1970) warned that one of the main dangers in the analysis of political interventions in relation to race lay in either the implicit or explicit adoption by social scientists of the dominant definitions of the problems in this field:

> It is no criticism of a field of study to say that it is concerned with social problems, but it is a criticism of that field to say that it defines its own sociological problems in accordance with the definition of social problems prevalent in that society. Thus, for a long time, race-relations research was primarily concerned with prejudice and discrimination, defined as problems by the 'liberal' agencies of the wider society. (Zubaida, 1970: 3)

Throughout this book we have attempted to show what the dangers may be of not heeding Zubaida's, and others', warning about this tendency to decontextualise the social problems which either the state or other institutions or individuals define as racial. In each chapter we have given an outline of a particular aspect of racialised politics, and have sought to problematise the ways in which these issues have been constructed in official political discourses, political debates and conflict situations.

As we saw in Chapters 8 and 9 there have been a number of changes in the political and popular discourses about race and nation within British society. This is not to say that recent developments can be seen as completely distinct from the themes that dominated political debate about these issues during the 1960s and 1970s. Immigration is after all still a constant reference point in political debates about racial issues. There is also an all-to-common tendency to perceive minority communities as a whole or specific groups within them as sources of social problems and as a potential source of social conflict. The recurrent theme of crime, and particularly the involvement of young Afro-Caribbeans in criminal activities, is but one case of how certain ideological images continue to influence political debates.

During the 1980s, however, political debates about racial issues have increasingly focused on two concerns. First, the phenomenon of urban unrest has been used to emphasise the danger that anger and resentment among the minority communities represented to social order. Second, the visible growth of multi-ethnic communities and attempts to challenge the hegemony of Anglo-Saxon cultural values in such areas as education has resulted in attempts to mobilise political support in defence of conservative and mono-cultural definitions of Englishness. In recent years the development of debates about anti-racism has shown the importance of ideological and political mobilisation around the meaning of both local and national identities.

The social and economic context

The interrelationship between racism and processes of economic, social and ideological change has been emphasised at a number of points in this book. This is not to say that we have provided a complete analysis of this vexed question, since it remains an issue that has to be researched in more detail at both a national and local level.

Two main points arise from the arguments developed in this book. The first is that if we conceive of racialisation as a process, we need to understand the complex ways in which racial relations are likely to be affected by the underlying processes of social and economic change in advanced capitalist societies. The research findings that we looked at in Chapter 9 point to the ways in which the restructuring of labour markets and regional economic spaces reproduces new forms of incorporation and division along racial and gender specific lines.

The second point to make is that in the present environment of fundamental restructuring of economic and social relations in British society racial and national symbols remain important and volatile for political mobilisation. The wholesale reorganisation of regions and localities in the pursuit of an enterprise culture has, if anything, helped to strengthen mythological claims about the national culture and the threats which it faces.

Equality or symbolic reforms?

The central arguments running through this book represent a critical and, in some ways pessimistic, assessment of the racialisation of British politics over the last four decades. This does not mean, however, that it points to a picture of the present situation which rules out the possibility of either radical or more limited reforms. Indeed one of the main conclusions of Chapters 4 and 5 was the need to develop a dynamic analysis of the policy environment within which race relations have been implemented over the past two decades which looks at both their achievements and their limitations.

The limits of existing policies which aim to tackle racial discrimination are threefold. First, legislation against discrimination has been passed on the basis of the taken-for-granted assumption that the enactment of legal measures outlawing discriminatory acts can produce changes in everyday discriminatory practices in employment. Little attention has been given to the need for wider administrative and political strategies against discrimination, or to the development of positive action programmes by central government. This has meant that anti-discrimination policies have operated in a vacuum and an environment which has been generally negative, if not hostile (Freeman and Spencer, 1979; Gordon, 1982).

Second, successive governments have promised reform, while actually doing very little to break down the structural separation and relative powerlessness of organisations such as the CRE to bring about fundamental changes. Thus there has been no cohesive plan linking the various elements of state intervention, even when this has been called for in various government reports since the mid-1970s. Referring to the situation since 1976, Bindman has argued that at best what has been achieved is the perpetuation of existing inequalities, and that this is unlikely to change short of a radical policy package covering the major policy areas:

The most pressing need . . . is not for change in the law but for a substantial strengthening of the legal and economic powers and inducements to apply effective equal opportunity policies. This will only come about if there is greater readiness by the courts and the law to enforce the law, if more resources are provided for law enforcement, and if the Government demonstrates its commitment to racial equality by using its executive powers. (Bindman, 1980: 258)

This analysis is remarkably similar to the CRE's own estimate of the problems it faces (CRE, 1985), and has also been supported by a number of other studies of the operation of the 1976 Race Relations Act (McCrudden, 1987; Jenkins and Solomos, 1987). What these studies make clear is the inherent difficulty of bringing about fundamental reform through piecemeal actions rather than co-ordinated public policies. Yet through the 1980s there has been little sign that new positive initiatives to strengthen anti-discrimination legislation are likely, although immigration controls have been strengthened by a number of measures.

Third, there is also a broader structural limit on the operation of the 1976 Race Relations Act, namely the impact of the economic and social policies pursued by successive administrations, particularly since 1979. Although, as argued above, the broader economic environment cannot be seen as determining the limits of government policies in a deterministic fashion, there is a linkage between what is happening within the state and the demands on resources placed by wider pressures, e.g. economic downturn, high levels of unemployment.

The lack of progress on this front seems to be confirmed in various research reports over the past decade. It seems quite clear from the experience of the past decade that the pursuit of equality of opportunity as a goal of government policy cannot be made sense of outside of the pressures placed on this stated objective by the economic and political forces of society as a whole (Offe, 1984).

It is interesting to note that, in this regard at least, the CRE's perception of the government's response to the Scarman Report on the 1981 disturbances in Brixton singles out this limit as crucial:

So far the response (to the Scarman Report) by the Government and others has been disappointingly inadequate. It lacks the sense of urgency that runs through Lord Scarman's report in particular. Of course, it is more difficult in a time of recession, when unemployment is high and resources are scarce, for a massively expensive effort to be made. But it is precisely at such a time that the vulnerable sections to society suffer most, and even steps that require only a comparatively modest outlay are not being taken by the Government. (CRE, Annual Report, 1981: 3)

Similarly while much was promised in the aftermath of the 1980–1 and 1985 riots, and some policy changes were implemented, it does not seem that these events have resulted in a major shift from the policies which have been pursued so far.

Given these three basic limits, there are still a number of questions that need to be asked. Are these limits an inherent aspect of social policies within a capitalist society, such that reform policies will always be symbolic in character? Or are there counteracting measures which can be used to change these limits and allow for a more radical package of social policies on race and other issues to be implemented?

There is a need for much more detailed research before these questions can be answered satisfactorily, but the weight of existing evidence would seem to support the thesis that race relations policies have functioned largely at the symbolic level since 1965, although slightly less so since 1976 (Brown and Gay, 1985). What is needed at the present time are detailed studies of the role of the state and government institutions in the development of race relations policies, the reasons why certain definitions of the race problem have gained currency, and the reasons why a major gap has developed between the promise of equality and the reality of high levels of discrimination and systemic racism. Such accounts will allow us to go beyond the limits of existing analyses and provide a basis for a more reasoned and critical account of different strategies for tackling the roots of racism.

This is all the more necessary in the context of the tendency in the popular media to blame the black communities themselves or the race relations industry as the source of the problem, rather than racism. The *Sun*, for example, responsed to a report from the Commission for Racial Equality which demonstrated high levels of racial discrimination by editorialising under the headline 'What Racism?' that:

Discrimination is not widespread. Sadly, there are racists in our society. But they are a tiny minority. The overwhelming mass of the

public want people of immigrant stock to have equal opportunities. This has enabled Asians to flourish in our society. (23 June
1988)

The logic of this argument is that racism is not endemic in the social,
economic and social institutions of British society, but merely a
question of the personal prejudices of a few individuals. From this
follows the claim that everybody in British society, regardless of
colour or ethnic origin, enjoys the same opportunity for social
advancement.

Of course, the views of popular papers do not necessarily reflect
general opinion on racial issues in British society. But it is important
to note that in the present environment the denial of racism as an
important determinant of social relations goes hand in hand with a
lack of a clear public policy commitment to the need to tackle racial
inequality. Since 1979 the social programme of the Thatcher
administrations has not included any major initiative in this field,
apart from the strengthening of controls on immigration.

Yet it should be clear that the policy changes in the past four
decades were not imminent ones, inherent in the natural trajectory of
racial relations in British society. Various actors and groups pressed
their interests as they saw them. It is important therefore not to lose
sight of the dynamic role that minority groups and the white majority
play in determining the course of political debate and policy change
in this field. As we showed in Chapter 8, for example, the black
communities are by no means the helpless victims of circumstance but
an active, though by no means unified, political force.

Protest and social change

The political language used to explain and respond to the 1980–1 and
1985 riots provides a clear example of the inherently contradictory
nature of political legitimacy when confronted by street violence,
particularly in a political context which allows only limited reform of
the fundamental social and power inequalities which structure the
fate of inner city residents. It may be argued that all political language
is about symbolic reassurance or promises that governments are in
control of the situation. But this does not mean that such promises
can succeed in providing legitimacy to unsuccessful policies on a
permanent basis.

This diagnosis seems to be further supported by events in the aftermath of the riots. Although symbolic reassurance, depoliticis- ation and promises of future reform helped to bring about a temporary truce in collective violence on the 1980–1 and 1985 model, the occurrence of smaller scale outbreaks of unrest during 1986 and in subsequent years is a pointer to the inherent limitations of such policy responses and the volatile nature of political mobilisation on racial issues.

This is not to say that no attempts have been made to deal with issues such as racism and racial inequality, urban decline, unemploy- ment, policy and community involvement. A number of attempts have been made to bring about reform in all these areas, particularly since 1981.

In the aftermath of both the 1980–1 and 1985 riots there have been, as pointed out in Chapters 6 and 9, numerous pronouncements by government departments and ministers about the need to tackle the law and order issue not in isolation, but alongside the questions of unemployment, inner city decline, the provision of leisure and social facilities and private enterprise. Indeed in the wake of her third election victory in 1987 Mrs Thatcher chose to put the question of inner city policy at the top of her agenda. During 1988 a number of initiatives on this issue were announced by the government.

Whether these more recent promises will be more successful in dealing with the underlying issues which structure forms of violent protest is the burning question of the moment. The experience between 1981 and 1985 would seem to indicate that it is the promise of reform which is the main concern of the state institutions rather than the implementation of a co-ordinated programme of change. Thus in relation to unemployment and urban decline promises were made in the aftermath of the July 1981 outbreaks to deal with the jobs crisis of the young, the decline of inner city areas, and to help push the economy out of the recession. The immediate publicity emphasised the broad objectives to be achieved but not the mechanisms through which they were to be implemented.

In a similar fashion the period after the September–October 1985 events has been full of promises of action to deal with these very same problems. In early November 1985 the *Guardian* reported that the riots had led to a review of inner city and employment policies. The emphasis on order as the first priority was, however, quite unmis- takeable. In fact the Government emphasised that the immediate response to the riots must be to re-establish law and order, since:

There can be no economic or sociological justification of throwing a petrol bomb. That is crime and must be dealt with as such, wherever it occurs. (*The Guardian*, 6 November 1985)

It should be noted also that whilst in 1980–1 it was quite often the Department of Environment that led the way in terms of public pronouncements, by 1985 it was the Home Office that served as the lead department. The social departments were called in to play their part in restoring order and preventing future disturbances, but only within the context that their actions were only part of the total answer.

This perhaps tells us something about the contradictions which are inherent in the logic of responses to urban unrest, whether it be in Britain during the 1980s or the US during the 1960s. Both sets of response represented an attempt to reassure the public that Government was still very much in control while minimising the political impact of the protests. In addition, and this has perhaps been more clear in Britain since 1985, the restoration of law and order has been achieved through the imposition of tough measures to support the police. Such a strategy has necessitated that the riots be branded as criminal acts, senseless outbursts or the work of drug barons. Against such expressive political symbols the language of liberal reform has found itself pushed into a corner.

Throughout the late 1980s there have been numerous calls to look more closely at the policy agenda of the Scarman Report and the reasons for its non-implementation, but it is perhaps not surprising that these have not been heard. The re-imposition of order on the streets is seen within the current dominant political discourse as an objective which can be achieved without the economic and political reforms which are called for by the liberal project, at least in the medium term. In the long term the strong free-market economy which the present Government aims to construct is seen as the best insurance against social disorder, rather than short term reform measures.

Caught between the repeated calls for reform voiced by liberals since 1980 and the logic of the free market and the strong state, the inner city areas which have witnessed violent protest seem to have little chance of any fundamental change in the medium term (Gamble, 1988). Given such a situation, and there is little evidence of change, the occurrence of violent protest is not merely a possibility – it is a likelihood. Promises of a better future in some future free-market paradise will do little to transform the economic and social fabric of inner city areas, overcome political powerlessness, or challenge the differential policing patterns which brand certain racial and ethnic groups as criminal. In such a situation the preservation of authority and order will be secured as much by force as by consent.

Rethinking the politics of racism

Few analytically clear attempts have been made to theorise the interrelationship between racism and the state in Britain or in other advanced capitalist societies. There are, by contrast, numerous accounts of the relations between class structure and the state, and even some accounts of gender relations and the state.

This omission has serious consequences for the adequacy of theoretical models of the state in capitalist society. For instance, how adequate are accounts of welfare and social policy, employment policy and housing policy which ignore the position of black and ethnic minorities? Yet there are numerous studies of these issues which ignore the question of racial inequality, and the role it plays in structuring social conditions in advanced industrial societies.

At the beginning of this book we argued that there was a need for greater theoretical clarity about the interplay between racism, politics and society. But as we have shown throughout this book the basic problem confronting any account of the complex relations between race, class and the state is to be found in the very nature of racism in contemporary capitalist societies. From the brief survey in Chapter 1 of the competing approaches to this question in sociological, neo-Marxist and political discourses it should be clear that there are at least two problems which have so far defied resolution. First, the question of the interplay between racial and ethnic categorisations and economic and class determination. Second, the role of the state and the political institutions of capitalist societies in the reproduction of racism, including the complex role of state intervention in many countries to control immigration, to manage race relations and, more broadly, to integrate racial and ethnic groupings into the wider society.

We have addressed aspects of these issues in the substantive chapters of this book, but it must be said that we have not sought to develop a polished theoretical framework. In the rest of this chapter, however, we want to outline some of the fundamental questions that arise from the substantive case studies of racialised politics in contemporary Britain.

Michael Omi and Howard Winant, in their analysis of the politics of race in the United States, have suggested that it is wrong to conceive of the state as an external factor in the shaping of racial relations. Rather, they argue that:

> The state is inherently racial. Far from intervening in racial conflicts, the state is itself increasingly the pre-eminent site of racial conflict . . . Every state institution is a racial institution, but not every institution operates in the same way. In fact, the various state institutions do not serve one co-ordinated racial objective; they may work at cross-purposes. Therefore, race must be understood as occupying varying degrees of centrality in different state institutions and at different historical moments. (Omi and Winant, 1986: 76–7)

Such arguments have been made in a number of other theoretical contributions to the analysis of the politics of racism. But whatever the merit of theoretical propositions such as these the difficulty has been that they have not been used systematically to inform historical and empirical analysis of particular racial situations. There have been some ad hoc attempts to do this, but they have been both partial and based on limited research on the dynamics of racism across historical and spatial boundaries. While not diminishing the importance of these studies, the relative absence of empirical analysis has left a major gap in existing writings on this subject. Without analysing the interaction between racist structures and other social structures in capitalist societies it becomes difficult to explain how certain types of racialised ideologies and inequalities develop and help to shape the fundamental institutions of a society.

Part of the problem has been the lack of a fruitful dialogue on theoretical and methodological issues between those involved in research on various aspects of the politics of racism in Britain and comparatively. Another problem is the absence of detailed studies of the genesis, development and transformation of racial institutions.

An example of this failure to integrate theory with research can be found in the work of Stuart Hall. In his account of the interplay between racism and other social relations in capitalist societies, he argues:

At the economic level, it is clear that race must be given its distinctive and 'relatively autonomous' effectivity, as a distinctive feature. This does not mean that the economic is sufficient to found an explanation of how these relations concretely function. One needs to know how different racial and ethnic groups were inserted historically, and the relations which have tended to erode and transform, or to preserve these distinctions through time – not simply as residues and traces of previous modes, but as active structuring principles of the present society. Racial categories alone will not provide or explain these. (Hall, 1980: 339)

Hall's approach implicitly criticises those approaches which assume that there is a harmonious articulation between racism and the capitalist mode of production. His emphasis on the ways in which racial and ethnic groups are incorporated historically in different societies, and how their position changes over time suggests that the relation between racism and wider social relations should be seen as historically and spatially variable and contradictory.

But such broad generalisations need to be tested out and analysed in accounts of processes of racialisation in particular historical situations. In order to develop a dynamic framework which can help us understand the historical and contemporary intersection between racism and politics in specific societies there is a need for an analytic framework that focuses attention on the processes that lead to the politicisation of racial and ethnic issues. Yet there is no attempt in Hall's work to go beyond general theoretical propositions by analysing the development of racism in particular societies. This failure to integrate theory with detailed historical and political analysis is to be found in much of the radical literature on racism.

This separation between theoretical analysis and political analysis needs to be overcome if we are to understand the history and present forms of racialised politics in British society. There is a need to move away from a notion of racialisation which is uniform across different historical formations or even particular societies.

The paradox of attempts to construct a uniform conception of racism is that they seem to lose the ability to explain the dynamics of change and conflict. In so doing they fail to analyse the processes which lead to the racialisation of social relations in particular societies.

This has been our main concern in this book. In particular we have focused on two broad questions. First, how do political structures and institutions in Britain function in relation to race and in what ways do they produce and reproduce or help overcome racism? Second, how does racism shape the ways in which class, gender and other social relations are actually experienced and how do they structure political action? The limits of one volume have allowed us to cover only the essential aspects of these issues, but in doing so we have tried to open up areas for further debate and analysis.

What kind of future?

The subject matter of this book represents one of the most controversial and volatile questions in contemporary British politics. Indeed, it is clear from the response to the outbreaks of urban unrest and disorder during the 1980s that race is a divisive issue at all levels of British society and is likely to remain so in the future. This makes it all the more important that the history of the past four decades is analysed fully and any lessons for the future are learned quickly.

The failure to tackle the roots of racism and racial inequality during the past four decades means that it is difficult to be optimistic about the likely futures of racial relations. As we enter the 1990s the need for urgent political action on this issue is clear, but there is no clear political basis for such action. Indeed, during the past decade the most notable features of governmental policy has been the further institutionalisation of immigration controls and a complete failure to promote positive measures to overcome racial inequality and injustice.

The political climate generated by Thatcherism is such that it is difficult to imagine a fundamental change in political priorities and policy change in this area in the medium term (Gamble, 1988). Certainly there are no signs that the third Thatcher administration will radically change the policy stance of the previous two.

At the same time the Labour Party and the other opposition parties do not seem able to offer a coherent radical alternative to the policies pursued by successive governments over the past four decades. Indeed the growing influence of the new right and the public attention given to the loony left and the anti-racist lobby has resulted in attempts by the Labour Party to distance itself from the actions of many Labour-controlled local authorities, and to reduce the identification of the party with minority causes.

Within the context of the present political climate, therefore, the prospects of a radical reorientation of policies remain slim. The 1980–1 and 1985 outbreaks of urban unrest resulted in a short-lived flurry of activity, but this did little to tackle the broader context of racial inequality and urban neglect. At the same time, although the election of four black MPs in 1987 may have a bearing on the nature of the parliamentary politics of race, their influence is likely to remain marginal, in the medium term at least. In the longer term increasing black political involvement and political representation, and alliances with other political forces, may help to fundamentally transform the terms of political debate about racial inequality in British society.

In the present political climate, however, it is all the more important for those interested in tackling the roots of racism and racial inequality in British society to look more deeply into the questions that have been discussed in this book. The lessons of the past four decades need to be learned and internalised if we are to move towards a more just and egalitarian society, one in which racism does not structure the life chances of Britain's black citizens. If this book has raised a few issues for further thought and debate on this question it would have achieved its task.

Guide to Further Reading

The object of this Guide is to point to specific works of relevance to the subjects covered in each chapter. It is not intended as an exhaustive literature review, although the references in the Bibliography provide an overview of the literature in the areas covered by this book. The object rather is to suggest works which give an up-to-date view of a specific topic and which allow you to come to terms with divergent perspectives. You may also find it useful to have a look at issues of the journals *Ethnic and Racial Studies*, *Immigrants and Minorities*, *New Community*, *Patterns of Prejudice*, *Race and Class*, and *Sage Race Relations Abstracts*. The Runnymede Trust publishes a monthly bulletin called *Race and Immigration*, which provides detailed coverage of current issues in this field.

Chapter 1

The literature on this area is vast. A useful overview of divergent theoretical perspectives is contained in J. Rex and D. Mason (eds) (1986). Other important texts are M. Banton (1987), P. Gilroy (1987), R. Miles (1989), J. Rex (1983).

A useful review of recent American debates can be found in M. Omi and H. Winant (1986). Other useful American studies are M. Marable (1985) and W. J. Wilson (1980).

Chapter 2

On the history of race and immigration in British society the best starting point is C. Holmes (1988). Two important collections of original papers are to be found in C. Holmes (ed.) (1978) and K. Lunn (ed.) (1980). On the history of Irish migration and attitudes towards the Irish see R. Swift and S. Gilley (eds) (1985) and L. P. Curtis (1968). On the politics of Jewish immigration see B. Gainer (1972) and L. P. Gartner (1973). P. Fryer (1984) takes a historical view of the black presence in British society, and two other sources on this subject are R. Ramdin (1987) and P. Rich (1986).

189

Chapter 3

There are no up-to-date studies of the politics of immigration since 1945. Two studies worth looking at are G. Freeman (1979) and Z. Layton-Henry (1984), though they are limited in their coverage. Other studies widely referred to are: P. Foot (1965); R. Miles and A. Phizacklea (1984); and A. Sivanandan (1982). The socio-legal context is covered fully in I. A. Macdonald (1983).

Chapter 4

This field is relatively neglected, though it has recently begun to attract more interest. An interesting overview of the early history of legislation on this issue can be found in A. Lester and G. Bindman (1972), while the papers in S. Abbott (ed.) (1971) look at various aspects of race relations policies during the 1960s. On the legal context since the passage of the 1976 Race Relations Act see the divergent perspectives of L. Lustgarten (1980), and C. McCrudden (1982) 303–67. On the political and social context see: N. Glazer and K. Young (eds) (1983); R. Hepple (1983) 71–90; R. Jenkins and J. Solomos (eds) (1987).

Chapter 5

A number of recent books have looked at various aspects of the local politics of race, the most important being G. Ben-Tovim, *et al.* (1986). A pioneering work in this area was J. Rex and R. Moore (1967). An analysis of policy change in this field can be found by K. Young (1985). For a critical look at more recent developments see G. Stoker (1988).

Chapter 6

Because of recurrent controversies about relations between black communities and the police there is a large literature on this subject. Good starting points for recent developments are R. Reiner (1985) and D. Smith and J. Gray (1985). Other important studies are: S. Hall. *et al.* (1978); D. Humphry (1972). On the history of police relations with young blacks see J. Solomos (1988). On the politics of urban unrest see: Lord Scarman (1981); J. Benyon (1984); and J. Benyon and J. Solomos (eds) (1987).

Chapter 7

Much of the literature on this general area is fairly limited in scope. It remains a relatively neglected topic. A good starting point of the theoretical aspect of this question is R. Miles (1989). Useful attempts to look at the changing political language about race and nation are to be found by G. Seidel in R. Levitas (ed.) (1986); P. Gordon and F. Klug (1986). On the politics of the extreme right see the papers in R. Miles and A. Phizacklea (eds) (1979) and the study by C. Husbands (1983). For a selection of new right perspectives on these issues see F. Palmer (ed.) (1986). You may also find it useful to look at copies of the journal *Searchlight*.

Chapter 8

Due to the relative neglect of this question there is no detailed up-to-date study of all the dimensions of this question. An early attempt to argue that this dimension had been neglected in traditional studies of this subject was CCCS Race and Politics Group (1982). Useful studies of aspects of Afro-Caribbean and Asian political mobilisation can be found in: D. Pearson (1981); M. Fitzgerald (1987); B. Jacobs (1986); T. Carter (1986).

Chapter 9

The experience of urban unrest and social change during the 1980s has led to a growing interest in the politics of protest and violent unrest. For an up-to-date review of some of the main issues see the papers in J. Benyon and J. Solomos (eds) (1987). For other perspectives see: M. Kettle and L. Hodges (1982) and H. Joshua and T. Wallace (1983). A discussion of some of the major problems in some popular discussions of urban unrest can be found in M. Keith (1987).

Chapter 10

The best starting point for the issue discussed in this chapter are the overviews provided by Z. Layton-Henry (1984) and M. Anwar (1986). For useful American comparisons take a look at M. Marable (1985) and W. J. Wilson (1988).

Bibliography

Abbott, S. (ed.) (1971) *The Prevention of Racial Discrimination in Britain* (London: Oxford University Press).

Alderman, G. (1983) *The Jewish Community in British Politics* (Oxford: Clarendon Press).

Alford, R. and Friedland, R. (1985). *Powers of Theory: Capitalism, the State and Democracy* (Cambridge University Press).

Anwar, M. (1986) *Race and Politics* (London: Tavistock).

Applebey, G. and Ellis, E. (1984) 'Formal Investigations: the Commission for Racial Equality and the Equal Opportunities Commission as law enforcement agencies', *Public Law*, Spring: 58–81.

Banton, M. (1955) *The Coloured Quarter: Negro Immigrants in an English City* (London: Jonathan Cape).

——(1959) *White and Coloured* (London: Jonathan Cape).

——(1967) *Race Relations* (London: Tavistock).

——(1983) *Racial and Ethnic Competition* (Cambridge University Press).

——(1985) *Promoting Racial Harmony* (Cambridge University Press).

——(1987) *Racial Theories* (Cambridge University Press).

Barker, M. (1981) *The New Racism* (London: Junction Books).

Beetham, D. (1970) *Transport and Turbans* (London: Oxford University Press).

Ben-Tovim, G. and Gabriel, J. (1979) 'The politics of race in Britain: a review of the major trends and of the recent literature', *Sage Race Relations Abstracts*, 44: 1–56.

Ben-Tovim, G., Gabriel, J., Law, I. and Stredder, K. (1986) *The Local Politics of Race* (London: Macmillan).

Benyon, J. (1986) 'A Tale of Failure: Race and Policing', *Policy Papers in Ethnic Relations*, No. 3 (University of Warwick, Centre for Research in Ethnic Relations).

Benyon, J. (ed.) (1984) *Scarman and After* (Oxford: Pergamon Press).

Benyon, J. and Solomos, J. (eds) (1987) *The Roots of Urban Unrest* (Oxford: Pergamon Press).

Berghahn, M. (1984) *German-Jewish Refugees in England* (London: Macmillan).

Berghe, P. L. van den (1967) *Race and Racism* (New York: Wiley).

Berkeley, H. (1977) *The Odyssey of Enoch* (London: Hamish Hamilton).

Bevan, V. (1986) *The Development of British Immigration Law* (London: Croom Helm).

Billig, M. (1978) *Fascists: A social psychological view of the National Front* (London: Academic Press).

Billig, M. and Bell, A. (1980) 'Fascist Parties in Post-War Britain', *Sage Race Relations Abstracts*, 5, 1, 1980, 1–30.

Bindman, G. (1980) 'The law, equal opportunity and affirmative action', *New Community*, VIII, 3: 248–60.

Bowles, S. and Gintis, H. (1987) *Democracy and Capitalism* (London: Routledge and Kegan Paul).

Bozzoli, B. (ed.) (1987) *Class, Community and Conflict* (Johannesburg: Ravan).

Brown, C. (1984) *Black and White Britain*, (London: Heinemann).

Brown, C. and Gay, P. (1985) *Racial Discrimination: 17 Years After the Act* (London: Policy Studies Institute).

Browning, R. P., Marshall, D. P. and Tabb, D. H. (1984) *Protest is Not Enough* (University of California Press).

Burgess, J. R. (1985) 'News from nowhere: the press, the riots and the myth of the inner city' in J. R. Burgess and J. R. Gold (eds) *Geography, the media and popular culture* (London: Croom Helm).

Butler, Lord (1971) *The Art of the Possible* (Harmondsworth: Penguin).

Carter, B., Harris, C., Joshi, S. (1987) 'The 1951–55 Conservative government and the racialisation of black immigration', *Policy Papers in Ethnic Relations*, No. 11 (University of Warwick, Centre for Research in Ethnic Relations).

Carter, T. (1986) *Shattering Illusions* (London: Lawrence and Wishart).

Casey, J. (1982) 'One nation: the politics of race', *The Salisbury Review*, Autumn: 23–8.

Cashmore, E. (1987) *The Logic of Racism* (London: Allen & Unwin).

Castles, S., with Booth, H. and Wallace, T. (1984) *Here for Good: Western Europe's new ethnic minorities* (London: Pluto Press).

Castles, S. and Kosack, G. (1985) *Immigrant Workers and Class Structure in Western Europe* (London: Oxford University Press).

CCCS Race and Politics Group (1982) *The Empire Strikes Back: race and racism in 70s Britain* (London: Hutchinson).

Cheetham, J. (1988) 'Ethnic Associations in Britain' in S. Jenkins (ed.) *Ethnic Associations and the Welfare State* (New York: Columbia University Press).

Clare, J. (1985) 'Time to dust off the Scarman report', *The Listener*, 3 October. 6–7.

Coates, D. (1984) *The Context of British Politics* (London: Hutchinson).

Cohen, P. (1988) 'The Perversions of Inheritance: Studies in the Making of Multi-Racist Britain' in P. Cohen and H. Bains, *Multi-Racist Britain* (London: Macmillan).

Colls, R. and Dodd, P. (eds) (1986) *Englishness: Politics and Culture 1880–1920* (London: Croom Helm).

Commission for Racial Equality (CRE) (1977–87) *Annual Reports* (London: Commission for Racial Equality).

——(1983) *The Race Relations Act 1976 – Time for a Change?* (London: Commission for Racial Equality).

——(1985a) *Review of the Race Relations Act 1976: Proposals for Change* (London: Commission for Racial Equality).

——(1985b) *Immigration Control Procedures: Report of a Formal Investigation* (London: Commission for Racial Equality).

Cox, O. C. (1948) *Caste, Class and Race* (New York: Monthly Review Press).

Crewe, I. (1983) 'Representation and the Ethnic Minorities in Britain' in N. Glazer and K. Young (eds) *Ethnic Pluralism and Public Policy* (London: Heinemann).

Cross, M. and Smith, D. I. (eds) (1987) *Black Youth Futures* (Leicester: National Youth Bureau).

Crossman, R. (1975) *Diaries of a Cabinet Minister*, Volume 1, (London: Hamish Hamilton & Jonathan Cape).

Curtis, L. P. (1968) *Anglo-Saxons and Celts* (Connecticut: University of Bridgeport).

——(1971) *Apes and Angels: The Irishman in Victorian Caricature* (Washington: Smithsonian Institution Press).

Curtis, L. (1984) *Nothing But the Same Old Story* (London: Information on Ireland).

Dangerfield, G. (1976) *The Damnable Question: A Study of Anglo-Irish Relations* (Boston: Little, Brown).

Deakin, N. (1965) *Colour and the British Electorate* (London: Pall Mall Press).

——(1968) 'The Politics of the Commonwealth Immigrants Bill', *Political Quarterly*, 391: 24–45.

——(1970) *Colour, Citizenship and British Society* (London: Panther).

——(1972) *The Immigration Issue in British Politics* (Unpublished PhD Thesis, University of Sussex).

Dean, D. (1987) 'Coping with Colonial Immigration, the Cold War and Colonial Policy', *Immigrants and Minorities*, 6, 3, 305–34.

Dear, G. (1985) *Handsworth/Lozells, September 1985: Report of the Chief Constable, West Midlands Police* (Birmingham: West Midlands Police).

Dearlove, J. (1973) *The Politics of Policy in Local Government* (Cambridge University Press).

——(1982) 'The Political Science of British Politics', *Parliamentary Affairs*, 35, 436–54.

Dearlove, J. and Saunders, P. (1984) *Introduction to British Politics* (Cambridge: Polity).

Deedes, W. (1968) *Race Without Rancour* (London: Conservative Political Centre).

Dijk, T. van (1988) *News Analysis: Case Studies of International and National News in the Press* (New Jersey: Lawrence Erlbaum).

DO 35/5219 (1957) 'Commonwealth Immigration: Social and Economic Problems' (London: Public Records Office).

Dunleavy, P. (1980) *Urban Political Analysis* (London: Macmillan).

Dunleavy, P. and O'Leary, B. (1987) *Theories of the State* (London: Macmillan).

Edelman, M. (1971) *Politics as Symbolic Action: Mass Arousal and Quiescence* (Chicago: Markham).

——(1977) *Political Language: Words that Succeed and Policies that Fail* (New York: Academic Press).

——(1985) Political Language and Political Reality', *PS*, XVIII, 1: 10–19.

Edgar, D. (1977) 'Racism, Fascism and the Politics of the National Front', *Race and Class*, 19, 2, 111–31.

Edwards, J. and Batley, R. (1978) *The Politics of Positive Discrimination* (London: Tavistock).

Elton, Lord (1965) *The Unarmed Invasion* (London: Godfrey Bles).

Evans, J. M. (1983) *Immigration Law* (London: Sweet and Maxwell).

Evans, N. (1980) 'The South Wales Race Riots of 1919', *Llafur*, 3, 1: 5–29.

——(1985) 'Regulating the Reserve Army: Arabs, Blacks and the local State in Cardiff, 1919–45', in K. Lunn (ed.) *Race and Labour in the Twentieth-Century Britain* (London: Frank Cass).

Evans, P. B., Rueschemeyer, D., Skocpol, T. (1985) *Bringing the State Back In* (Cambridge University Press).

Fielding, N. (1981) *The National Front* (London: Routledge).

Fitzgerald, M. (1984) *Political Parties and Black People* (London: Runnymede Trust).

Fitzgerald, M. and Layton-Henry, Z. (1986) 'Opposition Parties and Race Policies: 1979–83' in Z. Layton-Henry and P. Rich, (eds) *Race, Government and Politics in Britain* (London: Macmillan).

Flett, H. (1981) 'The Politics of Dispersal in Birmingham', *Working Paper on Ethnic Relations*, No. 14 (Centre for Research in Ethnic Relations, University of Warwick).

Flew, A. (1984) *Education, Race and Revolution* (London: Centre for Policy Studies).

Fogelson, R. M. (1971) *Violence as Protest* (Garden City, N.Y.: Anchor Books).

Foot, P. (1965) *Immigration and Race in British Politics* (Harmondsworth: Penguin).

Fredrickson, G. M. (1981) *White Supremacy: A Comparative Study of American and South African History* (Oxford University Press).

Freeman, G. (1979) *Immigrant Labor and Racial Conflict in Industrial Societies* (Princeton University Press).

Freeman, M. D. A. and Spencer, S. (1979) 'Immigration control, black workers and the economy', *British Journal of Law and Society*, 6, 1: 53–81.

Fryer, P. (1984) *Staying Power: The History of Black People in Britain* (London: Pluto Press).

Gaffney, J. (1987) 'Interpretations of Violence: The Handsworth Riots of 1985', *Policy Papers in Ethnic Relations*, No. 10 (University of Warwick, Centre for Research in Ethnic Relations).

Gainer, B. (1972) *The Alien Invasion: the origins of the Aliens Act of 1905* (London: Heinemann).

Gallagher, T. (1985) 'A Tale of Two Cities: Communal Strife in Glasgow and Liverpool Before 1914' in R. Swift and S. Gilley (eds) *The Irish in the Victorian City* (London: Croom Helm).

Gamble, A. (1981) *Britain In Decline* (London: Macmillan).

——(1988) *The Free Economy and the Strong State* (London: Macmillan).

Garrard, J. A. (1971) *The English and Immigration 1880–1910* (London: Oxford University Press).

Gartner, L. P. (1973) *The Jewish Immigrant in England 1870–1914* (London: Simon Publications).

Gates, H. L. (ed.) (1986) *'Race', Writing and Difference* (University of Chicago Press).

Gay, P. and Young, K. (1988) *Community Relations Councils* (London: CRE).

Gifford, Lord, Chairman (1986) *The Broadwater Farm Inquiry* (London: Karia Press).

Gilley, S. (1978) 'English Attitudes to the Irish in England 1789–1900' in C. Holmes (ed.) *Immigrants and Minorities in British Society* (London: Allen & Unwin).

——(1980) 'Catholics and Socialists in Glasgow, 1906–1912' in K. Lunn (ed.) *Hosts, Immigrants and Minorities* (Folkestone: Dawson).

Gilroy, P. (1987) *There Ain't No Black in the Union Jack* (London: Hutchinson).

Glass, R. (1960) *Newcomers: West Indians in London* (London: Allen & Unwin).

Glazer, N. and Young, K. (eds) (1983) *Ethnic Pluralism and Public Policy* (London: Heinemann).

Gordon, P. (1982) 'Racial Discrimination: towards a legal strategy', *British Journal of Law and Society*, 9, 1: 127–35.

——(1985) *Policing Immigration: Britain's Internal Controls* (London: Pluto).

——(1986) *Racial Violence and Harassment* (London: Runnymede Trust).
Gordon, P. and Klug, F. (1986) *New Right/New Racism* (London: Searchlight).
Goulbourne, H. (1987) 'West Indian Groups and British Politics', paper presented to Conference on Black People and British Politics (University of Warwick, November 1987).
Greater London Council (1984) *Racial Harassment in London* (Greater London Council).
Greenberg, S. B. (1980) *Race and State in Capitalist Development* (New Haven: Yale University Press).
Gregory, D. and Urry, J. (1985) *Social Relations and Spatial Structures* (London: Macmillan).
Griffiths, P. (1966) *A Question of Colour* (London: Leslie Frewin).
Hall, S. (1977) 'Pluralism, race and class in Caribbean society' in UNESCO, *Race and class in post-colonial society* (Paris: UNESCO).
——(1980) 'Race, Articulation and Societies Structured in Dominance' in UNESCO (ed.) *Sociological Theories: Race and Colonialism* (Paris: UNESCO).
——(1985a) 'Gramsci's Relevance to the Analysis of Racism and Ethnicity', unpublished paper.
——(1985b) 'The gulf between Labour and Blacks', the *Guardian*, 15 June 1985.
——(1987) 'Urban unrest in Britain' in J. Benyon and J. Solomos (eds) *The Roots of Urban Unrest* (Oxford: Pergamon Press).
Hall, S., Critcher, C., Jefferson, T., Clarke, J. and Roberts, B. (1978) *Policing the Crisis: Mugging, the State, and Law and Order* (London: Macmillan).
Harris, C. (1988) 'Images of Blacks in Britain: 1930–60' in S. Allen and M. Macey (eds) *Race and Social Policy* (London: Economic and Social Research Council).
Harltey-Brewer, M. (1965) 'Smethwick' in N. Deakin (ed.) *Colour and the British Electorate 1964* (London: Pall Mall Press).
Hechter, M. (1975) *Internal Colonialism* (London: Routledge).
Heineman, B. (1972). *The Politics of the Powerless: A Study of the Campaign Against Racial Discrimination* (London: Oxford University Press).
Henderson, J. and Karn, V. (1987) *Race, Class and State Housing* (Aldershot: Gower).
Hepple, R. (1968). *Race, Jobs and the Law in Britain* (Harmondsworth: Penguin).
——(1983) 'Judging Equal Rights', *Critical Legal Problems*, 36, 71–90.
Higgins, J., Deakin, N., Edwards, J. and Wicks, M. (1983) *Government and Urban Poverty* (Oxford: Basil Blackwell).
Hill, M. and Issacharoff, R. (1971) *Community Action and Race Relations* (London: Oxford University Press).
Hirst, P. (1985) *Marxism and Historical Writing* (London: Routledge).
Hirschfeld, G. (1984) *Exile in Great Britain: Refugees From Hitler's Germany* (Leamington Spa: Berg).
Holmes, C. (ed.) (1978) *Immigrants and Minorities in British Society* (London: George Allen & Unwin).
——(1979) *Anti-Semitism in British Society 1876–1939* (London: Edward Arnold).
——(1988) *John Bull's Island* (London: Macmillan).
Home Affairs Committee, Sub-Committee on Race Relations and Immigration (1981a) *Racial Disadvantage* (London: HMSO).
——(1981b) *Commission for Racial Equality* (London: HMSO).

Home Office (1975) *Racial Discrimination*, Cmnd 6234 (London: HMSO).
Home Office (1977) *A Guide to the Race Relations Act 1976* (London: Home Office).
Howe, D. (1973) 'Fighting back: West Indian youth and the police in Notting Hill', *Race Today*, December: 333–6.
Howe, S. and Upshal, D. (1988) 'New Black Power Lines', *New Statesman & Society*, 15 July 1988.
Humphry, D. (1972) *Police Power and Black People* (London: Panther).
Husbands, C. (1983) *Racial Exclusionism and the City* (London: Allen & Unwin).
Huxley, E. (1964) *Back Street New Worlds* (London: Chatto and Windus).
Institute of Race Relations, *Newsletter*, 1960–9.
Jackson, J. A. (1963) *The Irish in Britain* (London: Routledge).
Jacobs, B. (1986) *Black Politics and Urban Crisis in Britain* (Cambridge University Press).
Jenkins, R. and Solomos, J. (eds) (1987) *Racism and Equal Opportunity Policies in the 1980s* (Cambridge University Press).
Jenkins, Robin (1971) 'The Production of Knowledge in the Institute of Race Relations' (Unpublished paper).
Jenkinson, J. (1985) 'The Glasgow Race Disturbances of 1919' in K. Lunn (ed.) *Hosts, Immigrants and Minorities* (Folkestone: Dawson).
Jessop, B. (1982) *The Capitalist State* (Oxford: Martin Robertson).
Joshi, S. and Carter, B. (1984) 'The role of Labour in the creation of a racist Britain', *Race and Class*, XXV 3: 53–70.
Joshua, H. and Wallace, T. (1983) *To Ride the Storm: the 1980 Bristol 'Riot' and the State* (London: Heinemann).
Katznelson, I. (1976) *Black Men, White Cities* (University of Chicago Press).
——(1982) *City Trenches* (University of Chicago Press).
——(1986) 'Rethinking the silences of social and economic policy', *Political Science Quarterly*, 101, 2: 307–25.
Katznelson, I. and Weir, M. (1985) *Schooling for All* (New York: Basic Books).
Keith, M. (1987) '"Something Happened": the problems of explaining the 1980 and 1981 riots in British cities' in P. Jackson (ed.) *Race and Racism* (London: Allen & Unwin).
Kennedy, P. and Nicholls, A. (1981) *Nationalist and Racialist Movements in Britain and Germany Before 1914* (London: Macmillan).
Kettle, M. (1982) 'Will 1982 See More Riots', *New Society*, 18 February.
Kettle, M. and Hodges, L. (1982) *Uprising!* (London: Pan).
Kirp, D. (1979) *Doing Good by Doing Little* (London: University of California Press).
Knopf, T. A. (1975) *Rumors, Race and Riots* (New Brunswick, NJ: Transaction Books).
Labour Party Black Section (1988) *The Black Agenda* (London: Labour Party Black Section).
Lawrence, D. (1974) *Black Migrants, White Natives* (Cambridge University Press).
Layton-Henry, Z. (1980) 'Immigration', in Z. Layton-Henry (ed.) Conservative Party Politics (London: Macmillan).
——(1984) *The Politics of Race in Britain* (London: Allen & Unwin).
——(1986) 'Race and the Thatcher Government' in Z. Layton-Henry and P. Rich (eds) *Race, Government and Politics in Britain* (London: Macmillan).

——(1988) 'The Black Electorate and the General Election of 1987' paper presented at Conference on Black People and British Politics (University of Warwick, November 1987).

Layton-Henry, Z. and Rich, P. (eds) (1986) *Race, Government and Politics in Britain* (London: Macmillan).

Layton-Henry, Z. and Studlar, D. (1985) 'The Electoral Participation of Black and Asian Britons', *Parliamentary Affairs*, 38: 307–18.

Lebow, R. N. (1976) *White Britain and Black Ireland* (Philadelphia: Institute for the Study of Human Issues).

Lebzelter, G. (1978) *Political Anti-Semitism in England* (London: Macmillan).

——(1981) 'Anti-semitism: a Focal Point for the British Radical Right', in P. Kennedy and A. Nicholls (eds) *Nationalist and Racialist Movements in Britain and Germany Before 1914* (London: Macmillan).

Lee, A. (1980) 'Working Class Response to Jews in Britain, 1880–1914' in K. Lunn (ed.) *Hosts, Immigrants and Minorities* (Folkestone: Dawson).

Lees, L. H. (1978) *Exiles in Erin: Irish Migrants in Victorian London* (Manchester University Press).

Lenton, J. *et al.* (1966) *Immigration, Race and Politics: A Birmingham View* (London: Bow Publications).

Lester, A. and Bindman, G. (1972) *Race and Law* (Harmondsworth: Penguin).

Levitas, R. (ed.) (1986) *The Ideology of the New Right* (Cambridge: Polity).

Lewis, R. (1988) *Anti-Racism: A Mania Exposed* (London: Quartet).

Leys, C. (1983) *Politics in Britain* (London: Heinemann).

Lipman, V. D. (1954) *Social History of Jews in England 1850–1950* (London: Watts & Co.).

Lipsky, M. and Olson, D. (1977) *Commission Politics: The Processing of Racial Crisis in America* (New Brunswick, NJ: Transaction Books).

Little, K. (1947) *Negroes in Britain: A Study of Racial Relations in English Society* (London: Routledge and Kegan Paul).

Lunn, K. (ed.) (1980) *Hosts, Immigrants and Minorities* (Folkestone: Dawson).

——(1985) *Race and Labour in Twentieth-Century Britain* (London: Frank Cass).

Lustgarten, L. (1980) *Legal Control of Racial Discrimination* (London: Macmillan).

Macdonald, I. (1983) *Immigration Law and Practice in the United Kingdom* (London: Butterworths).

Macmillan, H. (1973) *At the End of the Day* (London: Macmillan).

Marable, M. (1981) 'Race, Class and Conflict, *Sage Race Relations Abstracts*, 6, 4, 1–38.

——(1983) *How Capitalism Underdeveloped Black America* (London: Pluto Press).

——(1985) *Black American Politics* (Verso).

May, R. and Cohen, R. (1974) 'The Interaction Between Race and Colonialism: A Case Study of the Liverpool Race Riots of 1919', *Race and Class*, 16, 2, 111–26.

McAdam, D. (1982) *Political Process and the Development of Black Insurgency: 1930–1970* (University of Chicago Press).

McCrudden, C. (1982) 'Institutional Discrimination', *Oxford Journal of Legal Studies*, 2: 303–67.

——(1983) 'Anti-discrimination goals and the legal process' in N. Glazer and K. Young (eds) *Ethnic Pluralism and Public Policy* (London: Heinemann).

McCrudden, C. (1987) 'The Commission for Racial Equality' in R. Baldwin and

C. McCrudden (eds) *Regulation and Public Law* (London: Weidenfeld and Nicolson).

——(1988) 'Codes in a Cold Climate: Administrative Rule-Making by the Commission for Racial Equality', *Modern Law Review*, 51, 4: 40941.

Messina, T. (1985) 'Race and Party Competition in Britain', *Parliamentary Affairs*, 38, 4: 423–36.

——(1987) 'Mediating race relations: British Community Relations Councils revisited', *Ethnic and Racial Studies*, 10, 2: 187–202.

Metropolitan Police (1986) *Public Order Review – Civil Disturbances 1981–1985* (London: Metropolitan Police).

Miles, R. (1982) *Racism and Migrant Labour* (London: Routledge and Kegan Paul).

——(1984) 'The Riots of 1958: notes on the ideological construction of "race relations" as a political issue in Britain', *Immigrants and Minorities*, 3 3: 252–75.

——(1986) 'Labour Migration, Racism and Capital Accumulation in Western Europe Since 1945', *Capital and Class*, 28, 49–86.

——(1987) 'Recent Marxist theories of nationalism and the issue of racism', *British Journal of Sociology*, XXXVIII 1 : 24–43.

——(1989) *Racism* (Routledge, 1989).

Miles, R. and Phizacklea, A. (1984) *Racism and Political Action in Britain* (London: Routledge).

——(eds) (1979) *White Man's Country* (London: Pluto Press).

Millward, P. (1985) 'The Stockport Riots of 1852: A Study of Anti-Catholic and Anti-Irish Sentiment; in Swift, R. and Gilley, S. (eds) *The Irish in the Victorian City* (London: Croom Helm).

Mishan, E. J. (1988) 'What Future for a Multi-Racial Britain?' *Salisbury Review*, 6, 4: 18–27.

Moore, R. (1975) *Racism and Black Resistance in Britain* (London: Pluto Press).

Moore, R. and Wallace, T. (1975) *Slamming the Door: The Administration of Immigration Control* (Oxford: Martin Robertson).

Moran, M. (1985) *Politics and Society in Britain* (London: Macmillan).

Mullard, C. (1985) *Race, Power and Resistance* (London: Routledge and Kegan Paul).

Murdock, G. (1984) 'Reporting the riots: images and impact', J. Benyon (ed.) *Scarman and After* (Oxford: Pergamon Press).

Murray, N. (1986) 'Anti-racists and other demons: the press and ideology in Thatcher's Britain', *Race and Class*, XXVII, 3, 1–19.

Mydral, G. (1969a) *Objectivity in Social Research* (London: Duckworth).

——(1969b) *The American Dilemma: The Negro Problem and Modern Democracy* (New York: Harper and Row).

Newman, K. (1983) 'Fighting the fear of crime', *Police*, September: 26–30; October: 30–2.

——(1986a) 'Police–public relations: the pace of change' (Police Federation Annual Lecture, 28 July).

——(1986b) *Public Order Review: Civil Disturbances 1981–85* (London: Metropolitan Police).

Newton, K. (1976) *Second City Politics: Democratic Processes and Decision-Making in Birmingham* (Oxford: Clarendon Press).

Nixon, J. (1982) 'The Home Office and Race Relations Policy: co-ordinator or initiator?' *Journal of Public Policy*, 2, 4: 365–78.

OECD (1986) 'United Kingdom', National Report for OECD Conference on the Future of Migration (Paris, February 1986).

Offe, C. (1984) *Contradictions of the Welfare State* (London: Hutchinson).

——(1985) *Disorganised Capitalism* (Cambridge: Polity).

Omi, M. and Winant, H. (1986) *Racial Formation in the United States* (London: Routledge).

O Tuathaigh, M. (1985) 'The Irish in Nineteenth Century Britain: Problems of Integration' in R. Swift and S. Gilley (eds) *The Irish in the Victorian City* (London: Croom Helm).

Ouseley, H. (1981) *The System* (London: Runnymede).

——(1982), 'A local black alliance' in A. Ohri, B. Manning and P. Curno, *Community Work and Racism* (London: Routledge).

——(1984) 'Local Authority Race Initiatives' in M. Boddy and C. Fudge (eds) *Local Socialism* (London: Macmillan).

Ouseley, H. *et al.* (1986) *A Different Reality: An account of Black people's experiences and their grievances before and after the Handsworth Rebellions of September 1985* (Birmingham: West Midlands County Council).

Palmer, F. (ed.) (1986) *Anti-Racism – An Assault on Education and Value* (London: The Sherwood Press).

Parekh, B. (1987) 'The "new right" and the politics of nationhood' in Runnymede Trust, *The New Right: Image and reality* (London: Runnymede Trust).

Park, R. (1950) *Race and Culture* (New York: Free Press).

Parkin, F. (1979) *Marxism and Class: A Bourgeois Critique* (London: Tavistock).

Parkinson, M. and Duffy, J. (1984) 'Government's response to inner city riots: the Minister for Merseyside and the Task Force', *Parliamentary Affairs*, 37 1: 76–96.

Patterson, S. (1963) *Dark Strangers* (Harmondsworth: Penguin).

——(1969) *Immigration and Race Relations in Britain 1960–1967* (London: Oxford University Press).

Pearson, D. (1981) *Race, Class and Political Activism* (Aldershot: Gower).

Phizacklea, A. and Miles, R. (1980) *Labour and Racism* (London: Routledge).

Pilkington, E. (1988) *Beyond the Mother Country: West Indians and the Notting Hill White Riots* (London: I. B. Tauris).

Piven, F. F. and Cloward, R. (1977) *Poor People's Movements* (New York: Vintage Books).

Pollins, H. (1982) *Economic History of the Jews in England* (London: Associated University Presses).

Powell, E. (1969) *Freedom and Reality* (Kingswood: Elliot Right Way Books).

——(1972) *Still to Decide* (London: Batsford).

PREM 11/1409 (1956) 'Immigration from the Irish Republic' (London: Public Records Office).

Preston, M. B., Henderson, L. J. and Puryear, P. (eds) (1982) *The New Black Politics* (New York: Longman).

Pryce, K. (1979) *Endless Pressure* (Harmondsworth: Penguin).

Race Relations Board (1973) *Race Relations Legislation in Britain* (London: Race Relations Board).

Ramdin, R. (1987) *The Making of the Black Working Class in Britain* (Aldershot: Gower).

Redford, A. (1976) *Labour Migration in England 1800–1850* (Manchester: Manchester University Press).

Reeves, F. (1983) *British Racial Discourse* (Cambridge University Press).
Reiner, R. (1985) *The Politics of the Police* (Brighton: Wheatsheaf Books).
Rex, J. (1973) *Race, Colonialism and the City* (London: Routledge and Kegan Paul).
——(1981) 'A working paradigm for race relations research', *Ethnic and Racial Studies*, 4 (1): 1–25.
——(1983) *Race Relations in Sociological Theory*, 2nd edn (London: Routledge and Kegan Paul).
——(1986) *Race and Ethnicity* (Milton Keynes: Open University Press).
Rex, J. and Mason, D. (eds) (1986) *Theories of Race and Ethnic Relations* (Cambridge University Press).
Rex, J. and Moore, R. (1967) *Race, Community and Conflict* (London: Oxford University Press).
Rex, J. and Tomlinson, S. (1979) *Colonial Immigrants in a British City: A Class Analysis* (London: Routledge and Kegan Paul).
Rich, P. (1986) *Race and Empire in British Politics* (Cambridge University Press).
Richmond, A. (1954) *Colour Prejudice in Britain: A Study of West Indian Workers in Liverpool, 1942–51* (London: Routledge and Kegan Paul).
——(1973) *Migration and Race Relations in an English City* (London: Oxford University Press).
Robinson, C. (1983) *Black Marxism* (London: Zed).
Rose, E. J. B. and Associates (1969) *Colour and Citizenship: A Report on British Race Relations* (London: Oxford University Press).
Rose, R. (1985) *Politics in England* (London: Faber and Faber).
Saunders, P. (1981) *Social Theory and the Urban Question* (London: Hutchinson).
Scarman, Lord (1981) *The Brixton Disorders 10–12 April 1981: Report of an Inquiry by the Rt Hon. The Lord Scarman* OBE (London: HMSO).
Seidel, G. (1986) 'The concept of culture, "race" and nation in the British and French new right' in R. Levitas (ed.) *The Ideology of the New Right* (Cambridge: Polity).
Select Committee on Race Relations and Immigration (1975) *The Organisation of Race Relations Administration* (London: HMSO).
——(1977) *The West Indian Community* (London: HMSO).
——(1978) *Immigration* (London: HMSO).
Sherman, A. (1973) *Island Refuge: Britain and Refugees from the Third Reich* (London: Paul Elek).
Sherwood, M. (1984) *Many Struggles: West Indian Workers and Service Personnel in Britain 1939–45* (London: Karia Press).
Shyllon, F. O. (1974) *Black Slaves in Britain* (London: Oxford University Press).
Silverman, J., Chairman (1986) *Independent Inquiry into the Handsworth Disturbances, September 1985* (Birmingham City Council).
Sim, J. (1982) 'Scarman: The Police Counter-Attack', in Eve, M. and Musson, D. (eds) *The Socialist Register 1982* (London: Merlin Press).
Sivanandan, A. (1982) *A Different Hunger* (London: Pluto Press).
Skolnick, J. (1969) *The Politics of Protest* (New York: Simon and Schuster).
Smith, D. (1977) *Racial Disadvantage in Britain* (Harmondsworth: Penguin).
Smith, D. (1987) 'Knowing your place: Class, politics and ethnicity in Chicago and Birmingham 1890–1983' in Thrift, N. and Williams, P. *Class and Space* (London: Macmillan).
Smith, G. (1987) *When Jim Crow Met John Bull* (London: I. B. Tauris).

Smith, D. and Gray, J. (1987) *Police and People in London* (Aldershot: Gower).
Smithies, B. and Fiddick, P. (1969) *Enoch Powell on Immigration* (London: Sphere Books).
Solomos, J. (1986) 'Trends in the political analysis of racism' *Political Studies*, XXXIV, 2: 313–24.
Solomos, J. (1988) *Black Youth, Racism and the State* (Cambridge University Press).
Sowell, T. (1981) *Markets and Minorities* (Oxford: Basil Blackwell).
Spencer, K. *et al.* (1986) *Crisis in the Industrial Heartland: A Study of the West Midlands* (London: Clarendon Press).
Stoker, G. (1988) *The Politics of Local Government* (London: Macmillan).
Studlar, D. (1978) 'Policy Voting in Britain: The Coloured Immigration Issue in the 1964, 1966 and 1970 General Elections', *American Political Science Review*, 72, 1: 46–64.
——(1980) 'Elite responsiveness or elite autonomy: British immigration policy reconsidered', *Ethnic and Racial Studies*, 3, 2: 207–23.
Swift, R. and Gilley, S. (eds) (1985) *The Irish in the Victorian City* (London: Croom Helm).
Tannahill, J. A. (1958) *European Volunteer Workers in Britain* (Manchester University Press).
Taylor, S. (1982) *The National Front in English Politics* (London: Macmillan).
Thompson, G. (1986) *The Conservatives' Economic Policy* (London: Croom Helm).
Thrift, N. and Williams, P. (eds) (1987) *Class and Space* (London: Macmillan).
Thurlow, R. (1975) 'National Front Ideology', *Patterns of Prejudice*, 9, 1: 1–9.
The Times (1968) *The Black Man in Search of Power* (London: Nelson).
Troyna, B. and Williams, J. (1986) *Racism, Education and the State* (London: Croom Helm).
Visram, R. (1986) *Ayahs, Lascars and Princes* (London: Pluto).
Walker, M. (1977) *The National Front* (London: Fontana).
Waller, P. J. (1981) *Democracy and Sectarianism: A Political and Social History of Liverpool 1868–1939* (Liverpool University Press).
Walvin, J. (1973) *Black and White: The Negro and British Society* (London: Allen & Unwin).
——(1984) *Passage to Britain* (Harmondsworth: Penguin).
Ward, R. (ed.) (1984) *Race and Housing in Britain* (Centre for Research in Ethnic Relations, University of Warwick).
Widgery, D. (1986) *Beating Time* (London: Chatto and Windus).
Wilson, H. (1971) *The Labour Government 1964–70* (London: Weidenfeld and Nicolson).
Wilson, W. J. (1980) *The Declining Significance of Race* (University of Chicago Press).
——(1988) *The Truly Disadvantaged* (University of Chicago Press).
WING (1985) *Worlds Apart: Women Under Immigration and Nationality Law* (London: Pluto).
Wolf, E. (1982) *Europe and the People Without History* (Berkeley: University of California Press).
Wolpe, H. (1987) *Race, Class and the Apartheid State* (London: James Currey).
Worsthorne, P. (1978) 'Too much freedom' in M. Cowling (ed.) *Conservative*

——(1985) 'End this silence over race' (*Sunday Telegraph*, 26 September).

Young, K. (1985) 'Racial Disadvantage' in S. Ranson *et al.* (eds) *Between Centre and Locality* (London: Allen & Unwin).

Young, K. (1987) 'The space between words: local authorities and the concept of equal opportunities' in R. Jenkins and J. Solomos (eds) *Racism and Equal Opportunity Policies in the 1980s* (Cambridge University Press).

Young, K. and Connelly, N. (1981) *Policy and Practice in the Multi-Racial City* (London: Policy Studies Institute).

——(1984) 'After the Act: Local Authority Policy Reviews under the Race Relations Act 1976', *Local Government Studies*, 10,1: 13–25.

Zubaida, S. (ed.) (1970) 'Introduction' in *Race and Racialism* (London: Tavistock).

——(1972) 'Sociologists and Race Relations' in *Proceedings of a Seminar: Problems and Prospects of Socio-Legal Research* (Nuffield College, Oxford, 1972).

Zubrzycki, J. (1956) *Polish Immigrants to Britain* (The Hague: Martinus Nijhoff).

Index